Final Appeal

Decision-making in Canadian Courts of Appeal

Ian Greene, Carl Baar, Peter McCormick,
George Szablowski, and Martin Thomas

James Lorimer & Company Ltd., Publishers
Toronto, 1998

James Lorimer & Company Ltd. acknowledges the support of the Department of Canadian Heritage and the Ontario Arts Council in the development of writing and publishing in Canada. We acknowledge the support of the Canada Council for the Arts for our publishing program.

Cover design: Kevin O'Reilly

Cataloguing in Publication Data

Main entry under title:

Final appeal: decision-making in Canadian courts of appeal

Includes index.
ISBN 1-55028-565-3 (bound)   ISBN 1-55028-564-5 (pbk.)

1. Appellate courts — Canada. 2. Judicial process — Canada. I. Greene, Ian.

KE8585.F56   1998   347.71'03   C97-930945-X
KF9058.ZA2F56 1998

James Lorimer & Company Ltd., Publishers
35 Britain Street
Toronto, Ontario
M5A 1R7

Printed and bound in Canada.

Contents

To Peter Russell
Father of the political science study of law and politics in Canada

Tables

Acknowledgements

This first-ever comprehensive study of appellate court decision-making in Canada would not have been possible without the assistance and cooperation of a great many Canadians — from our research assistants to the chief justices of Canada's appellate courts. Our colleagues in other countries are envious at the degree of cooperation that we received.

We are particularly indebted to Canada's appellate court judges who agreed to take time out of their busy schedules to be interviewed by us and to fill out our background questionnaire. We are especially grateful to the chief justices, all of whom not only were interviewed and filled out the background questionnaire, but also completed an additional questionnaire about their court's procedures. They were also extremely helpful in setting the stage for us to arrange interviews with the puisne judges. Several judges sent us articles that they though might be useful, and some others provided us with helpful comments about the manuscript for the book. The late Chief Justice Brian Dickson was good enough to read an early draft of Chapter 6 and to provide us with comments. We had always admired him for the clarity and succinctness of his decisions; we now more fully appreciate his passion for these qualities.

The registrars of all of the appellate courts deserve special thanks for allowing our research assistants to spend a good many days in their offices pulling out files and collecting data on the flow of cases from trial to appeal. They did their best to provide working space for our research assistants and were helpful in whatever ways they could be.

The data collection and the interviews would not have been possible without the financial assistance of a standard research grant from the Social Sciences and Humanities Research Council, and minor research grants, transcription support, and graduate assistant support from York University.

Most of the case-flow data were collected by Karen Atkin, our chief research assistant, as described in more detail in the Appendix. Our other research assistants responsible for data collection were Rosemary Graf, Elaine Ross, Tim Nicholls and Nadine Changfoot.

Annie Dionne did a great deal of work to input the data from the background questionnaires and to assist with data analysis. Other research assistants were Lorena Azucena, Michael Oliphant, Lucy Lorefice, Sonia Pascal, Jocelyne Praud, and Barry Yellin.

We had the benefit of comments on parts of the manuscript (or conference papers that were incorporated into the manuscript) from several of our colleagues, including Thomas Cromwell, Robin Elliott, Jacqueline Krikorian, Christopher Manfredi, Peter Russell, and Lorne Sossin. We are especially grateful for the good advice and patience of those at James Lorimer and Company who worked with our manuscript, especially Diane Young and Ward McBurney. And a special thanks to Jim Lorimer, whose faith in our ability to produce a manuscript kept us motivated, in spite of the faculty strike in 1997 at York University that threw a monkey-wrench into our publication schedule.

Most of all, we owe a debt of gratitude to our families for tolerating our time away from home on our research visits, and the many evenings and weekends we were not able to spend with them. On the other hand, the book would have been published sooner had we not tried to allocate "equal concern and respect" to our families. Christina and Philip Greene, just beginning their school years at the time of writing, will eventually judge for themselves whether their dad struck the right balance.

Peter Russell has had an incalculable impact on all of us. Beginning in the 1960s, his influential publications combined with his limitless energy and good will spurred Canadian political scientists to regard "law and politics" as a legitimate field of study within the discipline of political science. The research reported in this book simply would not have come about without the ground-breaking research he inspired and produced. He was the Ph.D. dissertation supervisor for Ian Greene, and his writings have had a major impact on all of us.

Ellen Baar was generous enough to read and to provide meticulous and insightful comments about several of our chapters, and we all deeply regret that she did not live to see the final version. Like Peter Russell, Ellen was a founding member of the Canadian Law and Society Association, and we will indeed be grateful if some of those whom Ellen has inspired will find this book a source for the kinds of intense but civilized debates that Ellen encouraged — and demanded — throughout her career.

Introduction

The purpose of this book is to shed light on what has been an unexplored element in Canada's system of democratic government: how our 125 or so appellate court judges make their decisions in the context of varying decision-making procedures in the provincial courts of appeal, the Federal Court of Appeal, and the Supreme Court of Canada.

Judges have power. Where the law allows for alternative resolutions, judges have the power to settle issues in whatever they consider to be the best way. The law can never be more than a general guide to decision-making, except in the situation where a law has been enacted to resolve a specific dispute, such as the laws that used to be enacted by Parliament to give effect to individual divorces in Quebec and Newfoundland.[1] The greater the number of fact situations that a law is intended to cover, the greater the scope of potentially valid interpretations between which judges may and must choose. Among the most general of the laws of Canada is the constitution, because it sits atop the entire legal structure. The 1982 amendment of the Canadian constitution to include the Charter of Rights and Freedoms increased the scope of judicial discretion so much that it made judicial power publicly visible for the first time. Supreme Court decisions about the Charter have had a well-publicized impact on public policy in areas like abortion law, conditions for rape victims when they testify in court, and human rights protection for gays.

Judicial power is commonly thought to be anti-democratic. Judges are appointed, and moreover they represent an elite group in society. Therefore, many people who are concerned about democratic practice in Canada have been troubled by the apparent transfer of power that occurred in 1982 from elected legislators to judges. We argue, however, that judicial power is not necessarily anti-democratic if judicial appointment procedures are appropriate and if judges exercise power in ways calculated to promote the basic principle behind democratic institutions: mutual respect.

Our book is based on three sets of data. First, we conducted hour-long interviews with 101 of the 125 or so appellate court judges in Canada,[2] including eight justices of the Supreme Court of Canada; each interview was based on a ten-page questionnaire. Second, we asked all judges we interviewed to fill out a four-page questionnaire about their backgrounds and their parents' backgrounds. Finally, we collected data from a representative sample of nearly six thousand cases moving from trial to appeal in the ten provinces and in the Federal Court.[3] Further information about our methods of data collection is presented in the Appendix. We collected a massive amount of data. This book analyses some of the key findings. We plan other publications that focus on specific findings that we did not address here.

At the top of the court hierarchy in every province is a court of appeal. These courts generally hear cases in panels of three, and the total number of judges from which these three-judge panels are selected ranges from three in Prince Edward Island to about twenty in Ontario and Quebec.[4] As well, one or two judges of the British Columbia and Alberta courts of appeal sit with a superior court judge in the nearest territory to form panels of the courts of appeal for the Yukon and the Northwest Territories. Then there is the Federal Court of Appeal that hears appeals from the trial division Federal Court — the court whose work is mostly composed of federal administrative law cases. At the very top of the appellate hierarchy sits the Supreme Court of Canada with its nine judges.

Decisions of the Supreme Court are final, although in most cases so are the decisions of the other appeal courts — hence the title of this book. The Supreme Court controls most of its own case load, because, with the exception of a few unusual criminal cases where the accused has a right of appeal, litigants must apply to the top court for permission or "leave" to appeal. The Supreme Court accepts only about a hundred of the five hundred plus applications for leave that it receives annually, meaning that 98.5 per cent of the cases heard by the provincial, territorial, and federal appellate courts are final appeals.

The courts are an integral part of our political system. John Locke was a seventeenth-century philosopher who is regarded as the first great proponent of the philosophy of liberalism. Locke considered the courts as part of the executive branch of government. It is, however, the threefold division of government into separate legislative, executive, and judicial branches, as proposed by Baron de Montesquieu in the eighteenth century that has become commonplace. Three common definitions of "politics" are the process of making decisions about who gets what, when and how;[5] private demands, displaced into the public arena, and rationalized in terms of the public good;[6] and the authoritative allocation of values for a society.[7] Courts, as well as legislatures and executives, can be said to fit into all three of these viewpoints.

The courts are viewed as less partisan and therefore less "political" than the other two branches of government. This is because of the constitutional expectations of judicial independence and impartiality. Thus the important political function of the courts as the formal dispute-resolution arm of government is very often underestimated. The political power of courts is assumed to be a quiet, humble, and unassuming one. The innocuous nature of the political power of the courts has always been a myth, but the myth was finally shattered once and for all with the advent of the Charter. The Supreme Court's decision to strike down Canada's abortion law in 1988 as violating the Charter,[8] the 1990 decision to stop prosecution of criminal cases that took longer than eleven months to get to trial unless the accused had caused the delay,[9] and the 1995 decision that same-sex couples are not entitled by the Charter to claim spousal old age pension benefits[10] cannot be thought of as non-political. Nor can the Ontario Court of Appeal's judgment that lap dancing is a criminal offence — upheld by the Supreme Court in June 1997 — be seen as other than an example of the political power of provincial appellate courts.[11]

Although such sensational cases are rare, and in fact the work of most provincial appellate courts is boringly routine, discretion nevertheless plays a much greater role in appellate decision-making, even in run-of-the-mill cases, than we had expected prior to this research project. We have concluded that this discretionary part of appellate decision-making is not necessarily evil or anti-democratic, but rather that judging is a "human process,"[12] and there are probably several different "just" solutions to every legal problem.

In Chapter 1 we take a closer look at the nature of and perceived "problem" of judicial discretion in relation to the thinking of critics of the judicial role in the Canadian democracy. Key to understanding how judicial discretion is used is the sense of "justice" developed over a lifetime by each individual judge. This sense of justice is likely to bear close relation to the backgrounds and family contexts of the judges insofar as these distinguish them from the general public, and this is the topic of Chapter 2. In Chapter 3 the institutional nature of the appellate process in Canada is analysed.

The next two chapters summarize how the penultimate appellate court judges described the decision-making process to us: their pre-hearing reviews of the relevant case materials, their own reasoning processes during and after the hearing, and the collegial decision-making process that either results in a unanimous decision, one or more dissenting decisions, or one or more separate concurring decisions. The decision-making processes in the various appellate courts demonstrate a surprising degree of variation, even in courts with similarities in size or legal tradition. Chapter 4 pays special attention to the penultimate appellate courts, especially in the purely common law provinces and in the appeal division of the Federal Court. Chapter 5 focuses on the Cour d'Appel du Québec (Quebec Court of Appeal), the only provincial appellate court that follows the European civil law tradition in addition to the English common law approach. The Supreme Court of Canada — an appeal court whose procedures and processes are unique in several important ways — is the topic of Chapter 6.

Appeal judges put considerable effort into their written decisions to persuade their readers, be they litigants, judges in the courts below, academic critics, or members of the general public, that their decisions are just. Chapter 7 explores the strategies developed by appellate judges for defending their decisions. One of the by-products of judicial discretion, and the concurrent discretion exercised by the legal profession, is that significant differences have developed in the appellate processes and patterns of decisions in each jurisdiction in Canada; in Chapter 8 we consider these differences.

The role of appellate courts in the policy process has become such a contentious issue since the Charter of Rights came into effect in 1982 that we devote Chapter 9 to a consideration of the role of appellate courts in a democratic society. Naturally, we take into account the judges' own thoughts about that role.

In our concluding chapter, we argue that many of the concerns that have been raised since 1982 about judicial legislation or judicial policy-making are ill-founded. The two main causes of these unnecessarily alarmist views are a lack of clarity in thinking about democracy and a failure to consider the broader role of discretion among members of all branches of government. We argue that a conception of democracy based on the principal of mutual respect, if taken seriously both by those sceptical about judicial power and by the judiciary, may help both to alleviate fears about a judicial "super-legislature" and to ensure more acceptable results when judicial discretion is employed.

1

Judicial Discretion and Democracy

It is an uncomfortable fact that no particular approach to justice, ethics, or governing can be proven, beyond any doubt, to be "right." Most of us probably wish that this were not so; we would like to think that there are some higher authorities that "get it right," if not all the time then at least most of the time.[1] Judges are high on the list of credible authorities among Canadians, and this is one reason why Canadians tend to hold them in such high esteem.[2]

A recent survey showed that 70 per cent of Canadians had some degree of confidence in the courts, compared with only 46 per cent who had the same confidence in Parliament. Fifty-two per cent rated the ethical principles of judges as higher than average (and 41 per cent said they were the same as those of most Canadians), while only 17 per cent rated members of Parliament as having higher than average ethical principles (and 41 per cent said they were the same as those of most Canadians).[3]

But judges make mistakes. For this reason, nearly all cases involving serious consequences can be appealed to a higher court that performs an "error correction" function.[4] But appellate court judges are human, too, and when they make errors, there is no appeal. One might expect, therefore, that the burden of error-avoidance would weigh much more heavily on their shoulders. And it probably would, if not for the fact that the burden is shared by a panel of judges. In any case, the higher the rank of the judge, the more we expect that judge to make "correct" decisions, both from a technical legal point of view and from the perspective of justice and ethics.

Even more important, judges have discretion to choose from an array of potential decisions, none of which could be shown to be "incorrect." For example, when the law is unclear, judges must, in a sense, make law to create the necessary clarity to decide cases. Moreover, judges have their own ways of arriving at and defending a particular decision. No two judges, after hearing the same case, follow exactly the same reasoning process to make a decision or write opinions using precisely the same words. Furthermore, judges might give different weights both to factual and legal matters, and in some kinds of cases these variations in weighting can result in different decisions about the same kinds of issues. What determines a particular judge's decision is the interplay of his or her personality, background, values, and legal education.

Second, because we live in a democracy, we expect judges to leave the process of lawmaking to our elected representatives. However, no matter how hard a judge may try to defer to the "will of the people," this general will as expressed in the law can rarely be absolutely clear. Sometimes, even when the general will is clear, it cannot be followed because it appears to contradict an important constitutional principle in the Charter or another part of the constitution. There is an apparent contradiction between the expectations we place on our judges, as a result of our democratic norms, and the reality of judicial discretion.

This chapter is intended to pursue two fundamental points. First, we argue that the debate about whether judicial lawmaking undermines democracy becomes far less important when democracy is considered not merely as lawmaking through elected legislatures, but more basically as government operating on the principle of mutual respect. A more important question for debate is whether judges tend to pursue decision-making strategies designed to give effect to democratic principles. Second, we argue that the extent of judicial discretion is broader than it is generally considered to be and that the importance of the human element in judicial decision-making is often underestimated. These misconceptions about judicial discretion have impoverished the debate about the optimal role of judicial policy-making in a democratic context. Judicial discretion is neither avoidable nor necessarily anti-democratic — it depends on how this discretion is exercised.

Judicial Lawmaking vs Democracy

It is useful to review the strands of thought concerning the relation between judicial activism and democracy in Canada, because underlying this intellectual activity there is either a divergence of views about the nature of democracy or just plain fuzzy thinking.

In the nineteenth century, following the example of the Austinian positivists, it was generally thought in common law countries that good legal reasoning had reached such a state of perfection that intelligent, experienced judges who followed the correct procedures would nearly always arrive at the "correct" legal answers in their cases.[5] Thus, there was no conflict between the judicial role and democracy, as judges merely applied the law as enacted by elected legislatures.

This school of thought, which had been adopted, among others, by A.V. Dicey, was attacked in the twentieth century by "legal realists"[6] who argued that legal rules can never be that clear. Their view was that the individual predisposition of judges must necessarily affect their decisions — the more so when interpreting constitutions, because constitutions are written in a general language to cover a very broad range of issues. (Compare the broad and general language in the seven-page Canadian Charter of Rights and Freedoms, with the tediously precise wording of the 800-page Income Tax Act, which nevertheless has spawned thousands of pages of regulations and legal interpretation bulletins.)

The realists' concern was with a small minority of cases in which the law was unclear because potentially conflicting laws governed a specific situation,[7] or no law clearly applied,[8] or a law contained internal contradictions,[9] or the law was worded very generally.[10] But even in these cases (often referred to as "hard" cases in the literature on jurisprudence), there were "better" and "worse" outcomes depending on whether the judge followed the commentator's preferred reasoning process.[11] So the problem for democracy was a small number of cases in which judges exercised policy-making discretion.

It is generally accepted that appellate judges have greater scope for discretion in legal interpretation than judges in the lower trial courts. This is because the appellate judges encounter a higher proportion of hard cases — those on which equally competent jurists may disagree — since these cases are more likely to be appealed than straightforward ones where nearly everyone agrees what the relevant law means. As well, the higher the position of the judge in the judicial hierarchy, the less encumbering are the rules of *stare decisis* — the common law doctrine of precedent — because there are fewer courts "above" whose decisions are supposedly binding. At the top, the Supreme Court of Canada is free to overrule its own precedents and those established previously by the Judicial Committee of the Privy Council in London, which was Canada's highest court until 1949.

The era of the Canadian Charter of Rights and Freedoms, beginning as it did in 1982, has created a great deal of *angst* among

Canadian academics about the role that judges ought to play in democratic institutions. The post-1982 literature on the Charter and the role of the judiciary could easily fill a bookcase or, to make the point in more up-to-date terms, a CD-ROM. This is because the Charter has made judicial discretion more publicly visible, and therefore, for the first time to any significant extent, generally troubling.

Peter Russell, professor emeritus at the University of Toronto, has encouraged analysis of the Canadian justice system from a political science perspective more than anyone else. Since the 1960s, he has produced a steady stream of influential books and articles that have provided deep insights into the nature of judicial discretion and what gives rise to "judicial power."[12] From Russell's perspective, judicial power is manifest primarily, but not exclusively, in hard cases and in higher courts. The Charter changed the degree, not the nature of judicial power. Judges do sometimes have a profound influence on public policy,[13] and because such influence is unavoidable, Russell advocated more democratic approaches to the selection of judges (he was the first chair of Ontario's Judicial Appointments Advisory Committee), more effective training programs for judges, and better mechanisms for ensuring judicial accountability.

Prior to 1982 Russell had been sceptical about whether the Charter of Rights and Freedoms would result in the enhanced protection of human rights for Canadians. He observed that judges were not better equipped than elected legislators to make decisions about how to protect human rights, except possibly legal rights like procedural safeguards in criminal prosecutions. Russell also pointed out that the legal–judicial system is not nearly as well designed as the legislative system to make good public policy in the area of human rights. According to Russell's evaluation of how the judges have handled Charter jurisprudence, they have not done as badly as had been feared by Charter sceptics like himself, but neither have they done as well as Charter enthusiasts had predicted.

In his controversial book *The Charter of Rights and the Legalization of Politics in Canada*,[14] Michael Mandel argued that the Charter gave birth to "the legalization" of politics. What he meant was that some of the most important public policy decisions had been taken out of the realm of democratic debate and placed into the hands of an elite class of unelected, unaccountable, and socially privileged individuals. Mandel claimed that nearly every important Charter decision has resulted in enhancing the status of social elites in Canada, of which judges and lawyers are an important segment, thus further diminishing the lot of the underprivileged. From Mandel's perspective, the legal–judicial process itself is biased towards the rich and powerful. Litigation is expensive, and lawyers with the highest fees tend to win the most cases. The rules of evidence filter out factors important to the underprivileged, factors that would have a greater chance of being heard in the democratic legislative process. Politics has become more "legalized," more the preserve of the advantaged classes. Mandel's advice to those with a progressive social policy agenda is to ignore the Charter, avoid the courts, and concentrate on effecting policy changes through the democratic process of elections and legislatures.

Many scholars and practitioners reject the legalization of politics argument.[15] They also question the proposition that judicial review is inherently undemocratic. We share this perspective, for several reasons.

First, as a category of judicial decision-making distinct from dispute resolution, judicial review accounts only for a small percentage of the workload of the trial and appellate courts. It does not therefore convert courts into political actors analogous to legislatures, government executives, or bureaucracies. When, in the course of judicial review, the courts are compelled to examine policy questions, the narrow and issue-specific scope of inquiry cannot be compared to the broad mandate that governments have to make comprehensive policies within their constitutionally defined jurisdictions. Senior government bureaucrats, who exercise overall much greater impact on policy and its implementation, are as unelected, unrepresentative, and socially privileged as judges, and their accountability to the public leaves a great deal to be desired. Most federal MPs and members of provincial legislatures have very little power compared with cabinet ministers or senior bureaucrats.[16]

Second, Charter review is only one of three types of review practised by the judges in Canada's courts. For many years before 1982, legislative and administrative review allowed courts to make important political and policy decisions, and the legitimacy of these decisions is now rarely questioned. Since 1867, in the course of legislative review, the courts have reshaped and redefined the political powers of Canadian governments to make laws, and they have significantly and permanently influenced the development of federal–provincial relations in Canada. Administrative review, which predates Confederation, has been responsible for many leading decisions directly affecting such policy areas as immigration, police powers, security, labour relations, and municipal government. In the words of Nicola Lacey, a British lawyer and academic, "No reasonably independent-minded and critical observer of the judiciary's activities in the areas of judicial review of administrative action ... could possibly imagine anything other than that judges already exercise substantial political power."[17]

Judicial review is a well-established practice that forms an integral part of the Canadian legal tradition, which is rooted in British constitutionalism and the rule of law. Judicial review was not invented with the Charter in 1982. On balance, it is fair to observe that the policy output of the Canadian courts pursuant to Charter review since 1982 still falls considerably short of their similar output pursuant to legislative and administrative review. It is thus plainly inaccurate to blame the Charter alone for the legalization of politics in Canada and to claim that the Constitution Act, 1982, has fundamentally altered the role of Canadian courts. Both trial and appellate courts are typically reactive institutions. Without a writ and a statement of claim or an inscription in appeal, the courts can do nothing. Unlike political executives and bureaucracies, they will not initiate or develop a policy process nor render a decision unless specifically and formally asked to do so in the context of existing litigation.

Finally, those who criticize the Charter and judicial review as undemocratic fail to recognize the essentially corrective role of the courts in a system of parliamentary majority rule where the executive dominates the policy process. This corrective role of the courts, exercised when human rights are in danger, is especially important in a country such as Canada with numerous minorities, which are unevenly distributed territorially and are often politically weak or unable to access the political establishment. In such circumstances, judicial review is clearly not undemocratic. On the contrary, it strengthens political pluralism and enriches democracy itself, and it is essential for the preservation of mutual respect.

Rainer Knopff and Ted Morton, whose book *Charter Politics*[18] was published in 1992, are the best-known critics of the Charter from the centre-right of the political spectrum. Like Mandel, they lament that the Charter has transferred power from democratically elected legislatures to judges. From their perspective this development is unfortunate because judges may become the unwitting pawns of either left-wing or right-wing social activists. They argue that the Charter is a two-edged sword — it can be used to slash either to the right or to the left — and the history of the U.S. Bill of Rights has shown that the pendulum tends to swing back and forth in response to both historical trends and the impact of particular personalities on the courts. In another volume, Rainer Knopff is sceptical about whether judges, or indeed any policy-makers, possess the wisdom to engage in "social engineering."[19] Knopff and Morton are considered to be on the right because of their scepticism about the possibility of success of social policy initiatives. They argue that policy activists have no moral right to impose their designs on society, and hence they advocate less government intervention.

Knopff and Morton spelled out the inherent danger of judges overstepping what ought to be the legal bounds of their authority and becoming "oracles" of social policy. Should judges deem themselves not to be limited by the intent of the framers of the constitution,[20] they would then be giving themselves *carte blanche* to rewrite the constitution from the perspective of their own limited wisdom, something that is not only foolhardy but also undemocratic.

Christopher Manfredi made a contribution to this debate about the proper role of judges in Canada's democracy in his 1993 book *Judicial Power and the Charter*. He suggested that all branches of government, whether judiciary, legislative, or executive (including the Cabinet and civil service), have responsibility for interpreting the constitution, including the Charter. The Charter recognizes this joint responsibility largely because of the infamous Section 33, the "notwithstanding" clause, which gives Parliament or a provincial legislature the power to enact a law, for five-year renewable periods, so that it can operate "notwithstanding" the sections of the Charter dealing with fundamental freedoms, legal rights, and equality rights. Thus, Section 33 is a signal that cabinets need not roll over and play dead in the face of important judicial interpretations of the Charter. Rather, cabinets ought to be encouraged to review these decisions and to challenge them, if necessary, through the introduction of a Section 33 override into the appropriate legislation.

Manfredi observed that the wording of the Charter gets the democratic balancing act about right, giving appropriate powers to each branch of government. However, as a result of a historical accident, Section 33 has lost, at least temporarily, its legitimacy. As it has turned out, the first time that Section 33 was used in a politically significant way[21] was by the Quebec government of Robert Bourassa in 1989. Bill 178 was spearheaded by Bourassa. He used the Section 33 override to uphold the provisions in Quebec's Charter of the French Language forbidding the use of English on outdoor commercial signs — contrary to an explicit decision of the Supreme Court of Canada that Bill 178 violates the Charter.[22] The reaction of Anglophone Canada to this manoeuvre was so negative that Section 33 was roundly condemned — unfairly, from Manfredi's perspective — and this situation became a major factor behind the eventual failure of both the Meech Lake and Charlottetown accords.

If it had not been for the Bill 178 fiasco, argued Manfredi, Section 33 might have been used by the federal government to counteract what many consider to be two bad decisions of the Supreme Court of Canada: *Askov*[23] in 1990 and *Seaboyer*[24] in 1991. The Charter of Rights and Freedoms guarantees Canadians the right to a trial without "unreasonable delay." *Askov* forced the Supreme Court to define "unreasonable delay." The decision was complex, but with the effect that criminal cases delayed for more than eleven months can be dismissed. Tens of thousands of cases in Canada's criminal courts were dropped because of the delay between arrest and trial if the delay was not caused by the accused person. In *Seaboyer*, the Supreme Court struck down the "rape shield" protections in the Criminal Code that protected rape victims from having to expose and defend their sexual history. The majority on the court felt that the rape shield provisions might result in unfair trials for those charged with sexual assault. Prior to these decisions, most of the Supreme Court of Canada's decisions on the Charter had met with general approval. Even the *Morgentaler* decision[25] — that struck down the sections of the Criminal Code dealing with abortion — did not prevent Parliament from introducing another abortion law that respected the procedural rights of women more effectively.

It is important to note that in 1997 the Parti Québécois government of Lucien Bouchard decided *not* to re-enact the Section 33 override to protect the provisions for French-only outdoor signs. Over the years since the controversy over Bill 178, Francophone opinion in Quebec had come to the conclusion that Bill 178 was too draconian and that the Supreme Court of Canada's recommendation for protecting the French language — that French could be predominant on outdoor signs but other languages need not be prohibited — was acceptable. Use of the Section 33 override had resulted in a democratic and public debate about the appropriateness of the override in this circumstance, as was indeed the intention in framing Section 33 with its built-in, five-year expiry period. Perhaps Anglophone opinion in Canada may yet come to accept that Section 33 can be useful both to provide a counterbalance to judicial decisions in a democratic context and to promote democratic debate.

In *Politics and the Constitution*, Patrick Monahan argued that in order to resolve the dilemma of the possibility of judicial fiat in a democratic setting, the courts ought to make decisions that wherever possible reinforce the democratic process.[26] If a court is faced with two alternate ways of resolving an issue, both of which could be considered legally correct, then it ought to choose the route that results in the greatest public input. For example, if the issue before a court is whether a particular municipal zoning by-law is within the jurisdiction of a municipality to enact, and if there are sound legal arguments on both sides of the issue, then the courts ought to consider whether the by-law promotes democracy through broad and fair public participation or whether it restricts democracy. If democracy is promoted, then this factor ought to be considered as a point in favour of upholding the by-law. Appealing as this approach sounds, however, there may not be many cases where considerations of participative democracy are relevant to the outcome of a judicial decision.

David Beattie stepped into the democracy versus the courts debate with his book, *Constitutional Law in Theory and Practice*. Beattie argued that in the current complex political environment, issues of individual fairness are liable not to get the attention they deserve from elected politicians. Therefore, a transfer of some decision-making power to the courts is not a bad thing in order to prevent the legitimate rights claims of individuals — claims legitimized by laws enacted by democratically elected legislatures — from falling into the cracks.[27] Judicial participation in policy-making is therefore essential to preserve fundamental democratic norms. Judges themselves ought to, and often do, approach constitutional adjudication in a way that reinforces the logic of the constitution. They do so by ensuring that legislatures have chosen the best available policy alternatives and by ensuring that legislative advances are not outweighed by cuts to personal rights and freedoms. Beattie argued that, as long as there is continued improvement in the process of selecting Supreme Court judges, and in making them more accountable and more responsible, there will be no inherent contradiction between judicial review and the democratic process.

Unlike the many courts versus democracy studies that have tended to focus on judges, Alan Cairns pointed out that a major impact of the Charter has been to fortify the political power of groups previously marginalized by the political process. These "Charter Canadians" include women, seniors, the disabled, visible minorities, and, to some extent, Aboriginal peoples. All of these groups had an impact on the wording of the Charter in the early 1980s; the Trudeau government formed alliances with them to get the Charter past the barriers being erected by a coalition of anti-Charter provincial premiers. As a result of their involvement in the process, members of these groups have come to see the Charter as an entrée to political influence, through the possibility of judges supporting their claims, that they could not have achieved as easily through the elected legislatures.[28]

This review of the debate surrounding the courts and democracy indicates fundamentally that the nature of democracy is often assumed to have something to do with policy-making through elected legislatures. More thought needs to be given to the nature of democracy itself in order to produce a clearer analysis of the role courts should and do play in the democratic process.

Democracy and Judicial Decision-making

The selection of leaders through elections and the approval of laws by elected legislatures do not in themselves define democracy. These are merely visible manifestations of an underlying principle. This notion was alluded to in the Supreme Court decision on Quebec secession in 1998:

> Democracy is commonly understood as being a political system of majority rule. [But] Democracy is not simply concerned with the process of government. On the contrary ... democracy is fundamentally connected to substantive goals, most importantly, the promotion of self-government.... [T]he Court in *R. v. Oakes*, [1986] 1 S.C.R. 103, articulated some of the values inherent in the notion of democracy (at p. 136):
> "The Court must be guided by the values and principles essential to a free and democratic society which I believe to embody, to name but a few, respect for the inherent dignity of the human person, commitment to social justice and equality, accommodation of a wide variety of beliefs, respect for cultural and group identity, and faith in social and political institutions which enhance the participation of individuals and groups in society." [Chief Justice Dickson wrote this opinion for a unanimous seven-judge panel.]

... [D]emocracy in any real sense of the word cannot exist without the rule of law.... Finally, we highlight that a functioning democracy requires a continuous process of discussion ... compromise, negotiation, and deliberation. No one has a monopoly on truth, and our system is predicated on the faith that in the marketplace of ideas, the best solutions to public problems will rise to the top. Inevitably, there will be dissenting voices. A democratic system of government is committed to considering those dissenting voices....[29]

The court listed a number of the important ingredients for democracy. But, we argue, behind all these the basic principle from which the notion of democratic government arises is the principle of mutual respect. Indeed, democracy can be thought of as government based on the principle of mutual respect.[30]

Samuel LaSelva, in his book *The Moral Foundations of Canadian Federalism*, sketched the development and interplay of various notions of democracy in Canadian history.[31] There is the Lockean approach based on individual rights that tends to be favoured in Anglophone Canada. There is the Rousseauian idea that emphasizes the importance of the cultural community that has drawn more support in Francophone Canada. There is the Aboriginal Canadian perspective that emphasizes consensual decision-making. There is the tension between proponents of local democracy and those who advocate more centralization of power at the provincial or national levels to ensure that "prejudice and intolerance are easier to combat and equal citizenship is more secure."[32] Finally, there are debates between those who prefer more participation by citizens in the development of public policy, and those who defer to policy-making through accommodation of elites, because they claim this method tends to maximize individual benefits. What all these strands of thought about democracy have in common is respect for the aspirations of all citizens, or a more or less unconscious conception of mutual respect. Our view is that more conscious thinking about the nature of mutual respect may lead to more effective refinements of democratic institutions and procedures.

Mutual respect is the notion that every human being in a society is equally deserving of respect. Every person is an end in himself or herself, not to be seen merely as a means to achieve someone else's goals. Each person's life is important. The right of all individuals to develop their potential and to make choices about their lives without interfering with the similar right of others is fundamental, along with the responsibility to contribute to the political conditions that make the implementation of mutual respect possible. Among contemporary political philosophers, John Rawls comes closest to describing what we mean by mutual respect with his emphasis on consideration for the needs of the least advantaged in society when democratic institutions must choose among competing notions of social equality.[33]

Definitions of democracy often begin with the principle of majority rule through fair and open elections. We consider selection of governments through election to be only one of several subprinciples of the basic axiom of democracy — mutual respect. The other important subprinciples[34] include:

- Decision-making through consensus where possible and practical, and, if not, according to majority rule;
- Respect for the principle of social equality, which, to use the words of Ronald Dworkin, means that "individuals have a right to equal concern and respect in the design and administration of the political institutions that govern them;"[35]
- Respect for minority rights, meaning that minorities are owed the same concern and respect as majorities;
- Respect for fairness, meaning both sides in a dispute about the application of law have a right to a fair hearing before an impartial tribunal;
- Respect for the rule of law;
- Respect for the value of freedom, or the right of citizens to determine their own priorities and to develop their human potential except in a way that interferes with the equal right of others to do so (including freedom of expression and of the media, which were described in the 1938 Alberta Press Case as "the breath of life for parliamentary institutions");[36]
- Respect for integrity, which we take to mean honesty implemented through compassion.

From this perspective, the alleged tension between democracy and judicial decision-making becomes less of a conundrum. One of the purposes of courts in a democratic context is to resolve disputes about the application of the law such that when there is judicial discretion, it acts to promote important subprinciples of democracy, such as procedural fairness and the impartial application of the law, and through these the democratic principles in the constitution, such as social equality, protection of minority rights, and freedom of expression.

What becomes important, then, is how well the courts perform functions involving discretion, rather than whether the lawmaking aspects of judicial decision-making can be considered as representing the majority views of the public at any particular time. As long as the judicial process is organized to promote mutual respect, there is no inherent contradiction between the lawmaking role of courts and democracy. There will always be legitimate debates about whether the existing rules and practices controlling the interplay between the legal–judicial system, the legislative–executive system, and the public results in the optimization of democratic norms, but the question about *whether* judicial lawmaking is democratic becomes much less important.

Judicial Discretion

When appeal court panels are split, it is frequently the case that neither the majority nor the minority decision can be held up as "the one right decision" according to an objective analysis of the law.[37] From a legal perspective, the majority decision is the enforceable one. Minority judges and judges writing separate concurring opinions also believe that their opinions are legally sustainable, and in most cases this is correct. Academics argue over which interpretation of the law is the most persuasive to them, but this discussion rarely demonstrates that there is one right answer to a particular question of legal interpretation.[38]

For example, consider the Supreme Court's decision on abortion in the *Morgentaler* decision of 1985[39]. The issue was whether Section 251 of the Criminal Code of Canada, the abortion section, violated the right of pregnant women to "liberty" or to "security of the person," both of which are guaranteed in Section 7 of the Charter of Rights. Section 251 prohibited abortions unless they were performed in a hospital designated by the provincial minister of health and approved by the hospital's abortion committee. The decision was heard by a seven-judge panel, and five of the judges decided that Section 251 was unconstitutional, but for three different sets of reasons. Altogether, then, there were four opinions delivered (three for Morgentaler and one against), and all of them are arguably legally correct.

Chief Justice Dickson and Justice Lamer concluded that Section 251 violated the procedural rights of women because "[f]orcing a woman, by threat of criminal sanction, to carry a foetus to term unless she meets certain criteria unrelated to her own priorities and aspirations, is a profound interference with a woman's body and thus a violation of security of the person." Justices Beetz and Estey agreed with this outcome, but would have found such a violation constitutional as long as the law was rationally designed to protect the fetus, which they concluded was not the case. Justice Wilson, the fifth judge writing for the majority, wrote that not only were the procedural rights of women violated, but their fundamental right to freedom of choice had also been negated. She said that "the basic theory underlying the Charter [is] that the state will respect choices made by individuals and, to the greatest extent possible, will avoid subordinating these choices to any one conception of the good life...." The two judges in the minority, McIntyre and LaForest, thought that the court should give more weight to some of the testimony in the courts below, which indicated that, in spite of the admittedly cumbersome wording of Section 251, "[n]one of the testimonies of medical doctors who had performed abortions produced examples of abortion applications ultimately refused, and no woman testified that her application for an abortion had been refused." Moreover, McIntyre and LaForest were of the opinion that because the Charter does not refer to abortion directly or indirectly, and because the framers of the Charter specifically rejected the urging of some interest groups to make such references, the Court ought not to disturb the judgment of Parliament.

All four decisions are compatible with the Charter of Rights and Freedoms because the Charter is worded generally and subject to varying interpretations. What is important to note is that the writer of each of the four opinions was obviously concerned with the value of mutual respect, but each emphasized different aspects of this value. Dickson and Lamer stressed the procedural rights of women; Beetz and Estey, the need to protect the foetus as well as the rights of women; Wilson, the freedom of choice owed to women; and McIntyre and La Forest, the evidence about the actual impact of the law, as well as the danger posed to democratic values by the Court unnecessarily extending its reach.

In holding that it is often the situation in hard cases that there can be a number of competing decisions that could all be considered theoretically "correct" according to law, we are not adopting a relativist perspective that holds that no particular ethical stance is better than any other. Nor are we assuming the view of legal positivism, which claims that standards of right and wrong are determined solely by elected legislatures, and the only role of judges is to accurately interpret the legislature's intent. Our position is that judicial decisions in hard cases can be placed on a continuum from excellent to poor, with the best decisions most in accord with the principle of mutual respect and the subprinciples associated with it.

With regard to the *Morgentaler* decision, three of us (Baar, Szablowski and Thomas) believe that the opinions of Dickson, Lamer and Wilson are more consistent with the principle of mutual respect and these decisions, taken together, deserve to be placed close to the excellent end of the continuum. First, unwanted pregnancy is an issue that effects pregnant women much more than anyone else. In such cases, mutual respect demands the recognition of "women's own priorities and aspirations" as paramount, except when they can be effectively accommodated with the express priorities and aspirations of others. Second, a judicial decision that enhances individual freedom of choice is, in principle, more democratic than the decision to enforce an existing legislative prohibition. If mutual respect is "the right of all individuals to develop their potential and to make choices about their lives without interfering with the similar right of others," then a criminal sanction limiting the exercise of this right is undemocratic unless the limit is demonstrably justified. In *Morgentaler*, the majority rejected as insufficient the justification advanced by those defending the abortion legislation in effect at the time. However, one of us (Greene), is more persuaded by the approach of Beetz and Estey because, although part of the majority, they at least make an effort to balance the respect that ought to be shown to women's priorities with respect for the unborn, a difficult issue that the other judges, for the most part, avoided because the law has never considered the fetus as a "legal person." Another of us (McCormick) leans toward the approach of McIntyre and La Forest because the legal process itself excludes too many factors that ought to be considered when thinking about how to apply mutual respect in a case like *Morgentaler*. The fact that we disagree among ourselves about which decision is closest to the "excellent" end of the continuum is not unlike the situation that judges on panels find themselves in when trying to decide among competing alternatives, all of which are arguably correct from a legal standpoint. There will always be debates about which are the "best" decisions. The genius of democracy is that it teaches us how to live with some degree of uncertainty; learning how to live with the openness of that uncertainty is essential to the preservation of mutual respect.[40]

To give due regard to the principle of deference to the majority, judges need to do their best to give effect to the intent of elected legislatures in their decisions, except when to do so would violate the principles of social equality, the protection of minority rights, and the fundamental freedoms as outlined in the Canadian Charter of Rights and Freedoms and the common law. Judges need to act with integrity, which includes attempting to be, and appearing to be, as impartial as humanly possible. From this perspective, judicial decisions are "right" to the extent that they pursue the sub-principles of mutual respect that underpin democracy. But there may be several right answers — answers that all attempt to implement mutual respect but are different from each other, perhaps because of different weights given to the sub-principles of democracy, as the *Morgentaler* decision exemplifies. The task of sorting through several potential "right" answers may seem less onerous when one considers that the number of potentially "wrong" answers is infinite.

The precise nature of a particular set of right answers developed by different judges may be determined by differences in their personality, values, or background and legal education, especially those aspects of their personal histories that affect how they reason and write about the nature of justice and democracy. Good judges may disagree about what constitutes the correct legal interpretation of a particular set of laws as applied to a specific factual situation, without this disagreement implying that any of them are incompetent or acting in bad faith.

We suspect that many Canadian judges, lawyers and legal scholars may not be as open as we are to the idea that there are often several possible solutions to legal dilemmas in hard cases that could all be considered potentially "correct." For example, our interviews with appellate court judges in the provinces and the Appeal Division of the Federal Court indicated that most of these judges were frustrated by the number of separate concurring decisions released in recent years by the Supreme Court of Canada. Our interviews with Supreme Court of Canada judges indicated that all those interviewed were aware of this desire in the lower courts for "one right answer," but the majority thought that it would be intellectually dishonest to move in that direction, because in most cases there were, in fact, several competing "correct" answers, and the development of the law is stimulated by exposing readers to alternate modes of reasoning.

Whether because of a need to deal with the problem of competing right answers with as much fairness as possible, given the need to settle disputes about the law, or because judges are human and will sometimes make wrong decisions, our judicial system has evolved so that what are usually considered to be the most important appeals are decided by panels of judges rather than one judge alone. These panels are composed of three or occasionally five judges in the provincial appeal courts, or by panels of five, seven, or nine judges in the Supreme Court of Canada. Several heads coming together to resolve controversial issues seems to make the decision more acceptable and persuasive, the more so when that decision is accompanied by the reasoned argument that supports and explains it.

The great majority of appellate decisions in Canada are unanimous. But dissenting, as well as separate concurring decisions, are acceptable. We suspect, however, that many jurists have been more heavily influenced by the legacy of the Diceyan notion of the rule of law than they might be willing to admit in casual conversation. A.V. Dicey was a late nineteenth-century professor of constitutional law at Oxford University who had an enormous impact on legal thought in the United Kingdom and other parts of the British Empire.[41] His writings on the nature of the rule of law provided the most thorough analysis of this important concept up to that time.[42] The basis of the rule of law is that public officials in democracies may act only according to laws authorized by elected legislatures and the law applies equally to everyone unless inequalities are built into the law itself. The rule of law is fundamental to any democracy because it reflects the principles of deference to the majority, equality, minority rights and freedom. However, Dicey developed a more specific version of the rule of law: First, there is ever only one "correct" interpretation of the law and, second, in countries that have adopted the British parliamentary system of government, superior court judges ought to have the final say as to the interpretation of the law, subject, of course, to amendment through legislation. Dicey had no time for separate administrative courts because they would allow several "right answers" to legal issues to co-exist in the separate court systems.

Thanks to the Diceyan tradition, voices in appellate courts that will not sing in unison are usually regarded either as exploratory attempts to find the right answer at the frontiers of legal reasoning or as necessary experimentation on the road to the right answer that will eventually materialize. Diversity is tolerated because it helps to "develop" the law to a higher state of correctness and justice. But, in our experience, there is little tolerance in the legal profession and especially in the Canadian public for the notion that several potentially different "right answers" can co-exist, except among some appellate judges, especially members of the Supreme Court.

In the debate about judicial discretion in Canada, the focus is on the extent to which judges — as opposed to elected politicians — ought to be involved in deciding important issues of public policy, rather than the *nature* of discretion itself. Our view is that because the nature of judicial discretion has not received enough careful analysis, the quality of the debate about the extent to which judges ought to exercise discretion over public policy issues has remained impoverished. Furthermore, we argue that judicial discretion plays a more significant role in the judicial process than is generally assumed. The common misconception that until the Charter of Rights and Freedoms, judicial discretion was so limited as to be nearly negligible is yet another reason for the poverty of the debate.

Extent of Judicial Discretion

Discretion is unavoidable in judicial decision-making in the following three situations. First, when the law is unclear, that is, in "hard" cases, judges must "legislate." This aspect of judicial discretion is now universally recognized, and, as already noted, the debate centres around whether, in a democratic setting, judges ought to pull back and legislate as little as necessary, or play a more activist role in order to deal with issues that legislatures are either too busy or too uninterested to handle.

Second, even when judges agree on the result, they have their own ways of getting to that result. No two judges, after hearing the same case, if locked in separate rooms would write exactly the same decision. For example, in the study of trial court decision-making conducted by McCormick and Greene, the authors found that trial court judges had four basic approaches to decision-making. We described the judges as "improvisers," "strict formalists," "pragmatic formalists," and "intuitivists."[43] We expected that these same approaches might be reflected in our interviews with appellate court judges, but, as we will show, because appellate decision-making is so different from trial court decision-making these "individualistic" discretionary factors were overshadowed by "collegial" discretionary factors.

Third, even in cases not considered "hard," different judges can give different weights both to factual and legal matters, and in some kinds of cases this different weighting can result in deciding the same kinds of issues in quite divergent ways. This aspect of discretion is illustrated by a study that Ian Greene conducted in 1990 of the "leave" decisions of judges of the Appeal Division of the Federal Court. At that time, part of the workload of these judges involved considering approximately two thousand applications per year for "leave" or permission to appeal that were filed by refugee applicants whose claims had been rejected by the Immigration and Refugee Board. The judges reviewed these claims singly, in their chambers. Each judge would consider one to two hundred of these applications a year, usually in batches of about fifty every few months. If the judges exercised little personal discretion, then we would expect that each judge would approve about the same proportion of leave applications, as long as there were no significant differences in the kinds of cases assigned to each judge. This was not what was found. As Table 1.1 shows, the average approval rate of the judges was 27 per cent. However, the "strictest" judge (who made 203 decisions) approved only 14 per cent of the applications, while the most "liberal" judge (who made 188 decisions) approved 48 per cent. The range of approval rates is nothing short of astounding.

When factors were tested that might explain the differences in the approval rates among the judges, such as the country of origin of the refugee applicants or the time period when the decisions were made, the differences among the judges remained.[44] A statistical test indicated negligible probability that the differences among the judges occurred by chance. Therefore, it was concluded that although the determination of merit was the major goal in the decision-making process regarding leave applications, it is possible for judges to give different weights to different relevant factors that affect conclusions about merit. The end result was that some judges appeared to be "stricter" than others in making decisions about applications for leave.

In addition, an independent expert was retained to conduct a "blind"[45] review of a random sample of 390 files. The expert would have approved about 35 per cent of the leave applications overall, as well as about 35 per cent of the cases from the dockets of *each* of the judges.[46] This is not to say that the independent expert's decisions were "right" and those of the judges were "wrong," but rather that when the same weighting of relevant factors is applied to all cases

					Table

Record of Dispositions: All Leave Applications

Leave Granted?	Pratte	Linden	Iacobucci	Stone	Décary	MacGuigan
Yes	29	20	20	33	57	69
%	14	16	18	21	22	23
No	174	101	92	125	200	228
%	86	84	82	79	78	77
Grand Total	2081*					

* Applications that were withdrawn by the applicant (44), dismissed for non-perfection (171) or were pending (1) were not included in this table. In addition, there were 7 files in which it was not clear which judge made the leave decision.

Significance of association = Less than .000005
Cramer's V = .23

through having the same person making the decisions, it appears that all the judges received about the same proportion of meritorious applications. There is no escaping the conclusion that given the same law and the same kinds of factual issues, some judges took a "strict" approach to granting leave to appeal, while others took a more "liberal" approach.[48]

There was also a test to find out whether the cases that received leave from the "liberal" judges fared worse at the substantive appeal, that is, the actual appeal considered by three judges of the Appeal Division of the Federal Court for the cases granted leave, than the cases that received leave from the "strict" judges. We were curious about whether the "strict" judges were better at screening out weak cases at the leave stage than the "liberal" judges. There was no statistically significant difference in rates of success in the substantive appeal between the cases granted leave by the "strict" and "liberal"

1.1[47]

Filed with Federal Court of Appeal in 1990						
Judge						
Hugessen	**Urie**	**Heald**	**Mahoney**	**Marceau**	**Desjardins**	**TOTAL**
59	16	43	60	73	90	569
27	28	30	36	44	48	27
157	42	98	105	92	98	1512
73	72	70	64	56	52	73

judges. Therefore, refugee applicants who were unfortunate enough to have their leave applications come before a "strict" judge may have had less access to justice in the long run than those who were lucky enough to have their applications come before a more "liberal" judge.[49]

The three discretionary factors we have described — that resulting from hard cases, that resulting from the decision-making and decision-justification process, and that resulting from giving different weights to relevant legal and factual matters — combine to make judging a very human process.[50]

Judicial Discretion and Democracy

In this chapter we have argued both that judicial discretion is not necessarily anti-democratic and that judicial discretion is a more important factor in decision-making in appellate courts than is generally recognized. This is not to say that we advocate that judges do, or ought to, depart from the law. On the contrary, we hold the rule of law to be an essential principle of democratic government. The law can usefully be thought of as a human instrument designed to promote the value of mutual respect. As such, there is often an array of potentially "right" answers to legal disputes, in addition to an infinite number of potentially "wrong" answers. The challenge of appellate courts is to weed out wrong answers from the courts below, while explaining why the particular answer that the court adopted was chosen as the best "right" answer from among competing alternatives.

In the chapters that follow, we analyse how the weeding and cultivating process of appeal courts works, using descriptions made by the judges themselves and an analysis of case flow from trial to appeal across Canada. However, precisely how judges choose to weed and cultivate depends to some extent on their backgrounds; in the next chapter we examine the backgrounds of Canadian appellate judges.

Personality and the Appellate Judge

The Chief Justice of New Brunswick was concerned that because one of his judges was ill, no interviews were scheduled for the last afternoon of Ian Greene's visit to Fredericton to interview the judges of the Court of Appeal of New Brunswick. On his own initiative, he arranged for Greene to interview a former chief justice in the time that had become available and also lent him his car to drive to the interview. (While driving out of the parking lot, Greene was almost arrested for stealing the Chief Justice's car.) It would be surprising if the Chief Justice's concerned and trusting nature was not reflected in some way in his judgments.

Biographies of judges are full of examples of how life experiences affect the views the judges hold about the nature of justice. For example, James McRuer, who was Chief Justice of the Ontario High Court from 1945 to 1964, was deeply committed to human rights, and aimed to ensure that the law would develop so as to serve the oppressed more effectively than in the past. His biography demonstrates that his passion for human rights and equality was connected with his experience growing up as a member of a poor, hard-working farm family that took religion and politics seriously. When he was fourteen, McRuer's father succeeded in pressuring the local school board to force an authoritarian schoolteacher to apologize for unfair discipline, leaving James with a poignant example of how, with persistence, justice could be done.[1]

Emily Murphy, an Edmonton social activist who became the first woman magistrate in the British Empire in 1916, had a deep interest in making decisions that were calculated to promote the rehabilitation of women and children who had run afoul of the law. She felt that her life experience prior to her appointment — for example, her love of intense discussions with the lawyers in her family about legal issues and her child welfare work — had been an ideal preparation for her role as a magistrate.[2] In a CBC interview in 1998, Madame Justice Beverley McLachlin mentioned how her own sense of justice had been shaped to some extent by the struggle of her fellow citizens of Pincher Creek, Alberta, to resolve a serious environmental problem related to sour gas when she was in high school.[3]

We are all products of the significant experiences that have helped to shape our values, work habits, and other aspects of our personalities. This chapter provides some general information about the backgrounds, training, and prior work experiences of appellate court judges in Canada and compares their backgrounds with those of elected officials and ordinary Canadians. From the perspective of the debate on democracy and judicial discretion, an interesting question is whether the judges' backgrounds might dispose them to use discretion differently than elected officials or ordinary Canadians would, were they in the judges' shoes.

For the sake of argument, let us imagine a democracy in which every citizen has precisely the same opportunity to become an appellate court judge. The most scientifically perfect system for the selection of a truly representative appellate judiciary might be to select a random sample of the population at birth, ensure that they are brought up as closely as possible to how they otherwise would be, but earmark them to become appellate judges. We will refer to this imaginary, perfectly representative group as the "imaginary representative judiciary."

Our background data about the appellate judges were obtained using a four-page questionnaire that we left with each of the appellate judges that we interviewed. We requested them to fill it out and send it back to us. Fifty-six judges did so, while another ten sent us their resumes instead, for a total of sixty-six responses out of 101 questionnaires. We also report some of the results of our interviews with appellate court judges in this chapter.

Gender

Canadian appellate judges are different from the imaginary representative judiciary in a number of ways that common sense would predict. Three-quarters are male, although the proportion of women judges on the appellate judiciary has been increasing steadily since the late 1970s. However, the overrepresentation of men in Canadian legislatures and cabinets tends to be about the same if not greater than the overrepresentation of men in the appellate courts.

Table 2.1

Percentage of Women Judges on Canadian Appellate Courts, 1997			
Court	# of Judges	# of Women Judges	% of Women Judges
Court of Appeal of Alta.	14	7	50
Court of Appeal of B.C.	17	6	35
Court of Appeal of N.S.	8	2	25
Court of Appeal of Sask.	8	2	25
Court of Appeal of Ont.	18	4	22
Supreme Court of Canada	9	2	22
Court of Appeal of Que.	21	4	19
Court of Appeal of Man.	8	1	13
Court of Appeal, Supreme Court of Nfld.	8	1	13
Federal Court of Canada, Appeal Div.	11	1	9
Court of Appeal of N.B.	6	0	0
Supreme Court of P.E.I., Appeal Div.	3	0	0
Total	131	30	23

Bertha Wilson was the first woman to be appointed to the Supreme Court of Canada, in 1982, sending a strong signal to women lawyers that women would henceforth be taken seriously as candidates for the highest echelons of the judiciary. At a public lecture at Osgoode Hall Law School at York University on February 8, 1990, she explicitly asked the question: do women judges approach the process of judging differently than men? She openly discussed "gender bias" in the courts and relied on studies conducted by University of California sociologist Norma Wikler that have shown that "in areas of tort law, criminal law and family law, gender difference has been a significant factor in judicial decision-making."[4] By 1988 a third of the judges on Canada's top court were women with the appointments of Claire L'Heureux-Dubé and Beverley McLachlin. But when Bertha Wilson retired in 1991, she was not replaced with a woman.[5]

Catherine Fraser became the first woman chief justice of a provincial appellate court in Canada when she became Chief Justice of Alberta in 1992. In 1996 the Court of Appeal of Alberta became the first appellate court in Canada where half the judges were women. Of the 132 Canadian appellate court judges in 1997, thirty, or 23 per cent, were women. However, the proportion of women on these courts varies enormously, from nearly half in Alberta and a third in British Columbia, to a quarter in Nova Scotia and Saskatchewan, to a fifth in Ontario, Quebec and the Supreme Court of Canada, to none in New Brunswick and Prince Edward Island, as shown in Table 2.1.

Age and Prior Experience

The average age of the appellate judges who completed our questionnaire is sixty-two, while the average age of adult Canadians is forty-five to fifty,[6] and the average age of MPs and members of provincial legislatures is also in this forty-five to fifty range.[7] A representative appellate court could not be much younger than the current Canadian appellate court judges are, if the current career path of appellate judges is considered appropriate. Even in European civil law jurisdictions, where the judicial career typically begins immediately after completion of specialized law training for judges, appellate judges have served for many years as trial judges prior to their promotion, and so they are somewhat older than trial court judges.

To be eligible for appointment to a superior trial court, or an appellate court, a candidate must have been a member of the bar for at least ten years. The 80 per cent of Canadian appellate judges in our sample whose pre-judicial career was primarily the practice of law spent on average fourteen years in private practice. The alternative pre-judicial career is an academic one, and nearly a fifth of the appellate judges had spent an average of fourteen years as a law professor prior to appointment as a judge. (A fifth of those who were appointed from private practice had also spent a year or more as a law professor.) Seventy per cent had experience on at least one court prior to their current position, and on average had spent nearly ten years on the lower court — typically the provincial superior trial court. Fifteen per cent of the judges had had experience on two lower courts prior to their current position.

A more important factor than age itself is career experience prior to becoming an appellate judge. Our conversations with judges during our interviews, and the anecdotes they related to us, underlined the importance of these prior experiences in affecting their approaches as appellate court judges. Several judges commented on how having practised for a number of years with lawyers of high reputation in a particular law firm had shaped their approach to particular issues. Nearly all of the judges with prior experience on a trial court commented on the value of that experience in being able to understand better the nuances of trials when interpreting the trial transcripts. The judges with academic backgrounds often mentioned how their academic research had shaped their approach to issues as diverse as the rights of the handicapped, gender equality, and *mens rea* (whether a criminal accused person has knowledge of a wrongful act).

Judges with significant experience as trial lawyers reported that the experience of presenting arguments before judges in court definitely affected their own approach towards appellate judging. They had gleaned examples of both "good" and "bad" styles of judging from observing appellate judges on the bench. The "good" judges were so described more for their personal qualities, such as patience, politeness, and openness to the arguments of counsel, than for their skills as legal practitioners. Often mentioned was the ability to signal to counsel, through questions in court, what the judges thought were the major issues that they wanted clarified during the hearing, as well as the ability to write clear and concise decisions. "Bad" appellate judges, on the other hand, were described as sometimes rude, impenetrable from the perspective of counsel in court, and poor writers.

Regarding the impact of previous experience, it is interesting that three-fifths of the appellate judges who had been legal practitioners considered themselves to have combined the roles of solicitor[8] and trial lawyer when in practice, while a quarter regarded themselves primarily as trial lawyers, and only 7 per cent said they had primarily been solicitors. Regarding areas of specialty, the judges had on average spent most of their time in a civil law practice (55 per cent), while criminal law accounted for about a third of their combined practice time, and administrative and family law the rest.

Judges come to court with a particular understanding of the law learned from their careers prior to appointment, and these careers nearly always involve a specialty in a particular area of law. In some provincial appellate courts, such as Ontario's, the chief justice takes into account this earlier experience when striking panels to try to ensure that at least one member of the panel is an expert in the area of law at issue. However, our data show that the chief justices who follow this model in striking panels may be short of judges with experience in criminal, administrative, or family law. In appellate courts like the Court of Appeal of Manitoba, where judges are selected for panels almost randomly, it is possible that there be no judges on a particular panel with significant experience in the area of law in question. However, our interviews indicated that few judges saw the lack of a relevant background specialty on a particular panel as creating a significant problem. Most Canadian appellate judges thought that any good judge can brush up on the relevant areas of the law that they need to know in order to make a good decision. Moreover, the judges often told us that lacking a specialty in the area of law relevant to a particular case can be seen as more of an asset than as a handicap, in that the judge is coming to that area of law with a fresh mind. It is interesting that the viewpoint about specialization on the English Court of Appeal is quite different. That court is divided into criminal, family, and civil sections, and judges are appointed to a section according to their background specialty.[9]

Admired Qualities

We asked the appellate judges what qualities judges have that earn the respect of fellow judges. Of the responses to this question, 30 per cent dealt with work-related skills, such as a good knowledge of the law, the ability to write well, promptness, and the quality of the reasoning — skills that we would take for granted that appellate judges ought to possess. A tenth of the judges said they admired other judges for their intelligence. However, 60 per cent of the judges' responses stressed the importance of personal qualities such as industriousness, honesty, humility, being collegial and helpful, and being compassionate and polite. The emphasis on personal qualities requires some explanation.

After completing our interviews, it was clear to us why the quality of industriousness was stressed so often. First, there is a need for every judge to be well prepared for each hearing. In every court we visited, stacks of materials were wheeled into judges' offices during the interviews by court officials; many of these stacks were one or two feet thick, or more, per case. We asked the judges how long they took to prepare for an average hearing, and the mean response was six and a half hours. However, the responses varied from one hour to forty hours, and there was a large variation in the range of responses on every court. Obviously, the judges cannot read every word of the factums, transcripts, and other supporting documents; they must focus on what they consider to be the most important points. If a particular judge does not pull his or her weight by being fully prepared for a hearing (either by spending too little time on each case, or too much time on some cases and too little on others), then that judge is not a terribly useful member of a panel. A number of judges mentioned to us that they frequently took files home on evenings and weekends to cram in as much preparation time as they could.

Second, there is a need for every judge to do his or her share of decision writing. In most courts, an important factor that the chief justice considers when assigning decision writing is who is available, meaning who is up-to-date with his or her decisions and ready to tackle another one. Judges who take inordinately long to write decisions are not always popular with their colleagues. It is obvious that the life of an appellate judge is anything but laid-back and unstressful, even in the less-busy courts. Appellate judges rely on each other to ensure that their court does a good job and maintains a good reputation with the bar and the public, and so it is no wonder in a collegial court that the quality of industriousness is so highly valued. We only encountered two or three instances where several judges in a court were clearly displeased with one of their colleagues for not working hard enough, but in these courts the judges may have valued their industrious colleagues more highly as a result.

When the judges said they valued honesty, they were not comparing honest judges with dishonest ones. Rather, they were referring to the willingness and ability of some judges to express their disagreement with their colleagues about particular questions of law with candour and clarity. It is not always easy to disagree openly with one's colleagues; it must be tempting at times to avoid what promises to be a difficult discussion in the conference after a hearing by remaining silent, and either pretending to agree with one's colleagues or writing a short but polite dissent or separate concurring opinion later on. But appellate judges tend to respect their colleagues more when they are open with their views and can express them in a way that is not self-righteous. Bora Laskin provides a good example of such a judge. Ian Greene conducted interviews with two retired Supreme Court judges in 1990 who had worked with Laskin, and both greatly admired his "brilliant" dissents, although they frequently disagreed with his reasoning. When Laskin saw things differently from the majority of his colleagues, he had the ability to express himself in a way that kept rekindling their respect for his intellect, without offending them.

The ability to express alternative viewpoints without offending is closely tied to another quality admired by the appellate judges — humility. In our earlier study that focused on trial court decision-making,[10] we found that according to the reports of the judges themselves, "judgitis" seemed to be as common as arthritis in their ranks. "Judgitis" is the term commonly used by judges themselves to describe a tendency to let the aloofness and high esteem of a judge's office cause a swollen ego. Any human being who finds himself or herself in a highly regarded and senior office is susceptible to developing a swelled head, and as we all know, it's not easy to work with someone who succumbs to this tendency. Therefore, the ability to resist developing a false sense of self-importance and maintain an attitude of humility is highly regarded by appellate judges.

Being "collegial and helpful" is closely related to the qualities of industriousness, honesty, and humility, but goes beyond these to include a personal dimension. The judges sometimes gave us examples of how their colleagues had supported them during a personal or family crisis, or how some of them had gone out of their way to find answers to a question about a legal issue casually mentioned at, say, lunch. As well, some judges mentioned to us that one or more members of their court — sometimes but not always including the chief justice — functioned as "social leaders" or persons whose personalities allowed them to promote good interpersonal relations on the court, boost morale during difficult times, and mediate occasional personality conflicts. That being "collegial and helpful" is so highly valued attests to the importance of good interpersonal relations in a small organization whose members spend so much time working with each other.

The quality of being compassionate and polite referred both to the way in which judges interacted with counsel and litigants in the courtroom and to their ability to empathize with people less fortunate than themselves. It seemed obvious to most appellate judges that in order for justice to be seen to be done well, litigants had to be treated justly, which meant with respect and requisite politeness. More than once when answering our question about admired qualities, a judge would describe a rude appellate judge before whom he or she had appeared as counsel. The respondent would then relate to us how little he or she thought of that judge and how important it was for appellate judges never to behave in such a manner. Even more important than surface politeness, however, was having real insight into the plight of the disadvantaged in society. Dry legal facts, several judges told us, cannot be properly understood without the ability to understand the social facts behind them. Compassion, to a judge, involves not only a broad knowledge of these social facts, but an openness to comprehend them and a willingness to try to understand situations from the perspectives of opposing litigants. We were told that this kind of compassion stems from a broad experience of life, and innate disposition. One-dimensional lawyers, law professors or trial judges who neglect their families and have few interests outside the law were not considered good candidates for a career as an appellate court judge.

Perhaps it is because the judges themselves realize the extent to which they have discretion that they stress the personal attributes of industriousness, honesty, humility, collegiality, and compassion so much. Current appointment procedures ensure that few, if any, who do not possess the requisite legal knowledge and experience will be considered for an appellate court position. But we are not so certain that the requisite personal qualities (requisite from the perspective of the judges themselves) receive the attention they deserve.

Law School

Before practice came law school, and the impact of the law school experience may be underrated by the judges we talked to. Few mentioned how their law school experience had shaped their approach to legal issues, although some mentioned the impact that specific law professors — perceived to be particularly able or wise — had had on them.

We suspect that law school has had an important impact. We teach courses about the political science study of law; a large proportion of our own students have gone on to law school, and we have made a point of keeping in touch with many of them. From what we have been told, law school is a major socializing event. Law school trains students to focus on the two factors that are important in the process of legal reasoning: statute law and judicial precedent. The broad-ranging analysis of social policy that our students learned from their political science courses becomes nearly irrelevant, and former students often complain that law school is too technical, emphasizing memory work and discouraging creativity. Yet most graduates of law school cannot help but be affected by the culture not only of law school in general, but by the particular approach of individual law schools. Law school in general is likely to impart the attitude that it is proper to decide issues taking into account only the factors that seem important from a legal perspective. Particular law schools will place different emphases on the importance of different lines of precedent. For example, professors at one law school may stress the merits of the centralist precedents in constitutional law courses, while professors at another may show a preference for the provincial rights precedents. But both law schools would place little weight on studies that analyse the impact that Supreme Court decisions on federalism have had on the Canadian economy or Canadian society, as these latter factors are considered non-legal.

The impact of the varying approaches of different law schools is not as obvious to judges as it might otherwise be because of the limited number of law schools in particular regions. Most members of the B.C. Court of Appeal, for example, were graduates of the UBC law school; the Alberta Court of Appeal was dominated by University of Alberta graduates, and Dalhousie graduates dominated the appeal courts in the Atlantic provinces. It was only in the courts of appeal in Ontario and Quebec, the Appeal Division of the Federal Court, and the Supreme Court of Canada that a particular law school did not account for the majority of members of the court, and in these courts the possible effect of different approaches to the law in different law schools was sometimes mentioned by the judges. The impact of differential legal training was often celebrated by the judges as bringing new insights into judicial decision-making.

The jury is out, however, regarding the impact of training in civil versus common law. On the two courts where some judges have had training in common law, and others in civil law — the Appeal Division of the Federal Court and the Supreme Court of Canada — we asked thirteen of the judges (seven on the Supreme Court) whether civil law judges have a different approach to the application of precedents. According to legal theory, common law judges ought to pay closer attention to matching relevant precedents to the cases before them, while civil law judges ought to place greater emphasis on the deductive reasoning process of applying general principles of particular situations. Only four judges (two on the Supreme Court) said that this legal theory described reality. Three concluded that the different training made very little difference, and five said it made no difference at all. Two of the judges who said that the civil law

training made an important difference were civil law trained Francophone judges, but two of those who said that training in civil law
made no difference at all were also civil law trained Francophones.
What these responses may indicate is that although a legal education
in common or civil law could possibly lead to differences in approaches to legal issues by the judges, it is a judge's personal choice
that determines to what extent the favoured paradigms of the law
schools are adopted by the judges and affect their decisions.

Ethnicity and Religion

We suspect that ethnicity and religion account for fewer of the
differences among the approaches of the current judges than might
be imagined. Of the judges, 90 per cent described their ethnic background either as "Canadian," or as French, English, Irish, or Scottish.
Four per cent said they were Jewish, and only 6 per cent said that
they were members of one of the more recent ethnic groups to arrive
in Canada. Only three judges reported that they had been born outside
of Canada, and one of these was born in the United States. Thus, it
is the "new Canadians," along with Aboriginal Canadians, who are
underrepresented on Canadian appellate courts.[11]

Ethnicity was not mentioned by a single judge as a cause of
differences of opinion about the law, and we suspect that this is
because, in fact, ethnicity does not explain differences of opinion
among judges from the more long-established ethnic groups. Ethnicity might make a difference, however, if there were a greater proportion of appellate judges from more recent immigrant groups. This is
because members of these groups would have lived through the
experience of becoming accepted as Canadians and everything that
entails — something that longer-established groups took for granted.
In this respect, elected members of Parliament and legislatures in
Canada are more representative of Canadians than appellate judges
are.

Three-quarters of the judges reported a religious affiliation, 40 per
cent with the Roman Catholic Church and a quarter with the major
Protestant religions. Six per cent said they were Jewish, and 5 per
cent said they were agnostic or had no religion. Thus, appellate
judges are broadly representative of the major religions in Canada,
as are elected parliamentarians. However, it is the general consensus
of the literature on Canadian judges that although religion might have
been associated with differences in judicial outcome decades ago,
this is no longer the case.[12] This does not mean that a predisposition

to religion is not a factor that affects judicial decision-making, only that *particular* religions may no longer make a difference.

If we assume that appellate judges need to follow a certain career pattern — a university education culminating in graduation from law school, followed by nearly twenty years in private practice or private practice and on a lower court — the main differences between the current Canadian appellate judiciary and the imaginary representative one, from the perspective of categorical indicators, are gender[13] and ethnicity, and these gaps are narrowing. (In one appellate court, the gender gap has closed.) However, to conclude that once the gender and ethnicity gaps are closed that Canadian appellate judges can be considered more or less representative would be shortsighted. If we look at orientation towards achievement, Canadian appellate judges are anything but representative.

High Achievers

Compared both with average Canadians and elected parliamentarians, Canadian appellate court judges are very high achievers. This propensity for achievement would set them apart in a number of respects from our imaginary representative judiciary,[14] and also (though to a lesser extent) from trial court judges and elected parliamentarians.

First, appellate judges have always tended to excel academically. Most undergraduate students know how difficult it is to get accepted into a Canadian law school without having at least a B+ average in two years of undergraduate work; law students therefore come from among the highest 10 per cent in achievement among undergraduate students, and they are certainly among the top 1 per cent of Canadians as a whole.[15] By way of comparison, about a third of Canadian MPs, and half of Canadian cabinet ministers,[16] have law degrees. A disproportionate number of non-lawyer MPs and cabinet ministers are business persons or professionals, but nevertheless in every legislature and Parliament, perhaps a fifth to a quarter of the elected members would not be considered exceptionally high achievers from an academic perspective.

Appellate judges tend to be among the highest achievers of law school graduates. For example, we asked the judges to list the significant awards and honours they had received. Only 10 per cent did not report anything significant. Most of the rest reported at least two significant awards, either for academic achievement or for exemplary community service. In addition to the mandatory law degree, 70 per cent had completed a bachelor's degree, 17 per cent a master's degree, and 9 per cent a doctoral degree. A third had been law professors or had participated actively in a teaching capacity in continuing legal education. A third listed one or more academic publications (books or academic journal articles), and only six reported that they had no publications, academic or otherwise. Moreover, a quarter had received honourary degrees — a symbol of esteem in the academic world.

If the education of appellate judges is compared with that of trial judges, Canadian cabinet ministers, Canadian MPs and members of provincial legislatures, appellate judges are the highest achievers of these four groups. Appellate court judges score higher on every measure of achievement and educational attainment than their superior and provincial trial court counterparts.[17] A third of Canadian cabinet ministers since the 1970s have had no education beyond an undergraduate degree, and a smaller proportion than the appellate judges have completed more advanced university degrees.[18] The average educational attainment of Canadian MPs and members of provincial legislatures is about midway between that of cabinet ministers and ordinary Canadians, and significantly below that of appellate judges.[19]

Appellate judges are not just bookworms — they tend to combine academic achievement with community service. Three-fifths listed one or more executive positions that they had held in a professional organization before becoming judges — most often in a provincial law society or in one of the bar associations — and a fifth had been a president or chair. Two-thirds listed community organizations in which they had been active, and 90 per cent had been members of community associations other than the professional associations. Nearly half of those who filled out the background questionnaire said they had been active or semi-active in a religious organization. In addition, they had all moved up in their firms when practising law; all who filled out the questionnaire said that they had become a partner or associate in their law firms.[20]

Forty per cent of Canadian marriages end in divorce,[21] but the divorce rate of appellate judges is much lower. More than 90 per cent of the appellate judges were or had been married; but only 7 per cent reported that they had remarried after a divorce *or* after having been widowed. Some may consider that the low rate of divorce among appellate judges is an achievement; it certainly sets them apart from the imaginary representative judiciary. Moreover, 90 per cent of the judges who were married had children, and two-thirds of these had three or more children.[22]

Political Affiliation

The proportion of appellate judges who previously held a political affiliation is much higher than in the general Canadian population. Sixty-two per cent reported that they had been a member of a political party at some time prior to judicial appointment, and a sixth of these reported having held an executive position in the party. A third said that they had been a candidate in an election — federal, provincial, or municipal — and six had served as a federal or provincial member of parliament.[23] In the general population, only 5 to 10 per cent have been members of a political party, and less than 1 per cent have ever run for a federal, provincial or municipal elected office.[24]

The tendency for appellate judges to have a history of political involvement might be viewed in a positive light as community service. It could more cynically be viewed as an attempt to position oneself for a judicial appointment, given the fact that patronage still plays a part in the appointment process — though much less now than it did several decades ago. We are inclined towards the former perspective. As noted above, 90 per cent of the appellate judges were active in their communities — and two-thirds were very active — in a number of respects not connected to partisan politics. In other words, nearly all appellate judges have played a community leadership role at some point in their lives, and for many of these this role was played out, in part, through service to a political party.

It likely comes as no surprise to federal ministers of justice — the people who recommend the appointments of the appellate judges in consultation with the Prime Minister — that most appellate judges place as much, if not more, emphasis on personal qualities as they do on legal expertise. Community service helps to develop these personal qualities, and to the extent that service to a political party can be considered community service, political party experience is not necessarily something that should be frowned upon in considering candidates for the appellate judiciary. As one judge we interviewed put it, "my colleagues who were active in politics seem to have a pretty good grasp on the day-to-day problems that ordinary people face. That's an important asset for a judge to have." It all depends on whether the appointment process treats political experience as just another form of valuable community service, or whether a particular party affiliation provides an advantage over another, or over otherwise more qualified candidates. Thus, it is important to consider the impact of the judicial appointment process.

The Appointment Process

Of the appellate judges, 70 per cent were promoted from trial courts or another appellate court; the other 30 per cent were appointed to an appellate court directly from law practice, or, occasionally, from a university position. When Pierre Trudeau was Minister of Justice in 1967, he initiated a system of consultation with the Canadian Bar Association for new federal judicial appointments. During his Prime Ministership, the office of the Minister of Justice developed more sophisticated methods of gathering the names of good potential candidates for federal judicial appointments than simply relying on the advice of top federal party officials in the provinces.[25] "New" appointments include appointments to the superior trial courts[26] (there are about 700 such positions in Canada) and appointments to the appellate courts that are not promotions from superior trial courts. A committee of the Canadian Bar Association would comment on whether candidates suggested by the federal Minister of Justice for judicial appointments (subject to the Prime Minister's input and approval) were qualified or not, and nearly always the cabinet would appoint only those deemed qualified. Patronage still played an important role, however, because those who got on the list in the first place were those acceptable to the minister. The review by the bar association did act, though, to screen out questionable patronage appointments.[27]

This system was revised by the Mulroney Conservatives in the 1980s, in an effort to catch up with the reforms made in the previous few years to the procedures for the appointment of provincial court judges. Most provinces had set up committees to screen judicial appointments, and these committees were more representative and systematic in their screening than the Canadian Bar Association system. The most thorough system, and arguably the best, was implemented in Ontario in the late 1980s by Attorney General Ian Scott. The fifteen-member committee that eventually resulted from Scott's reforms, and which was initially chaired by one of Canada's leading authorities on the judiciary, Professor Peter Russell, was composed of a nearly equal number of lawyers and non-lawyers, of men and of women. It advertised extensively for qualified persons to apply for judicial positions and was particularly proactive in encouraging women and members of minority groups to apply. Applicants had to fill out a comprehensive application form, and those who appeared to be best qualified were interviewed. The committee's recommendations were forwarded to the Ontario Judicial Council and from there to the Attorney General, and those appointed by cabinet were nearly always those recommended by the committee. Most appellate judges we interviewed thought that the quality of provincial court judges had increased during the previous decade, and clearly this was at least partly attributable to the new judicial appointments process.

As a result of the improvements at the provincial level, the federal government was pressured by lawyers' associations and interested members of the public to improve its system of judicial appointments, and the Ontario model was generally held up as one to emulate. The system that the Mulroney government devised represented only a small step in this direction. In each province, federal judicial appointments committees were established that included lawyers and non-lawyers, but their names were not made public and they were not given responsibility for recruiting candidates. All they could do was to react to names presented by the Minister of Justice. The Liberal election platform of 1993 included a promise to improve this system, and there have in fact been a number of enhancements since then. Advertising now occurs to encourage a broader range of applicants for the federally appointed judiciary, applicants must now fill out application forms that are remarkably similar to those used in Ontario, and the committees may interview applicants. (The federal government has promised to make public the names of committee members, although at the time of writing this has not yet occurred.)[28]

All but four of those in the appellate courts in our study received their initial judicial appointments during one of the periods described above.[29] It is important to note that only those appellate judges who were appointed "off the street" (the rather dramatic way the profession refers to those who are appointed without prior judicial experience) were screened by one of the federal appointments committees. Those elevated from a lower court — in recent years, the majority of appellate judges — do not go through a new screening process. Thus, the Minister of Justice is left with an enormous amount of discretion about elevations to an appellate court, as opposed to "off the street" appointments. And "off the street" appointments to the Supreme Court of Canada are not evaluated by any appointments committee, although officials in the office of the Minister of Justice collect a great deal of information about prospective Supreme Court appointees for the minister and the Prime Minister to consider.

The improvement in the appointments process to reduce the impact of patronage is a welcome development. Canadians deserve to have a judiciary composed of the most highly qualified candidates, not just the most highly qualified people from the current government's own political party. A survey in 1996 by Maureen Mancuso and her colleagues reported in *A Question of Ethics* found that only 4 per cent of Canadians approve a judicial appointments process that favours loyal party supporters; two-thirds of the remaining 96 per cent prefer judicial selection through a non-partisan committee. But one impact of the new appointment process has surely been to ensure that the courts are composed of an even higher proportion of high achievers than before the reforms.

Why Become a Judge?

One of the questions that we put to the judges was why they had accepted a judicial appointment in the first place. As well, we asked those who had held a prior judicial appointment why they had accepted the promotion to the appellate court. By far the most common response to both questions was that the challenge appealed to them. Several years earlier, McCormick and Greene had asked a sample of judges in Alberta and Ontario, who were primarily trial court judges, why they had accepted a judgeship. About a third said they had been "pushed" to the bench as an attempt to escape the stress of the practice of law, while about two-thirds said they had been "pulled" by the challenge or the prestige.[30] Only a tenth of the appellate court judges said they had been "pushed" to the bench. Of the remaining 90 per cent who were "pulled," a fifth were attracted by the honour of being an appellate judge, and the others were divided between those who were attracted by the challenge, and those who considered themselves duty-bound to accept the appointment when it was offered. It is noteworthy that more than 80 per cent of the appellate judges reported that their income had dropped after their appointment to the bench, and the average reported drop was 40 per cent. (In 1998, the puisne judges on the appellate courts earned $162,300 a year, and the chief judges and associate chief judges earned $177,700. Supreme Court of Canada judges earned $192,900, while the salary of the chief justice was $208,200[31]) It is interesting that the salaries of provincial appellate court judges are the same as those of superior trial court judges — a practice established in the days when appellate courts were not separate courts, but were made up of panels of judges from the superior trial court. Clearly, appellate judges are motivated more by career challenge than the desire for an even higher income.

We suspect that an imaginary representative judiciary would not be such high achievers as the current appellate judiciary in Canada. It is our view that appellate court judges are high achievers primarily because of the influence and opportunities provided by their parents and by the examples of family connections.

The Impact of Family

Children respond to the expectations of their parents, and clearly the parents of the those who eventually became appellate court judges not only had high expectations for their children, but usually also had the means to provide them with educational and developmental opportunities. Nearly half of the appellate judges' fathers, and 30 per cent of their mothers, had education beyond high school, which is much higher than we would find in an imaginary representative judiciary. (In 1986 only 21 per cent of Canadian men and 22 per cent of women had some postsecondary education;[32] these proportions would have been much lower in the 1930s and 1940s, when the appellate court judges were children.) A quarter of the fathers had obtained a bachelor's degree, two of fifty-six had graduate degrees, and another two had done some graduate work. More than half had been professionals or business persons, while only a sixth had been labourers or farmers.

Thus, the great majority of appellate court judges grew up in advantaged Canadian families. Because of the status, income, and educational level of their parents, they undoubtedly had numerous opportunities to develop their skills and talents, through, for example, music classes and opportunities to participate in sports events that had extra costs attached.[33] But it was not just having relatively privileged parents that contributed to the appeal court judges' propensity for high achievement. They also had the example of other family members. Nearly half of the appeal court judges reported having judges as part of their extended families (father, uncle, cousin, sibling, or in-law), and two-thirds reported lawyers in their extended families. As well, the appeal court judges' parents had often been active in community affairs, with some having been cabinet ministers, deputy ministers, or mayors.

Not only did appeal court judges generally grow up in families that presented ideal opportunities for high achievers, but they had the careers of other family members to aspire to. Very few of our imaginary representative judiciary would have ended up in families with such opportunities for high achievement.

A Representative Judiciary?

It should be kept in mind that it will never be possible, or even desirable, to select an appellate judiciary that has a more average approach to achievement. Appellate judges in our complex legal system require a certain skill set that is not likely to be obtained by any but the highest achievers. The point is that if there has been a shift of policy-making responsibilities from parliamentarians to appellate judges because of the Charter of Rights and Freedoms, then knowing about the backgrounds of judges might help to explain why and how the policy decisions of appellate judges are different from those of an imaginary representative judiciary, or from elected members.

We might suppose that the policy preferences of an imaginary representative judiciary would be similar to those of the average Canadian, as represented by opinion polls. The policy preferences of elected members are exemplified by the legislation they approve, while the policy preferences of the appellate judiciary — where they differ from those of elected members — are represented in part by the decisions in which legislative enactments, or parts of them, are struck down.

Elected members do not have the luxury of straying very far from public opinion polls, even if they would like to, because of the simple truth that politicians generally want to get re-elected. The fact that elected members, do on occasion, take positions that they know are unpopular — capital punishment is a good example — indicates that conscience and personal values can play an important role in the public policy process in legislatures, just as they do in some appellate decisions. The judiciary does not need to worry about re-election, although at least some judges believe that it is dangerous to stray too far from popular sentiment.[34]

Appellate judges are older than the average Canadian, and among the highest achieving Canadians, with a history of greater-than-average involvement in community and political organizations. They are more representative of men and the established Canadian ethnicities than of women and the less-established groups. Elected members have similar unrepresentative characteristics, but appellate judges are even higher achievers, and the problem of the underrepresentation of women appears to be correcting itself more rapidly among the appellate judiciary than among elected representatives.[35]

Taking into account both the backgrounds of appellate judges and the fact that judicial independence gives them an unparalleled freedom to decide, the appellate judiciary seems relatively well positioned to provide a "sober second thought" review to the decisions of elected members. They are certainly better positioned to do so than is the current Canadian Senate. That judges have a history of community involvement, combined with a record of high achievement, is an asset. Appellate judges are in a good position to give social problems a thorough and thoughtful consideration, and because of their intellectual prowess are well situated to take into account the complex factors that determine social issues. On the other hand, the current underrepresentation of women and of the less-established ethnic groups is a problem, but with the gradual improvement in appointment procedures, these obstacles might well be tackled sooner among appellate judges than among elected members.[36] There is also the danger that because appellate judges are such high achievers, and because they tend to grow up in advantaged families, they may not understand the problems of average Canadians as well as we might hope.

It is critical to understand that the differences in policy preferences between the appellate judiciary and elected members are a function not only of differences in personal backgrounds, but also of differences in decision-making procedures and institutional settings. In the next chapter we describe the nature of the cases that end up in the laps of appellate judges, and in Chapter 4 we review the procedures that the various appellate courts have developed to process these cases.

3

The Appellate Process

In this chapter we discuss the business of the Canadian appellate courts: the nature and volume of the cases they handle. As well, we analyse the flow of these cases through the courts. We highlight the similarities and differences between provinces in the volume of criminal and civil appeals brought to those courts, and the flow of appeals from initiation to hearing. If the discretion of judges and lawyers played no part in the appellate process, we would not expect to find significant differences from province to province in patterns of case flow or the proportions of criminal and civil appeals. Variations that do emerge, particularly in criminal appeals that arise under the same Criminal Code throughout Canada, suggest the importance of differing provincial practices and legal cultures.

From Trial to Appeal

It is important to understand the context in which appeals arise. This chapter will focus on the work of the "first appeal" courts — the ten provincial appeal courts and the appeal division of the Federal Court of Canada — because these courts primarily hear appeals "as of right" rather than "by leave." It is considered a matter of fundamental fairness in legal systems throughout the world that the party who loses at trial — whose case does not succeed in the court of first instance — is entitled to an appeal.[1] Sometimes the appeal is in the form of a trial *de novo* (new trial), especially if the court of first instance keeps no verbatim record of its proceedings or is staffed by a lay (non-lawyer) judge. Sometimes the appeal involves a rehearing of evidence presented at trial. In Sweden, for example, both trial and appeal courts meet in panels that include a combination of legally trained judges and lay assessors. Sometimes — and this is the typical pattern in Canada, Australia, England, and the United States — appeals are confined to questions of law arising out of the trial and do not extend to factual determinations. In these jurisdictions, trial judges, who actually see and hear the witnesses, are in a better position to judge the facts than an appellate judge who must rely on transcripts.

The losing party certainly does not appeal in every case, or even in most cases. Two factors make appeal cases much smaller in number than cases in trial courts. First, most cases completed in trial courts are not, in fact, completed as a result of a full adversary trial. For example, both sides may agree on the outcome. In civil cases, this is simply referred to as a settlement agreement between the parties. In criminal cases, the more specific term often used is "plea bargain." Furthermore, many cases brought to trial courts are abandoned, either when a plaintiff in a civil case does not serve his, her, or its claim on the defendant, or when a Crown attorney in a criminal case drops the charges against an accused. Finally, many cases are uncontested, as when a plaintiff in a civil case wins a default judgment after the defendant does not respond, or when a petition for divorce is granted when the other party does not challenge it, or when an accused person enters a plea of guilty to a criminal charge without any prior discussion of the sentence with the Crown attorney. In all, less than 5 per cent of all civil claims and less than 10 per cent of all criminal cases go to trial. So the cases in which a losing party is likely to appeal are few in number.

Second, a majority of trial decisions where there is a full adversary trial are not appealed. While the losing party has a right of appeal, a number of factors combine to discourage the exercise of that right. Appeals add to the cost of the litigation. While legal aid is available for persons who wish to appeal their conviction for a criminal offence, it is not automatic. Throughout Canada, legal aid agencies are under increasing budget constraints, and they will screen requests for assistance to see whether the convicted person has a strong enough case to justify the cost of a lawyer and the preparation of a trial transcript (often one of the major expenses). Even parties that can afford to appeal will consult first with their lawyer (counsel), and one of the duties of counsel is to make the client aware of the probability of succeeding on appeal. The client can proceed even if counsel thinks success is unlikely, but that response is not typical.

Despite these barriers and filters, well over ten thousand cases are appealed every year across Canada. While trial judges make every effort to conduct their trials in a way that does not raise legal objections by either party, many trials require rulings on questions of law that are important enough to the parties that even the most conscientious and fully researched conclusions of the trial judge will be

Table 3.1

Civil and Criminal Appeals Filed, 1990, 1995, and 1997

Province/Court	Civil Appeals			Criminal Appeals		
	1990	1995	1997	1990	1995	1997
B.C.	1,263	1,284	1,122	536	590	580
Alta.	674	669	613	1,007	759	580
Sask.	326	314	269	389	269	279
Man.	228	289	215	248	184	204
Ont.	904	1,321	1,229	2,090	1,543	1,225
Que.	2,750	2,556	—	669	667	—
N.B.	263	210	—	—	119	—
P.E.I.	36	33	31	47	—	20
N.S.	194	163	203	214	132	92
Nfld.	106	—	122	87	—	81
Federal Court	1,068	857	943	N/A	N/A	N/A
Totals	7,812	7,696*	4,747	5,287*	4,263*	3,061

Source: Canadian Judical Council's annual statistics on delays. Quebec Court of Appeal figures for 1995 were not included in the Council report, but were prepared by the clerks of that court in Montreal and Quebec City.
*Given missing data, "totals" are less than actual total for the year.

appealed. For example, a trial judge interviewed by Carl Baar for an earlier study recalled that in his early days on the bench, he would often reserve judgment and study the matter for many days before rendering a decision on a question of law. "Now I decide quickly. That's what the parties want. If they want the right answer, they'll appeal — especially when my decision was right in the first place."

Table 3.1 shows the number of civil and criminal appeals filed in each provincial court of appeal and in the Federal Court of Canada in 1990, 1995, and 1997, as reported by those courts to the Canadian Judicial Council. We caution that the number of appeals filed does not necessarily reflect workload. As we show in Chapter 8, cases collapse at different rates across the provinces; a high rate of filing may mean that litigants in some jurisdictions have more funds available to file frivolous appeals. With this caution in mind, and although some data are missing, it is possible to make several general observations:

- First, civil appeals consistently outnumber criminal appeals. The overall national ratio varies from year to year. It is as low as 1.5 to 1, and as high as 1.8 to 1. That the Federal Court hears only civil and not criminal appeals accentuates the difference, but even when examining the provincial appellate courts alone, civil cases outnumber criminal cases by ratios that range between 1.2 to 1 and 1.6 to 1.[2]

- Second, the total number of civil appeals across the country appeared relatively stable during the 1990s, despite fluctuations within individual provinces. Between 1990 and 1997, three provinces experienced increases (Ontario, Newfoundland and Nova Scotia), while five provinces and the Federal Court of Canada experienced declines. But within these jurisdictions, appeals increased and then decreased in some (Ontario and Manitoba), and decreased and then increased in others (Nova Scotia and the Federal Court of Canada). Three provinces recorded declining numbers of civil appeals each time (Alberta, Saskatchewan and Prince Edward Island).

- Third, the number of criminal appeals appears to have declined substantially across the country. While British Columbia shows an overall increase of 8 per cent, the other seven provinces for which both 1990 and 1997 figures are available all show declines, and many of those declines are substantial: 57 per cent in both Nova Scotia and Prince Edward Island, 42 per cent in Alberta, 41 per cent in Ontario and 28 per cent in Saskatchewan.[3]

There are a number of possible explanations for this decline. It could be that the number of criminal charges has declined. However, there is no evidence to support this. A review of Ontario data shows Criminal Code charges received by the Provincial Court[4] in the 1989–90 fiscal year stood at 390,394, and in the 1996–97 fiscal year remained at 393,426. The numbers fluctuated both above and below those figures in the intervening seven years. Charges under the Narcotics Control Act (a federal statute separate from the Criminal Code) went from 32,762 in 1989–90 to 30,268 in 1996–97, and were usually lower in the interim.[5] While other provinces may not exhibit the same pattern, the stable number of criminal charges coming into the original trial court in Ontario by itself strongly suggests that the 41 per cent decline in criminal appeals requires a different explanation.

Two other explanations deserve further study. First, it may be that government cutbacks in legal aid funding have reduced the number of criminal appeals. The expense of preparing trial transcripts adds further to the cost of appeals, and legal aid bodies typicaly screen applications for appeal to ensure that the expense is justified. At the same time, if cost constraints alone account for the decline in criminal appeals, it would be regrettable that defendants who might otherwise go to appeal are denied the opportunity, especially if changes in reporting and recording technology and practice could reduce transcript preparation costs.

Second, it may be that the decline of criminal appeals is related to changes in criminal practice at the trial court level. On the prosecution side, Criminal Code amendments between 1990 and 1995 increased the number of offences in which the Crown could proceed by summary conviction rather than by indictment, reducing in turn both the maximum penalties for those offences and the ability of accused persons to obtain trials by jury. To the extent that prosecutors try more offences before a provincial court judge rather than a superior court judge and jury, fewer appeals may arise. On the defence side, there is evidence that after merger of trial courts in Ontario, British Columbia, and Nova Scotia in the early 1990s, persons charged with indictable offences (crimes with higher potential penalties) were increasingly likely to elect trial in provincial court rather than trial by judge and jury in a superior court.[6] It may also be that the proportion of criminal cases disposed of by a plea of guilty rather than a full trial has increased; in fact, it has been government policy in Ontario since 1994 to encourage early pleas of guilty.[7]

Some of these changes may also be related to financial constraints surrounding legal aid, this time at the trial rather than at the appelate level. While Ontario data show that there has been no decline in criminal charges in the 1990s, there may have been a decline in the total number of full criminal trials, or the number of superior court trials, or the number of jury trials, or a combination of all three — any of which could contribute to the decline in criminal appeals.

The fourth and last observation about Table 3.1 is that the ratio of civil to criminal appeals varies sharply from province to province. In

British Columbia, civil appeals are double criminal appeals, while in Quebec, civil appeals outnumbered criminal appeals by four to one. Conversely, criminal appeals outnumbered civil appeals in Ontario in 1990 by over two to one, and were virtually identical in 1997. Alberta showed a similar but more moderate pattern, with criminal appeals 50 per cent higher than civil appeals in 1990, and slightly lower than civil appeals by 1997. Saskatchewan and Manitoba have no pattern — civil appeals are lower one year and than higher the next.

There are a number of possible explanations for these interprovincial differences, and a review of those hypotheses will highlight some important characteristics of appellate adjudication in Canada.

First, it is essential to remember that while we refer to some courts as trial courts and others as appeal courts, the division of labour is not as sharp or as uniform as the names suggest. On the criminal side, for example, while appeals from convictions and sentences for indictable offences (more serious crimes, analogous to felonies in England and the United States) go directly from trial courts to the provincial court of appeal, appeals from trials for summary conviction offences (less serious crimes, analogous to misdemeanours, but punishable in many matters by up to eighteen months in jail) are heard initially by a trial judge in the provincial superior court. Only after that hearing can the losing side take an appeal to the provincial court of appeal, and that second appeal is not a matter of right, but is available only by leave of the court. Similarly, provincial offences, for example, traffic tickets, liquor law violations, and environmental offences, are also appealed first to a trial judge sitting alone.[8] That summary conviction offences and provincial offences are appealed first to a judge in a trial court is one of the key reasons why there are fewer criminal appeals than civil appeals in the provincial appellate courts, and the prosecutor's increased authority to use summary conviction procedures in the 1990s may therefore account for the general decline in criminal appeals across Canada.

On the civil side, even small claims are appealed from the trial judge directly to the provincial court of appeal, with one important exception. In Ontario any civil appeal involving less than $25,000 goes not to the Court of Appeal, but to a court known as the Divisional Court of Ontario. The Divisional Court is in fact made up of superior court judges — trial judges of the Ontario Court of Justice (General Division) — who sit in panels of three for the purpose of hearing appeals from administrative tribunals and appeals in some kinds of civil cases.

Ontario's Divisional Court was given appellate jurisdiction in some civil cases precisely to reduce the case load of that province's appellate court. The reduced number of civil cases heard in the Court of Appeal for Ontario partly explains why Quebec and British Columbia's civil appeal case loads are so large when compared with the case load in Ontario, despite Ontario's larger population. For the three fiscal years from 1989 to 1992, the Divisional Court received 857, 796, and 913 civil appeals, enough to bring Ontario's total civil appeals close to the 2,090 criminal appeals heard in 1990 (as shown in Table 3.1). Given this large share of civil appeals that do not go directly to the Court of Appeal, the substantial growth in the Ontario Court of Appeal's civil cases from 1990 to 1995 — an increase of over 40 per cent, the largest in Canada — may reflect that the monetary limit of $25,000 has remained the same while the size of judgments has increased.[9]

Even with this adjustment in Ontario, however, the mix of civil and criminal cases in its appeal court is quite different from the mix in Quebec and British Columbia. Why? Another factor that may affect the case mix in provincial courts of appeal is their handling of sentence appeals. One of the most important tasks of provincial appeal courts in Canada is to review the length and nature of sentences given by trial courts. Convicted persons may not only appeal a verdict that they are guilty, but they also argue that, regardless of their guilt, the sentence imposed by the trial judge is too harsh. Furthermore, the Crown can also appeal that a sentence is too lenient. In contrast, review of sentences by appellate courts is virtually unknown in the United States, in spite of frequent controversy over both the nature and the length of individual sentences in that country's courts.

Some judges and lawyers we interviewed believe that appellate judges approach sentence appeals differently from province to province. Quebec and British Columbia are sometimes mentioned as less willing to alter the sentence imposed by the trial judge. We sometimes heard that in Quebec, unless an argument can be made to the appellate court that the sentence imposed by the trial judge is either at least twice as long or, at most, half as long as it ought to be, the case should not be appealed. Conversely, Ontario is are seen as more amenable to making smaller changes in sentences, or, in the words of some lawyers who criticize this practice, the appeal court in

Ontario tends to "tinker" with the trial judge's sentence.[1] In Ontario it is said that if a sentence appeal takes a long time to be heard, and the accused has only a few months left on his or her sentence, the court will reduce the sentence to time served.[11]

While different sentencing practices may encourage more appeals in one province than in another, the differences highlighted here do not explain why Quebec would have more civil appeals than the combined total in both the Divisional Court and Court of Appeal in Ontario, given the fact that Ontario's population is more than 30 per cent greater than Quebec's. One plausible explanation is that in Quebec's system of civil law, the judgments of an appellate court are not binding on trial courts as precedents in future cases. Appellate judgments do contribute to the clarification of "doctrine," but this indirect impact is different in theory from the binding character of appellate judgments in the common law provinces. The less robust body of precedent may mean that the appropriateness of the trial judge's decision is more likely to be questioned.

At the same time, however, the Quebec Code of Civil Procedure requires that trial judges prepare written reasons for judgment in cases under the Code. No similar requirement exists for civil cases in other provinces, where written reasons are provided in onl a minority of cases. This requirement has meant that judges of the Superior Court of Quebec sit in court only two weeks out of every four in order to prepare their judgments, while superior court judges in other provinces[12] sit in court for three weeks out of every four. The effect of this difference is not clear. It may be that the existence of written reasons following a trial in Quebec encourages appeals by providing more opportunities for the losing party to construct an effective legal argument in the Court of Appeal. Or, it may be that explicit written reasons effectively address what would otherwise have been grounds for appeal.

While practices in Quebec may explain why there are more civil appeals per capita there than in Ontario, we would expect the same difference to be seen when comparing Quebec with other common law provinces. Yet the rate of civil appeals in British Columbia is just as high, per capita, as the rate in Quebec.[13]

It is clear that one of the factors that affects the varying volumes of appeals is the thinking of the judges on a particular court about what structures are best to handle the appeal case load, and whether it is best to take a stricter or a more lenient approach to the particular issues. For example, consider the approach of the Ontario appellate courts to sentence appeals. The greater willingness of the judges to contemplate smaller changes in sentences than of judges in the other provinces may have led to a higher volume of sentence appeals. As well, the Alberta appeal court has developed a policy of "starting point sentencing," meaning guidelines set out in case law that indicate the appropriate length of sentences for certain offences, given particular situations. This policy may have led to a higher volume of sentence appeals in Alberta because of concern from either the convicted person or the Crown that that trial judge did not apply the starting point sentence appropriately.

This particular explanation of how different approaches to sentence appeals may affect case loads suggests a broader lesson about the fundamental importance of judicial discretion. It is a truism about courts and judges that they cannot choose their work. Constitutions and legislatures set the parameters of their jurisdiction, what kinds of cases they can hear, and what issues they can deal with in those cases. The parties determine what cases they must hear, and what issues they are asked to address. The Supreme Court of Canada could not enter into the national debate on Quebec secession if that issue had not been placed before it by the parties in a case. Conversely, the court cannot avoid this issue once a party (in this case, the federal government) has invoked the court's jurisdiction (in this case, by sending specific legal questions to the court as a reference under the Supreme Court Act of 1875) and brought the case forward. From this perspective, the courts are passive recipients of cases brought before them.

Interprovincial differences in the volume and handling of sentence appeals suggest that this passive view of the courts' workload is too simplistic. By their very decisions and practices, appellate judges signal to litigants a willingness or unwillingness to respond to certain types of claims. Thus, while the flow of incoming cases confines the discretion of judges, the discretion that judges exercise within those confines can expand or contract the flow of future cases.

While our analysis of sentence appeals attributes some part of the differences between Ontario and Alberta on one hand, and Quebec and British Columbia on the other, to the effect of individual judges' views and behaviour, that explanation by itself is also too simplistic. To say that judicial discretion is important and the law is not formal and monolithic is not to say that every judge follows his or her own private muse. Differences from one appeal court to the next are more than the sum of their parts. They go beyond the aggregate differences between individual judges who sit on those courts at any particular time. They represent the accumulation of formal and informal practices nurtured or resisted by appellate judges over a period of many years. In turn, these appellate practices are encouraged or resisted by the lawyers and trial judges who are affected by them. The reactions of lawyers and trial judges, in turn, may affect the thinking of the appellate judges about these practices.

Scholars have increasingly come to refer to these practices in a court as the "legal culture" of a court and its community. This term was first popularized by a study of trial court delay in twenty-one urban trial courts in the United States, and was used to explain why judges and lawyers in one city found a certain pace of litigation normal and even inevitable, while judges and lawyers in another city found the same pace of litigation unacceptably slow. These diverse expectations were labeled the "local legal culture."[14] Canadian provincial appellate courts clearly vary in their legal cultures, for example with regard to the expectations of the judges and lawyers about how sentence appeals should be dealt with. In turn, a court's legal culture evolves and changes as individual judges both adapt to and alter the norms and expectations of their courts over time. Thus, the exercise of discretion by individual judges must be placed in context, as both a dependent and an independent variable. We need to understand the factors associated with the exercise of judicial discretion, and the impact or results of its exercise.

As well, different systems are in place in the various provinces for handling the total appeals case load; Ontario has shifted part of its appellate case load to a divisional court made up of erstwhile superior court trial judges. In Alberta, the appellate judges support the concept of trial court judges sitting on an ad hoc basis with appellate sentencing panels, and the appellate judges in Alberta have told us that they have benefitted from being able to "keep in touch" with the thinking of trial judges about sentencing policy. But, as we show in Chapter 4, this view is definitely not shared by most other Canadian appellate judges.

Thus, structural changes and assignment practices are themselves shaped by the legal cultures of the various provinces. In Ontario, there has been for decades a sharp division between superior court trial judges and appellate judges. In order to cope with extreme case load pressures, Ontario's judges were willing to support the shift of a segment of cases from the Court of Appeal to a divisional court made up of a series of panels of three superior court trial judges. In

Alberta, superior court trial judges and appellate judges were considered to be divisions of the same superior court prior to structural changes in the late 1970s. In the old system in Alberta, there was less social distance between appellate and trial judges and more joint activity. In that setting, Alberta's judges were ready to support the shift of judges from trial to appeal panels on temporary assignment, rather than a shift of cases to a divisional court, as in Ontario. Not surprisingly, past formal structures and operating practices have shaped present institutions and methods.

The human factors that contribute to the diverse ways judicial discretion is exercised may also increase the complexity of relations between court structure and court operations. The pre-1980 example in Alberta of a single court with appellate and trial divisions parallels the present Federal Court of Canada, with its Trial Division and Appeal Division. Under the Federal Court's first chief justice in the early 1970s, Wilbur Jackett, the two divisions often exchanged judges to ensure that both trial and appellate work would be handled expeditiously. When the court expanded in the 1980s, the exchange of judges occurred much less often. Recent controversies in the Federal Court between trial and appellate judges, especially regarding the handling of cases involving accused war criminals, show sharp differences and even animosities that would not have been anticipated a generation ago.[15]

The point is that structural innovations like the Divisional Court in Ontario, or trial judges sitting ad hoc with appellate sentencing panels as in Alberta, are unlikely to come about without the tacit approval of a substantial number of the judges, and so judicial discretion plays a role in determining appellate structures.[16]

But the impact of the views of judges is only one of many factors that affect the volume and flow of cases. For example, available evidence points to the cuts to legal aid budgets as having had a big impact on reducing the volume of criminal appeals across Canada during the early 1990s, a change the judges had nothing to do with. Nevertheless, we wish to underline that the impact of the judges' views about how the appeal case load ought to be handled has not received enough attention in the literature on court administration.

The Funnel of Appeals

What is the relationship between appeals filed and appeals decided, and is this relationship connected in any way with judicial discretion? We are familiar with the phenomenon that most cases filed in the

Table 3.2

When Criminal Cases are Disposed of in Provincial Courts of Appeal

	#	%
Before documents are filed	1,249	43.5
After documents are filed but before the hearing is completed	127	4.4
After hearing	1,498	52.1
Total	2,874	100

trial courts are settled rather than tried, whether that settlement re-sults in a plea of guilty in a criminal matter, an agreed-upon payment in a civil matter, or an agreement on terms of custody and access in a divorce. Does anything comparable happen in appellate courts? The Supreme Court of Canada, like its U.S. counterpart (and the courts of last resort in many other countries), gets to choose its cases and denies leave to appeal to a large majority of those who bring matters before it.[17] The other appellate courts in Canada are, for the most part, courts of first appeal, and our legal tradition assumes that the losing party in a trial court is entitled to one appeal as of right — the opportunity to argue its case in a second neutral forum.

Thus, we would expect that an appellant who files a first appeal and has the right to be heard will typically move the case forward to a hearing. In fact, this view is mistaken. As shown in Table 3.2, a healthy proportion of appeals in criminal cases — 47.9 per cent of our national sample — drop out before the hearing is completed, and fully 43.5 per cent drop out before the documents needed for hearing are even filed. Thus, in the language of Canadian appellate courts, more than two out of every five appeals are not "perfected"; that is, factums summarizing the legal arguments of both sides, and an appeal book containing a copy of the trial transcript and photocopies of key precedents or "authorities" on which the contending lawyers will base their arguments, are never submitted.

The data on civil appeals that were part of our national sample suggest that in some provinces an even higher proportion of civil appeals drop off, including as many as two-thirds of the civil appeals filed in British Columbia.

We can therefore observe in the appeal courts of the various provinces the filtering out of appeals and their disposition by means other than a full hearing and a judgment by a panel of judges. As in trial courts, although apparently not in as high a proportion, appeals drop off along the way, so that a chart plotting their progress would resemble what Ernest Friesen, describing this pattern in the United States, termed a "reverse telescope."

Why do appeals get dropped so often? In some respects, it reflects the very nature of the appellate process. The rules for launching an appeal are determined by each province, but they always require that an appeal be filed within a short period of time, typically thirty days, after the trial court's judgment. This provides winning parties with the assurance that they can make life or business decisions in accordance with the holding of the court. It also means that losing parties may find themselves filing an appeal in order to preserve their options, but before doing a thorough analysis of whether there are adequate grounds for appeal.

For example, in criminal cases it is not unusual for an appeal to be prepared and argued by different lawyers than those who conducted the trial. Provincial prosecution departments normally assign appeals to a central legal office, after the trial is conducted by the Crown attorney's office in the local county or region. Even the defence bar has become increasingly specialized, with trial lawyers seeking out appellate counsel for their clients. In the process, the appellate specialists may not have the opportunity to review the case critically until after trial counsel have filed a notice of appeal.

As noted earlier, the legal aid screening procedure has become increasingly important in filtering out appeals by persons convicted and sentenced for an offence, as fiscal constraints lead to tougher assessment of the chances for success on appeal. Critics of legal aid, however, say that this type of assessment was more widely made before the expansion of legal aid provided a financial basis for lawyers to argue that individuals should have a broad scope to appeal their conviction and sentence. On the Crown side, fiscal constraint would be expected to play a role as well, but Crown appeals have always been less frequent than appeals from defendants. Crown counsel usually give more weight to the implications that an appellate ruling might have for future cases. In other words, the concern is for development of law as well as correction of error.

Table 3.3

Stage When Criminal Case Dispositions Occurred in Courts of Appeal, by Province

Province	Before Documents		After Documents		After Hearing		Row Total
	#	%	#	%	#	%	#
B.C.	217	48.4	43	9.6	188	42.0	448
Sask.	75	27.7	1	0.4	195	72.0	271
Man.	57	21.6	6	2.3	201	76.1	264
Ont.	471	58.3	3	0.4	334	41.3	808
Que.	226	51.6	28	6.4	184	42.0	438
N.B.	34	36.6	3	3.2	56	60.2	93
P.E.I.	12	20.0	3	5.0	45	75.0	60
N.S.	68	21.8	19	6.1	225	72.1	312
Nfld.	62	52.5	4	3.4	52	44.1	118
Total							2,812

In civil cases, an appeal by the losing party may simply begin the next stage of bargaining and negotiation. In Canadian provinces, filing an appeal can also postpone the effective date of a judgment and preclude its enforcement. In the United States, where civil juries have been known to award unusually large sums of money at trial, court rules often require the losing party to deposit an amount equal to all or a percentage of the judgment, so an appeal will not be used partly to delay paying the judgment. For many civil litigants, both launching and continuing an appeal becomes more a matter of weighing costs and benefits than analysing what result is just.

This broad discussion of how the requirement to file an appeal shortly after trial leads a large proportion of appeals to drop out before hearing, must be balanced by a different approach. Instead of asking why a large proportion of appeals do not move to a full hearing, we need to ask whether there are variations in the drop-out rate.

First, do drop-out rates vary by province? Table 3.3 shows that they do.[18] While criminal appeals drop out in every province (at least

Table 3.4

Stage When Criminal Case Dispositions Occurred in Courts of Appeal, Brought by either the Crown or the Accused

Stage	Appellant			
	Crown		Accused	
	#	%	#	%
Before Documents	179	32.4	1,028	46.5
Before Hearing	28	5.1	79	3.6
After Hearing	345	62.5	1,105	50.0
Total	552	100.0	2,212	100.0

in the nine provinces for which adequate data have been collected), there are substantial differences across provinces. An examination of the "after hearing" column — looking at the cases that have moved all the way through the appeal process — we see what statisticians call a bimodal distribution. Four provinces are bunched together with percentages between 41 and 44, while four other provinces are in a second group with a much larger proportion of appeals, between 72 and 76 per cent, going through the full process. Only one province (New Brunswick at 60.2 per cent) falls between the two groups.

Note that the highest drop-out rates are found in the three largest provinces. Ontario has far and away the highest percentage of criminal cases that do not reach the documents stage, while British Columbia and Quebec eliminate a higher proportion at the next stage. By the end of the process, less than half of the original appeals in all three provinces have resulted in a judgment by the court after a full hearing. Despite differences in both the legal culture of the three provinces and the approaches of each court to reviewing sentences, the pattern of filing more than twice as many appeals as the number that proceed to judgment can be observed in all three.

The different drop-out rates in large and small provinces (with Newfoundland as an anomaly, its pattern resembling the three largest provinces) suggest two competing explanations. Perhaps Crown and defence counsel in larger provinces have more difficulty reviewing files immediately after trial, leading those lawyers to file appeals and later decline to pursue them. Or there may be more pressure on counsel in larger provinces to avoid presenting relatively weak cases for review. Saskatchewan, for example, with a smaller population than Manitoba, has substantially more criminal appeals than Manitoba (Table 3.1), but only a slightly higher drop-out rate (Table 3.3). Saskatchewan's Court of Appeal, with eight full-time justices rather than the six on Manitoba's Court of Appeal, is more likely to have the time to hear and decide a high proportion of appeals. The decline in criminal appeals between 1990 and 1997 illustrated by Table 3.1 suggests that initial screening by counsel may have increased, perhaps as a result of reduced legal aid funding (assuming no decline in trials for indictable offences.)[19]

Another factor that may be associated with variation in the drop-out rate is whether the appeal is filed by the Crown or the defendant. Throughout the country, defendants file more appeals than the Crown. In fact, 80 per cent of the cases in our sample of criminal appeals were filed by the defendant. While this may reflect the outcome of trials (criminal trials end in conviction more frequently than acquittal), judges, lawyers, and court officials who deal with criminal appeals generally believe that the Crown is more selective in its appeals than are defendants. This would follow from the likelihood that an individual defendant would be more interested in correcting an error in the judgment or sentence of the court than would the Crown, who would be more concerned about establishing or maintaining a legal standard for future cases.

If this logic is valid, appeals from defendants would be more likely to drop out before hearing or judgment than Crown appeals. In fact, Table 3.4 shows that this is exactly what does happen. While only 50 per cent of defence appeals go through to hearing and judgment, 62.5 per cent of Crown appeals do so.

What are the implications of the funnel of appeals — both the universal pattern of appeals dropping away before they are heard or decided and the particular variations between provinces and between the Crown and the defendant?

Those who are involved in the work of any court on a daily basis are aware of the gap between the public's perception of what courts do and what actually happens in them. (The public perception, for those who have never set foot in a court, is that judges hear cases on a leisurely basis, and that hearings involve fascinating issues of law presented by eloquent Parry Mason clones. The reality is that both trial courts and appellate courts are backlogged, judges feel pressure to hear and decide cases as expeditiously as possible, and most hearings are anything but exciting.) However, the funneling of appeals suggests that the court may not look the same to its judges as it does to those who use its services. Defendants are likely to see the process coming out against them more frequently than the outcome of appellate hearings and judgments would suggest, since a much larger number and proportion of defendants' appeals than Crown appeals fail to move forward.

In a sense, accused persons would have already "lost" 1,028 appeals in our sample (Table 3.4) that did not even proceed to the stage of producing a full set of documents, since those appellants would not have argued their case and had an opportunity to secure a judgment in their favour. At the same time, the crown would have "lost" only 179 appeals in our sample at the same stage, or less than 15 per cent of the 1,207 cases that dropped out at the earliest stage of the appellate process. Chapter 8 below shows that appellants win a higher proportion of the cases (perhaps double the percentage) when cases proceed to hearing. Stated another way, the outcome of the deliberations of appellate judges will be more even-handed in quantitative terms than the outcome of all appeals filed in the court. As a result, judges on the court may perceive the exercise of their discretion differently than litigants before the court, since many — perhaps even most — of the appeals litigants bring to court will fail long before any judge or any panels sees them.

This gap in perceptions is a reminder of the need to take a broader view of the administration of appellate courts. Pressed by the list of perfected appeals awaiting hearing, and reserved appeals awaiting reasons for judgment, appellate judges focus on the end of the process. This is where judicial time is spent. However, the litigants' and the public's perception of the process may also be shaped in part by the number of appeals that are filed, and then neither perfected nor argued.

One of the fundamental lessons of case flow management in trial courts has been the need for trial court administrators and judges to be aware of all of the court's work — not only the cases set for trial, but also the cases languishing at earlier stages in the process, perhaps staying on the lists even after being settled or abandoned. Increasing, the quality as well as the timeliness of trial court adjudication requires an understanding of the cases that never reach trial.

It would be valuable for courts of appeal to consider analogous questions about their operation. If the losing party in a civil trial appeals for tactical reasons, hoping to force the winning party into a post-trial settlement rather than re-arguing important legal issues, perhaps the appellate courts need to tighten their time standards for perfecting an appeal, or need to make a inquiry within, say, 90 or 180 days about the status of the case. If criminal appeals are filed to meet a thirty-day deadline, but before opportunity for reviewing legal issues or completing a legal aid application, perhaps that time deadline needs to be lengthened. The essential point here is to broaden the way we look at and think about the appellate process, and expand the issues and questions that need to be asked to ensure that appellate courts act in the interests of justice even with regard to those cases that never reach the final stages of hearing and judgment.

An examination of those appeals that are initiated but never carried further in the process seems to shift our focus away from the exercise of judicial discretion, and highlight the discretion of litigants and their counsel in the appellate process. In practice, however, the ability of lawyers and litigants to manipulate court processes at any stage (pretrial, trial or appellate) is a function of judicial tolerance, and the refusal of judges to interfere with the parties' conduct of the litigation. The common law judiciary traditionally allows litigants and counsel to carry their cases, and rarely intervenes. In contrast, judiciaries in civil law countries, particularly in continental Europe, intervene more aggressively both prior to and during court hearings. Current observers frequently note that these two contrasting approaches are increasingly converging. Civil law systems are opening up the litigation process so that litigants and their lawyers can play a larger role in ensuring fair proceedings. Conversely, however, common law systems are finding that judicial ignorance of the course of litigation prior to a pretrial, trial or appeal hearing may exacerbate delay, encourage legal gamesmanship, and undermine fairness. As a result, the past practice of declining to exercise judicial discretion prior to hearing a case is giving way to new uses of judicial discretion that, properly exercised, could enhance the quality of justice on appeal as well as at trial.

This chapter has provided an overview of the work of the penultimate appellate courts. We now turn to a consideration of how the judges describe the decision-making process both individually and collegially.

The Process of Collegial Decision-making

The decision-making steps and procedures adopted by the penulti-mate appeal courts immediately below the level of the Supreme Court — the ten provincial and two territorial courts of appeal, and the Federal Court of Appeal — are sometimes strikingly different from each other. In Alberta, the Court of Queen's Bench routinely provides the third judge on sentencing panels and frequently on conviction appeals, a procedure viewed with suspicion by judges on some other appellate courts.[1] In Quebec, the Court of Appeal has developed the practice of selecting rotating "lead judges" to prepare the first draft opinion for the panel to discuss. This practice raises judicial eyebrows in other provinces, where some judges have told us that this might not be the best way to ensure that all the judges on a panel are equally prepared for a hearing. Do these differences between the appellate courts lead to unfairness, in that litigants in one jurisdiction may have advantages or disadvantages that litigants in another jurisdiction do not have? Are differences in appellate procedures compatible with the basic democratic principle of mutual respect?

Before tackling these questions, we note that in many respects, the basic processes by which the various penultimate appellate courts make their decisions are remarkably similar to each other. After an appeal is filed, there is a period during which the appellants must submit the necessary documents outlining their positions. Sometimes the appellant fails to file, and the appeal is considered abandoned. If the appellant submits the documents, the respondent is then given time to prepare a written response to the appellant's arguments. Once that time has expired, the hearing is scheduled, even if the respondent has not submitted any documents. The court's chief justice assigns a panel of judges (nearly always three) to hear the appeal. In Prince Edward Island this assignment is easy because there are only three judges on the court. But in Ontario, Quebec, British Columbia, and Alberta, which have appeal courts composed of more than fifteen full-time judges, plus one to five retired judges working part-time (supernumerary judges), a procedure is established by the chief justice for creating individual three-judge panels and assigning particular cases to them. Supernumerary judges have been employed from time to time in every province except New Brunswick and Manitoba; in 1991 the full-time judges outnumbered the supernumerary judges by about four to one.[2]

After the judges on a panel get the list of cases assigned to them for a particular week, they receive copies of the documents that have been filed, and sometimes their law clerks do additional work to assist them in preparing for the appeal. During the appeal hearing lawyers for both sides can explain their positions, and the judges usually question the lawyers about legal points that they feel are critical to the decision. After the lawyers are through, the panel meets in a "conference" to decide the appeal. Once the direction of the decision is worked out, there is another decision to make: whether the decision will be "oral," that is, announced in court within the next few minutes, or "reserved." A reserved decision is one that is written and includes an elaborate justification of the judges' reasoning.

If the decision is reserved, then this fact is announced in court.[3] Within the next few weeks, one of the judges writes a draft of the decision for the other two judges to consider during his or her next "judgment writing week." Most often, the other two judges make relatively minor suggestions, and after brief negotiations about whether or how these suggestions will be implemented, they sign on to the revised decision. Occasionally, one of the judges cannot agree with the outcome, and writes a dissenting opinion. Sometimes a judge who agrees with the outcome but disagrees with the reasons in the main opinion will write what is known as a separate concurring decision.

This basic process masks a myriad of differences about precisely how the courts proceed between the filing of the appeal and the release of the decision. Until recently even the appellate judges were not aware of the extent of the differences between the courts. McCormick and Greene were invited to observe the first-ever seminar for Canadian appellate judges, organized by the National Judicial Institute in Victoria in 1991. The main purpose of the meeting was to allow appellate judges to discuss differences in procedures and approaches and to learn from these comparisons what might be considered "best practices." At the beginning of the three-day seminar, it was clear that most judges thought that few differences in procedure existed, and whatever differences did exist must be slight and unimportant. Midway through the seminar, there was a palpable sense of amazement when the judges realized that the differences between the courts were in some cases quite pronounced. In the end there was a consensus that the judges could learn from each others' experiences to improve procedures in their own courts.

But even if we find that the mechanical procedures in two different appellate courts are exactly the same, there is still what we call the "human factor" to consider. In all the penultimate appeal courts, the judges read the case materials in advance and most have a sense of how they will decide prior to the appeal hearing. Fairly often, the oral arguments of the lawyers in court, together with the question-and-answer session between the judges and the lawyers, result in one or more of the judges changing his or her mind about the preferred outcome. It is not only the skill of legal counsel and their ability to think on their feet that can tip the balance, but also their ability to press the right buttons to appeal to the judges' personal sense of justice.

As another example, in all the provinces the judges meet after the hearing to vote on the outcome. Sometimes a judge who is initially in the minority can persuade one or both of the others to change their minds. Again, it is a case of appealling successfully to reason. The point is that even exactly the same processes can yield different results depending on the values and skills of the human beings involved.

In line with our argument that there is no "one right answer" to most hard legal questions disputed at appeal — although there are many possible wrong answers — our position is that there is no "one right appeal process" either. The bottom line is whether one process might be more fair and cost effective to the litigants than another — providing greater opportunities for presenting arguments and having them considered impartially, and maximizing efficiency in terms of timeliness and use of human and physical resources.

There are three periods during which decisions are made that help determine the outcome of the appeal: the pre-hearing stage, the hearing itself, and the post-hearing stage. The information we have used to portray these stages is from three sources. These include interviews with each of the chief justices about his or her role in administering the court, the general survey of appellate judges about the decision-making process on the court, and questionnaires about appeal court procedures that were filled out by the twelve chief justices of the provincial and territorial courts of appeal in 1991.[4] Because of the time elapsed since our research began, changes have occurred in procedures that we are not aware of. Nevertheless, it is inevitable that there will be important differences in procedures between one court and another. Since the beginning of the 1990s, appellate court judges have become more interested in experimenting with innovations from other provinces; these experiments seem to be resulting in greater fairness and efficiency.

We arranged the interviews with the judges by writing to the chief justice of each court to explain our project, request an interview and get advice on how best to contact the other judges on the court (they are known as "puisne" judges) to request interviews. In most cases, the chief justice would offer to contact the other judges on our behalf, and to schedule interviews with the judges who wanted to participate during a mutually convenient period of days. In other cases, we would be advised by the chief justice to write to each judge on the court and to make individual arrangements. In the end, all of the chief justices agreed to be interviewed, and we were able to interview three-quarters of the puisne judges. Very few judges turned down our request but we were unable to find a mutually acceptable time to meet with several of them.

We scheduled the interviews to last for one hour, and we made every effort to complete them during that time. However, occasionally we had to skip some of the questions that we had designated as less important to our project, and we frequently had to move on to other questions from some that the judges wished to elaborate on. When it was clear that we were going to be short of time, and that judge wished to give us additional comments, a number of the judges were kind enough to suggest that the interview be extended or continued at another time. Most of the judges agreed to allow the interviews to be tape-recorded.

We sent all of the judges a copy of the questionnaire in advance. Our previous experiences in conducting interviews with judges taught us that they frequently will not agree to be interviewed unless they have had the chance to see the questionnaire. As a result, the judges were well prepared for the interviews and able to provide us with considered responses.

Pre-Appeal Period

Once certain key documents have been filed in the court registry, a date is set for a hearing, but the point at which this occurs varies widely. In Manitoba, the appeal is scheduled when the transcript of the trial is received along with the appellant's factum, while in the Calgary office of the Alberta appeal court a hearing can be tentatively scheduled earlier on if the appellant provides an undertaking that the factum will be filed by a specific date. The "lead time" before the hearing occurs is also variable. In Newfoundland hearings are set for less than two months after the appellant has filed the necessary documents, while in Ontario dates are set for six to fourteen months after the documents are received for criminal and civil cases respectively. (This difference between Newfoundland and Ontario is explained by the much higher volume of cases per panel in Ontario.)

The process of assigning cases to particular panels is usually fairly mechanical and follows procedures that were established by previous chief justices, although in every court the current chief justice has modified the process to some extent.[5] To begin with, a clerk makes a list of all of the different combinations of three-judge panels that are possible. In Manitoba these mathematical combinations are rigidly adhered to. Every seven weeks different panels are struck, and these changes in panel composition continue every seven weeks until every possible combination of panels has heard cases. In most other provinces, however, the chief justice makes modifications to a perfectly random combination of panels to take into account factors such as a mix of well-seasoned and less experienced judges, gender balance, regional location,[6] the perceived need to have a judge on a panel who is an expert in the areas of law related to the cases on the panel's docket,[7] and, in some provinces, whether the judges get along with each other. In Ontario the chief justice ensures that each panel that is assigned a criminal case has at least one judge experienced in criminal law, and the same principle is followed for civil cases.

In every province the judges are assigned specific weeks in which to write judgments. The patterns for establishing "judgment-writing" and "sitting weeks" vary greatly. In Alberta, Newfoundland, and Ontario, the judges typically have two sitting weeks followed by two judgment-writing weeks. In British Columbia the judges are assigned two sitting weeks followed by one judgment-writing week, while New Brunswick judges have three sitting weeks per month. Nova Scotia has all its judges sitting during six-week terms, and there are five of these per year. In Ontario and Quebec each judge is assigned two to four weeks per year to hear motions in chambers.[8] However, this "normal" schedule can change depending on whether more time is required for preparation prior to hearings, writing judgments, or hearing cases. The greatest part of the judges' work involves reading materials to prepare for hearings, and writing decisions following hearings. Even during the "sitting weeks," the judges will try to use all the available time when they are not in hearings to prepare for upcoming hearings or to write decisions.

Quebec and Alberta routinely give counsel advance notice of the composition of the panel that will hear particular cases. In some other provinces the judges fear that providing such information may lead to "judge avoidance." Judge avoidance is the practice of inventing an excuse to request a rescheduling of the hearing, if counsel is uncomfortable with the perceived track records of one or more of the judges on a panel. A lawyer may invent an excuse to request an adjournment of the hearing, with the hope that the case will be assigned to a different panel next time around.[9]

It would be possible for the chief justice to influence the outcome of cases through his or her selection of judges on the hearing. However, we found none of the judges that we interviewed saw this as anything more than a hypothetical possibility, or suggested any concerns that any current chief justice in Canada uses his or her panel assignment powers in this way.[10]

In Alberta, superior court trial judges are assigned as the third member of panels that hear sentence appeals. This system of "ad hoc" judges is defended as carrying three significant advantages. First, it allows trial court judges to get to know appellate judges and the problems they face. Thus, it is hoped that there will be less grumbling among the trial court judges about what they might otherwise perceive to be inexplicable decisions from the Court of Appeal. Second, this is a way of reducing some of the workload pressure of individual Court of Appeal judges, thus lessening the need to expand the size of the court. Third, appellate judges are provided with an opportunity to hear the concerns of trial court judges. It is hoped that these contacts will prevent the appellate judges from developing sentencing guidelines that are not grounded in the real world of the trial experience. This third perceived advantage itself underlines the importance of the role of individual judicial perception in appellate court decision-making.

In Ontario and British Columbia no ad hoc judges at all are used, and some judges in these two provinces consider Alberta's practice to be dangerous because it might affect the impartiality of the appellate judges. In the other provinces ad hoc judges sit occasionally on the appeal court on an as-needed basis, but not nearly as frequently as in Alberta.

Virtually all of the appeals are heard by three-judge panels, but occasionally a case is important enough to justify a five-judge panel.[11] In Ontario and British Columbia up to half a dozen five-judge panels might be struck in a year, and in Quebec perhaps two or three. In the other provinces (except in Prince Edward Island, where only a three-judge panel is possible), a five-judge panel might be struck once or twice a decade. Five-judge panels are employed for cases of unusual public importance (for example, the Roman Catholic High School Funding case in Ontario[12]), for cases where the court is considering overruling one of its own precedents, or for cases where there is an important matter of law and the chief justice realizes that there is a greater divergence of views on the court than could be represented by a three-judge panel.

We asked all the judges how far in advance of the hearing they received the documents they needed to prepare for it, that is, the transcript of the trial and the factums of the appellant and respondent. The great majority received these about two weeks in advance, but the range of responses was two days to sixty days.[13] In most jurisdictions, when the factums were distributed to the judges depended on when the lawyers for the litigants had them ready.[14] In British Columbia, Ontario, Quebec, and Nova Scotia, the factums sometimes arrived only a few days in advance of the hearing.

In a preliminary study of the Ontario Court of Appeal, we learned that the judges were sometimes frustrated by being presented with appeals that had absolutely no hope of succeeding. So we asked the judges in the current study in what proportion of cases the result was so obvious that one wondered why the appellant had bothered with the appeal. The average response of eighty-six judges to this question was 21 per cent, and the range was from 1 per cent to 85 per cent. In all the penultimate appeal courts, the estimate of the proportion of "useless" appeals varied among the judges, but those courts with the highest estimates overall were Quebec, the Federal Court of Appeal, Manitoba, and New Brunswick. The most common reason suggested by the judges for these apparently pointless appeals was an attempt to delay the inevitable or, in cases funded by legal aid, to provide some extra income to the lawyer taking the appeal. However, several judges suggested that on occasion the client would simply not believe counsel's advice that an appeal was useless, or the appeal represented an opportunity for an unscrupulous lawyer to earn more money even when legal aid was not involved.

The judges were asked how much time they took to prepare for the "average" hearing. The average or mean response to this question was six and a half hours. But the range of responses was enormous: from one hour, to forty hours, and the median[15] time was two and a half hours. It was in Quebec, Ontario, and British Columbia where the judges tended to take less time to prepare. However, even in the smaller, less busy courts like New Brunswick's, some judges said they took an average of an hour to prepare for each case, while others said they took a full week. Again, personal styles influence work habits.

We should mention that nearly all of the judges pointed out that there is no such thing as an "average" hearing. There is a great variety of case types ranging from sentence appeals for minor offences, to murder cases, to complex Charter of Rights and Freedoms cases. Our response to this inevitable protestation from the judges was, "We understand. However, if you could average the amount of time it takes you to prepare for all of your hearings, what is your best guess as to what that average would be?" In "guesstimating" this average the judges invariably mentioned some relatively straightforward cases (sentence appeals were sometimes mentioned) that took them only fifteen minutes to prepare for and other, very complex cases that took several weeks of preparation time: "There are lots of cases I can prepare for in fifteen minutes or half an hour. I've had enough experience that I know where to look for the key issues. But I had a case just last week that took me a whole month to prepare for, reading several hours a day. It was a very complex tort case involving millions of dollars in liability, but I must add that it was also a very interesting case."[16]

Three-quarters of the judges said that all judges on a panel were about equally well prepared for a hearing. Only in British Columbia did the majority of judges say that the judges were not equally well prepared.[17] In a couple of instances, the judges were aware of colleagues who did not "pull their weight." Even in Quebec, which has a system of "lead judges" (judges selected on a rotating basis to take responsibility to prepare the first draft opinion), most judges thought that all judges were equally prepared by the time of the hearing.

On average, the judges said that they had enough time to prepare for the hearing three-quarters of the time. However, it was only in the smallest and less-pressured courts where nearly all the judges felt they had enough time to prepare adequately for all the cases. In the four biggest appeal courts — British Columbia, Ontario, Quebec, and Alberta — several judges on each court did not feel that they had enough time to prepare for most cases, but on the same courts at least as many judges felt that they had time to prepare adequately for all cases. This variation in response indicates value differences among the judges about what constitutes satisfactory preparation, and more broadly about the nature of the judicial role. For some judges, it is a case of zeroing in on the important points, which they feel they can easily pick out, and that reading all the materials carefully is a waste of time. For others, it is important to read all the materials carefully just in case something that's not obvious turns up. For still others, there are troublesome legal issues that they hope to resolve, and this means studying carefully some issues in the appeal materials that other judges might think unimportant. Here are two contrasting comments:

> I feel that I'm well prepared for every single case. It is not necessary to read every word in the factums and transcripts. I focus on the main issues and I always satisfy myself that I'm ready for them in court.
>
> I hardly ever feel completely prepared. There is always more preparation that could be done for most cases. But the reality is that we have limited time, and this will always be the case, and so we have to use our preparation time in what appears to be the most productive way.[18]

In British Columbia, Alberta, Manitoba, Quebec, and Prince Edward Island, the senior judge on a panel (usually the chief justice, or the court staff person known as the "list manager") would very occasionally meet with counsel prior to the hearing to talk about narrowing the issues or to discuss the probable length of the hearing. But this happened so infrequently that most other members of these courts were not even aware of this practice. However, about half the judges we interviewed thought that these kinds of pre-appeal meetings might be useful at least occasionally. Quite recently, the Alberta and Quebec appellate courts have experimented with offering pre-appeal mediation with the consent of both parties. This innovation, according to our interviews, appears to be quite successful in either narrowing the issues, or settling an appeal without the parties having to go through the entire appeal process.

In most appeal courts the judges on the panels routinely meet prior to the hearing to touch base with each other about the issues in the appeal. They often ask each other, "Do you think anything's there?" Or in other words, does the appellant have any credible arguments that the judges need to pursue? (In some courts these meetings are considered a formal part of the decision-making process; in others, the judges meet informally with each other ten or fifteen minutes prior to the hearing while they're gathering to go in, but these informal meetings almost always occur.) In the courts where the more formal meetings occur, the judges invariably find them useful. In Ontario and in the Appeal Division of the Federal Court these pre-hearing meetings are the exception, and some judges consider them improper because they may bias the judges. In British Columbia, most of the judges engage in these pre-hearing meetings and consider that they are part of the process. However, a third of the judges there do not participate in these meetings.[19] Only in the Supreme Court of Canada are these pre-hearing meetings rare, but even in that court, most judges thought that they were occasionally useful.

In all the courts there are law clerks to assist the judges. They are bright young graduates of law schools who have applied to do their articling in the appeal court. Unlike the situation in the Supreme Court of Canada, the judges in the penultimate appeal courts must share a pool of law clerks. It is in the pre-hearing stages where the clerks are put to most use, summarizing the issues in the cases and doing relevant legal research.

We asked the judges whether there were particular factors that often led to a reversal of a trial court decision. We were able to put this question to only twenty of the judges, but half said that there were particular trial court judges (not many, they said) who had a reputation of being wrong fairly often. A quarter of them cited the charge to the jury in criminal cases as a common reason for reversing the trial court.

As the foregoing analysis shows, what happens prior to the hearing is every bit as important as what happens during and after the hearing. By the time the judges come into the hearing, nearly all of them have a sense of how they think "the case will go," for all but the most complex of cases. But the way the judges approach their pre-hearing work is not mechanical: it depends on the work-related values of the individual judges and the processes that have become traditional in their court — processes that are themselves the result of the accumulation of years of decisions by previous judges and, in particular, chief justices, about how the court's workload should be tackled.

The Hearing

Several cases are scheduled for a morning or an afternoon sitting of a panel if it appears that the cases can be heard relatively quickly. For example, sentence appeals and summary conviction appeals are usually quick. It is not unusual in these kinds of cases for the hearing to take twenty to forty minutes from start to finish. At the other extreme are complex hearings that can take weeks.

By far the most common kind of hearing is the short variety.[20] These compose a third or more of the case loads of the penultimate appellate courts, but account for 10 per cent or less of the courts' hearing time.[21] Typically in a sentence appeal or summary conviction appeal, the panel of judges will walk into the courtroom from a door at the back of the room near their dais. Their entry is announced by the clerk, and all present must stand while the judges walk in. When the judges sit, everyone else follows suit. (The ceremony is based partly on church rituals, dating from the end of the twelfth century when all superior court judges in England were clerics, and partly on the etiquette of the royal court of that time.) Then the senior judge, who is in the middle of the panel that sits on a raised dais, will call counsel for the appellant to speak. He or she will point out the grounds for appeal. Sometimes the senior judge will interrupt and point out that the judges have read the submissions and that they would like the lawyer to summarize what he or she feels is the main point of the appeal as briefly as possible. When the lawyer for the appellant has finished, and for the short cases the appellant's lawyer may take no longer than five to thirty minutes, the judges will sometimes have questions. The question-and-answer session may add another minute or two to the proceedings. Rarely are any of the litigants present; they are represented by their counsel.[22]

The longer hearings follow the same steps, but each step takes longer. Whether the hearing is short or long, after the appellant's lawyer has finished, the three judges look at each other and exchange head signals. If the appellant's lawyer has not convinced the judges that there is some merit to the appeal, the lawyer for the respondent is told that it will not be necessary for the court to hear from him or her. If any of the puisne judges nod to the senior judge, or if they

Table 4.1

Proportion of Criminal Cases Reserved

	% Reserved	% Not Reserved
B.C.	13.4	86.6
Alta.	23.5	76.5
Sask.	12.3	87.7
Man.	11.9	88.1
Ont.	17.8	82.2
Que.	40.7	59.3
N.B.	80.4	19.6
P.E.I.	72.7	27.3
N.S.	32.3	67.7
Nfld.	25.0	75.0
Total	23.5	76.6

have decided in their pre-hearing meeting that the respondent needs to be heard, then the lawyer for the respondent is asked to speak. Most often, the response does not take more than two to three minutes in the short hearings, but in the longer hearings the respondent's lawyer's presentation tends to be proportionate in length to that of the appellant's lawyer, except that it is nearly always shorter. At this point, there may be another brief question-and-answer period.

In about a fifth of all cases, the judges' reading of the documents has persuaded them that the appellant has a compelling case, and so the onus of persuasion is reversed. In these cases, it is essential to hear what the respondent's lawyer has to say. Very occasionally, the appellant has such a strong case that the judges have decided in their pre-hearing meeting that it is not necessary even to hear from the appellant's lawyer. In these cases they will ask the respondent's lawyer to present first.[23] The respondent's lawyer is then under tremendous pressure, having just realized that his or her client has lost unless the lawyer's performance is exceptionally good.

After the judges have finished their questioning of counsel, they stand (and so does everyone else) and leave the courtroom. In the

Table 4.2

Proportion of Civil Cases Reserved

	% Reserved	% Not Reserved
B.C.	30.8	69.2
Alta.	40.5	59.5
Sask.	16.3	83.7
Man.	41.3	58.7
Ont.	36.6	63.4
Que.	50.0	50.0
N.B.	80.4	19.6
P.E.I.	95.8	4.2
N.S.	43.6	56.4
Nfld.	61.5	38.5
Total	40.6	59.4

case of short hearings they reappear in three or four minutes, and in the large, busy courts like Ontario's they nearly always announce their decision in the court. In the smaller, less pressured courts like New Brunswick's, nearly all the decisions are reserved. In all the appellate courts, if the case has some complexities, the judges will announce that they have decided to reserve their decision. If the appellant in a criminal case or sentence appeal is present and has lost the appeal, the judges will sometimes reserve the decision in order to spare the appellant the immediate disappointment or prevent a potentially ugly scene.

As Tables 4.1 and 4.2 show, the proportion of cases reserved varies enormously from province to province.[24] In general, the busier and more pressured the court, the fewer the cases reserved. But this is not consistently the pattern, so factors other than case load are needed to explain the varying rates of reserving. After our visits to Canada's appellate courts, we suspect that critical to understanding these differences are the judges' values about how to approach reserved decisions, as passed on from one generation of judges to another.

We cannot tell from our data whether a higher proportion of reserved decisions results in "better" justice, in that the judges have had more time to think about a case and therefore are more likely to produce a higher proportion of either "right" answers or "better" answers. However, this is certainly a question worth pursuing, now that the extent of the variation is known.[25]

In the lengthy cases lawyers for both sides, as well as lawyers for intervenors[26] may take days to present their clients' cases, from time to time being questioned by the judges. The decisions in these lengthy cases are almost always reserved because of their complexity. There are very few of these lengthy hearings, but they account for a third to a half of the courts' hearing time. In between, there is another group of cases that take up the better part of a morning or afternoon, or sometimes a day, to hear. They account for the final third of the courts' case loads and also for about a third of the courts' total hearing time.

It is the responsibility of counsel on both sides to give the court staff an estimate of how much time they think the hearing will take, and this information is used for scheduling purposes. The judges told us that Crown counsel were pretty reliable in estimating the time required, although 10 per cent of the time they would underestimate it. Those who tended to be the most unrealistic were the generalist lawyers, who underestimated the time required just as often as they presented accurate estimates. In between were the lawyers who were civil law specialists and criminal law specialists, and the latter tended to be more accurate than the former. Experienced hearing coordinators who work in the courts will take into account the mistakes that lawyers tend to make in estimating the hearing time, but sometimes their guess is wrong and hearings scheduled on a particular day will have to be postponed, or the judges are finished early and can go back to their chambers to work on their reserved judgments. (Not all judges are workaholics; one former appellate court judge used to go hunting on days when the court's case load collapsed early.)

The most important factor determining the time the hearing takes is the competence of counsel. Eighty per cent of the judges said that the length of the hearing depends on the quality of counsel; only half said that it depended on the type of case. Good counsel can identify the major issues and cover them succinctly. Poor or inexperienced counsel are not as skilled in this area and can waste a good deal of judicial time. Three-quarters of the judges said, however, that the quality of legal representation is generally good.

The judges are almost unanimous in their perception that civil cases generally take longer to hear than criminal cases. This is because the issues, both legal and factual, are usually more complex. This is not to say, however, that the civil cases are more difficult; most judges told us that they found civil and criminal cases to be about equally challenging.

Occasionally, judges will be troubled after hearing from counsel, because particular legal issues have not been thoroughly researched. In such cases, counsel are sometimes asked to make additional submissions. The most common approach is to adjourn the case until after lunch or until the next day to give counsel time to do their homework. But the judges say that they try to catch a problem in a factum in advance of the hearing, and the senior judge will sometimes write to counsel on both sides asking for additional submissions about a particular point of law. Altogether, the judges told us that counsel are asked for these additional submissions, either prior to the hearing or during the hearing, less than 5 per cent of the time.

Canadian appellate courts represent a halfway house between British and U.S. appellate courts with regard to reliance on oral argument. In the United Kingdom, appellate judges tend to be suspicious of written submissions, believing that oral argument in court is the best way to understand the case. This tradition is so strong that full-fledged factums of the Canadian variety, thirty to forty pages long or more,[27] are not allowed. Rather, only the "skeleton" argument can be given to the judges in advance.[28] In the United States, on the other hand, decisions based on written submissions alone are the norm in most final appeal courts in the state. Lawyers wishing to present arguments in person must apply to the court for permission to do so, and oral arguments occur in a minority[29] of the cases.

From this perspective, we were curious about how often the judges changed their minds as a result of oral argument. Their responses varied from 5 per cent to 55 per cent, with both the mean and median at 20 per cent. Many judges remarked that they never ceased to be amazed at how often they changed their minds as a result of oral argument. There would clearly be very little sympathy among these judges for a U.S.-style appellate system that relied only occasionally on oral argument. Conversely, there would be little appeal for the British system of discounting the value of written factums which allow the judges to prepare themselves for the main issues in advance of the hearing. Nevertheless, conversations we have had with U.S. and British appellate judges indicate that they are as firmly convinced that their system results in the most just outcomes for appellate justice. It is a human tendency to think that unless there are obvious deficiencies in the procedures we are used to, then those procedures are inherently the best.

Most judges regarded the question-and-answer part of the hearing to be one of the most helpful parts of the entire process. All but one of the judges said that this part of the hearing was valuable. We asked them how much of the hearing time was taken up by judges putting questions to counsel and counsel replying; on average the judges said that it took up a quarter to a third of the hearing time.

We asked the judges if they could describe to us the thought process they had developed for deciding on the outcome of appeals. More than half (55 per cent) said that they had developed no particular thought process for deciding cases. The rest described their thought process, but we could not discern any distinct patterns. At first we found this result surprising, because we had put the same question to a sample composed primarily of trial court judges in an earlier study[30] and found that nearly all of them had a personal strategy worked out. We were able to divide these patterns into three distinct types.[31] Those appellate judges who sketched out a personal thought process simply described a very general approach to appellate court decision-making: identify the main issues, check the precedents, form a tentative opinion, listen to counsel, and decide. A few said that the key part of the process for them was the balancing of the individual's interest against general principles.

In retrospect, perhaps we should not have been so surprised by the judges' general inability to describe a personal strategy for appellate decision-making. They are supposed to be team players, and at key points before, during, and after the hearing they need to consult with their colleagues on the panel. The system does not allow them to develop more than the most general idiosyncratic approach.

We asked whether some combinations of judges are able to work better together than others, and three-fifths said that some combinations did work better than others. However, a third of the judges said that particular combinations of judges made no difference at all — we suspect that they were the kinds of people who made it a point to get on well with everyone. There was a range of responses to this question on every court except the New Brunswick Court of Appeal and the Supreme Court of Canada, where the judges reported that all combinations of judges worked equally well together on their *current* court. They prided themselves on having a court composed of team players.

We asked the judges if the judges on their court could be divided into philosophical groups. A third said yes (a small-l liberal versus small-c conservative split was often mentioned), and only two judges said no. However, half said that they can't be neatly classified because the philosophical issue changes for each case. A judge might be a "liberal" on human rights issues, and at the same time might be a "conservative" on criminal law matters. The key point is that personal values do make a difference.

The Post-Hearing Period

The post-hearing period is arguably the most important of the three decision-making periods. This is the time when the judges decide as individuals whether the arguments they've heard in court have changed their initial impressions from the first decision-making period about the outcome of the case, and as a group whether they can come to a consensus decision. In the end, about a quarter of the appellants whose cases proceed to a hearing win their appeals.[32]

In all courts there is a post-hearing meeting, commonly called a "conference."[33] This is typically short, one to twenty minutes, and it serves three purposes. First, the judges vote informally about the outcome of the appeal, and by this time the judges have nearly always made up their minds. Second, they decide whether the decision will be reserved and a written decision produced. Third, if there is to be a written decision, they decide who will write the draft of it. Most often, someone representing the majority volunteers to write the decision (subject to the senior judge's agreement) based either on having the time to do it (perhaps they had just finished writing another decision that day so were prepared to tackle another one), or based on unusually high interest in the legal issues in that particular case. If there are no volunteers, the senior judge will either assume the responsibility for decision-writing or will ask one of the other judges to take it on, a request rarely resisted.

Nearly half of the judges said that the nature of the conference after the hearing changes if they decide to reserve. They said they usually discuss the main legal issues and how they ought to be handled, in order to provide some guidance to the judge who will draft the opinion. However, half the judges said that the nature of the discussion was about the same for reserved and oral decisions. In British Columbia and Quebec the consensus was that the decision to reserve did not change the nature of the conference. In Manitoba, New Brunswick, and Nova Scotia, the judges said that the decision to reserve did make a difference. We suspect that the differences between these courts are based on patterns of interpersonal behaviour being passed on from one generation of judges to the next.

We asked the judges what kinds of cases were the most likely to be reserved. They told us that cases that represented new areas of law were the most likely to be reserved,[34] followed by Charter of Rights cases.[35] Some of the less important factors included the time and cost to litigants of the delay while the opinion was being written,[36] the reputation of legal counsel involved,[37] and the impact of the delay on mounting interest in civil cases.[38]

We were curious about whether of a consensus, as opposed to dissenting or separate concurring decisions, depends on the type of case involved. Three-fifths of the judges said that, in their experience, consensus depends on the type of case; the rest said that this makes no difference. In fact, our case-flow data set confirms the views of the majority of judges: there is a higher rate of dissent in criminal cases dealing with persons than with property, and in civil cases, there is a higher rate of dissent regarding damage awards.[39]

Very few judges thought that dissenting opinions ought to be avoided, although 80 per cent thought that there was nothing wrong with appellate judges trying to promote consensus on a panel during the conference after the hearing. However, most thought that panels ought to try to avoid separate concurring decisions, as these were often confusing to the litigants.

The judge assigned to write the decision in reserved cases[40] writes a draft decision and sometimes requests one of the court's law clerks to assist with the legal research involved. At the penultimate appeal level, law clerks are rarely used to draft part of the decision, as they sometimes are at the Supreme Court of Canada level.

The judges told us that about a quarter of the time, they would consult judges outside of their panel when writing the draft decision. A few judges said that they might occasionally consult persons outside the court. In these consultations, the details of the case are never mentioned; what the judge is seeking is expert advice on legal issues.

The draft is then given to the other judges on the panel for their comments. We asked the judges to rate how extensive the changes were that the other judges suggested. The average result was 2.5 on a scale from 1 to 5, in other words, not very extensive.[41]

For writers, who they have in mind as their reading audience affects the tone and style of their writing. Consequently, we asked the judges who they perceived their "audience" to be for their written decisions. The most common audience mentioned was the parties to the dispute (55 per cent), followed by the judges below and the bar jointly (18 per cent), then the judges below alone (12 per cent), then the bar alone (5 per cent). Most of the judges had taken judgment-writing courses, and most said that these were valuable in helping them to write clearer and more concise decisions. A number of judges also told us that their certainty about the outcome of the case either firms up during the writing process, or it occasionally falls apart because the decision simply can't be written as envisioned. If the latter occurs, and the judge has changed his or her mind about the outcome, then what was originally meant to be the majority decision sometimes becomes the dissenting opinion.

In some provinces, such as Quebec, the draft judgement is circulated to all judges on the court, who may comment on it, although it is the panel's choice whether to accept that advice. In other provinces, such as Ontario, it is considered wrong to circulate draft decisions to judges who were not on the panel and therefore are unaware of the facts of the case.

At every step in this third stage of the process there is judicial discretion about matters that are not strictly legal, such as whether a case should be reserved, how best to reach a consensus, who will write the decision if it is reserved, what audience to write for, how many editorial or substantive changes to suggest to the draft decision, and whether it is worth writing a dissent or a separate concurring decision. All of these discretionary matters affect the nature and flavour of the court's final decision, most particularly with regard to reserved decisions.

Discussion

For some it may seem that this chapter is moving from the scenic highlands of general observations to the murky swamplands of insignificant detail. In a way, that is precisely our point. Appeal cases, like court cases more generally, have two rather different sides to them. One side is that of the parties. For them the appeal case is often the critically important culmination of a major crisis: an emotionally (and sometimes financially) draining prolongation of the dramatic confrontation that began with the trial process itself and that has now dragged on for months or even years.[42] This is particularly true for those litigants that Marc Galanter has called "one timers" —parties who seldom venture into litigation, let alone appellate litigation, and for whom the personal stakes can be very high.[43]

The one thing that stands out about the appellate docket of most provinces is the small scale of many of the issues. "John Q. Public" (and increasingly "Jane" as well) is frequently represented with intensely human dramas with which we can all identify. Provincial courts of appeal of course hear many cases in which large dollar values are at stake and which involve oil companies, banks, insurance companies, and government regulatory agencies pleading their cases with batteries of lawyers and thousands of pages of documents. They also look at child custody cases, personal bankruptcies, and criminal convictions for which the sentences are measured in months or even weeks rather than years. These cases are often earth-shakingly important to the parties, even though the legal issues around which they revolve may be rather small, and the case itself virtually indistinguishable from dozens or hundreds of other similar cases. This introduces the second side of many appeal cases, the side of the judges.

John Wold and Gregory Caldeira have written about the rather surprising extent to which appeal court dockets tend to be cluttered with routine cases — "faint hope" (or even "no hope") appeals which consume appeal court time with little chance of success and even less prospect of having an impact on the general direction of the law.[44] One of the judges we interviewed spoke of cases tending to be governed by a "rule of three," one-third of the time you reverse the trial decision, one-third of the time you hesitate a little but uphold the trial decision, and one-third of the time you wonder why these people are wasting your time.[45] The success rate of appeals in the provincial courts of appeal is in fact usually very close to the "predicted" one in three.

The implications of this phenomenon are aggravated, especially in the high case load provinces, by time pressures. There are only so many (and never, in ideal terms, enough) judicial "person hours" to go around. The more time is consumed by the routine cases, the less the judges can concentrate on researching, arguing, and articulating the ground-breaking and lower court leading decisions. Conversely, the only way that they can devote sufficient time to those "larger" cases is to proceed expeditiously, and sometimes very expeditiously, on the "smaller" ones. To be sure, this is not a happy trade-off, because all parties are entitled to courteous attention, careful deliberation, and a reasoned outcome. Procedures such as "There will be no need to hear from you, Ms. Smith," despite embarrassing the lawyers and annoying the parties, are one way of saving time by not hearing the refutation of arguments that have not been convincing even prima facie.

The parallel is so obvious that we cannot avoid making it. As university professors, we are all accustomed to receiving stacks of final examinations at the end of each semester. Given the recent collision between rising enrolments and falling university budgets, these stacks are getting larger all the time, even while the time pressures (in the form of deadlines for getting grades in to the dean's office) remain constant. On the one hand, we realize that most of our students have prepared assiduously for the exam and have wracked their brains for hours to write careful, thoughtful, and thorough answers that respond seriously to the more provocative issues that we tried to raise. These students rightly expect careful consideration and equally thoughtful response. On the other hand, simple mathematics suggests that we only have so many minutes to spend on each answer; and if we can break more time free, we are more likely to direct it to the exam booklets from the higher level courses. For professors and judges, that which is traumatic excitement for students and litigants is often mind-numbing routine. For professors, as for judges, a balance has to be struck between courteous professionalism and mundane time pressures. We are not always able to strike this balance in a way that satisfies students and litigants, or even ourselves. We must make tough choices, and these depend on our values, our stamina, and the demands on our time on a particular day. Sometimes we make what others consider to be the wrong choices. Thus, it is not surprising that the Supreme Court of Canada grants appeals from the decisions of the penultimate appellate courts 20 to 30 per cent of the time.

One important principle to bear in mind when studying the courts is that judges are people, although they are usually highly trained and dedicated overachievers. Another is that judging is (to some extent) just a job, although a very important job, and one with very important consequences. It is in the way that appeal courts deal with the procedural details of high case load that this second consideration plays itself out.

At the beginning of the chapter we asked whether the differences in procedures in the various appeal courts might lead to unfairness. In cases where a party is clearly disadvantaged, the answer is yes. For example, in the *Singh* case of 1985, counsel for the Government of Canada argued that administrative convenience could justify the determination of refugee claims without giving the claimant a chance for an oral hearing. The Supreme Court disagreed: administrative convenience cannot justify denying a refugee claimant the fundamental justice of an oral hearing.[46] In many other cases, however, it is not a case of cutting corners in a way that obviously disadvantages a party. It is a question of which set of procedures, among several good alternatives, is best. It is our position that if the judges were to ask which set of procedures is likely to be the most effective in furthering mutual respect, this approach may help in finding a resolution.

To the extent that judges remember that the procedures they invent to process cases more effectively or efficiently have real implications for people's lives, and therefore must be designed to maximize fairness, they are using the discretion they possess over procedure to further the principle of mutual respect. To the extent that judges allow court procedures merely to serve administrative convenience, they contribute towards the erosion of the courts and therefore to their weakening as a key institution of democracy.

Cour d'Appel du Québec[1]

The Quebec Legal System and the Practice of Judging

In the preceding chapter we have attempted to describe and explain the uniformities and the differences in appellate court decision-making, including in Quebec. Here, we take a closer look at the appeal process in Quebec in the context of its civil law heritage and its relation with common law jurisdiction in Canada.

The Quebec Court of Appeal functions in a legal system which, in many respects, differs significantly from the other provincial systems in Canada. As a territorial jurisdiction derived from the Constitutional Act, 1867, Quebec may appear to be no different from the other provincial jurisdictions. However, as a legal system which uniquely provides a historical and doctrinal link to the French customary laws and institutions prevailing in *Nouvelle France* prior to the British conquest in 1760, it is unlike any other provincial jurisdiction in Canada.

The continuity of the French civil law was re-established in 1774 by the Quebec Act "in all matters relative to property and civil rights." The first codification of the then existing customary laws (Coutume de Paris), based on the French Napoleonic Code, was completed in 1865 and adopted in 1866 as the Civil Code of Lower Canada (Quebec) with a bilingual text containing over 2,600 articles.[2] A new text of the Civil Code of Quebec came into force on 1 January, 1994, after a lengthy process of comprehensive reform and modernization.

The Code establishes fundamental principles of the law of persons, successions, property, contracts (obligations), and torts (civil responsibility) which are widely considered to be the building blocks of legal education and legal practice. In the common law provinces these principles and "building blocks" are found in the common law precedents, that is, in the reported leading decisions of the highest courts. Not surprisingly, in these fields of private law the articles of the Code serve very much the same purpose as the common law precedents, which is to maintain the stability, continuity, and pre-dictability of the authoritative and established principles of law.

The authority of a common law precedent is based on the propo-sition that, everything else being equal, what has been laid down in the past should also govern in the future. The authority of an article of the Civil Code is based on the same proposition. These conserva-tive, past-oriented features of the Code and of common law are in striking contrast to the objectives of statute laws and regulations that are steadily being churned out by contemporary legislative and bu-reaucratic lawmaking "factories." New statute laws and regulations invariably aim to change the status quo, to fill a legal vacuum, to disturb the existing legal stability and continuity, and to introduce new principles and rules often specifically intended to modernize or set aside established common law precedents or articles of the Code.

It is, of course, up to the judges to decide which is to prevail in a particular situation: the Code or common law principle, the new policy articulated in government legislation, or a combination of both. The tension between the past-oriented Code or common law, on the one hand, and newly enacted and apparently conflicting gov-ernment legislation or regulation, on the other, constitutes the very essence of the task of interpretation performed by the appellate judiciary, whether in Quebec or elsewhere in Canada.

This brings us to an important observation. The distinctiveness of the Quebec legal system notwithstanding, the functions, tasks, and decisional activities of the appeal court judges in Quebec are largely the same as those performed by the other appellate judges in Canada. In other words, substantive law, that is, the civil law contained in the Code, taken in its historical context, does not significantly affect the process of appellate decision-making determined by the Canadian judiciary. This institution possesses its own culture consisting of values, norms, rules of behaviour, expectations, procedures, and style of routine activity. The pattern of behaviour of the Quebec appellate judges is fully congruent with this national professional culture.

The Quebec legal system, of course, is not entirely centred on the Civil Code. In fact, it is *par excellence* a mixed system where com-mon law and civil law traditions live side by side and influence each other. A Quebec judge must be familiar with both traditions. He or she must be prepared to examine leading case law and to follow or distinguish a common law precedent when the case before him or her involves an interpretation or application of either labour law, administrative law, constitutional law, criminal law, international trade law, taxation, or any other field of law (federal or provincial) rooted in the common law tradition that may be relevant in a particular case. Case law is regularly cited even in the interpretation of the articles of the Civil Code. But most Quebec judges will not observe the doctrine of *stare decisis* (precedent) with the same degree of rigidity as their colleagues trained in the common law tradition.[3]

Substantive differences between Quebec civil law and common law in force in the other provinces are, obviously, highly significant. The practice of judging, as a professional discipline, is moving unmistakably from divergence to convergence throughout Europe and North America. Here are some brief illustrations of how this remarkable process of convergence is nourished and how it influences the judicial process in modern democracies:

- At the request of the national courts of the European Union member-states, the European Court of Justice in Luxembourg renders "preliminary rulings" on the interpretation or validity of EU laws in domestic court cases. These reference decisions now account for nearly 30 per cent of the court's case load and are generally accepted by all national courts as precedents. They promote the uniform interpretation and application of EU legislation in all fifteen member-states and facilitate the convergence of the judicial processes in Europe.[4]

- The accession treaties negotiated between the European Union and the new members (most recently, Austria, Finland, and Sweden) require a significant degree of harmonization of their laws, procedures, and judicial processes with the laws of the EU, including the decisions of the European Court of Justice. The new members must also accept all EU *acquis communautaires*.[5] This represents another step on the road to European legal and judicial convergence.[6]

- The association agreements (Europe Agreements) negotiated between the EU and the post-communist states of East-Central Europe provide for the same type of harmonization and offer these countries financial and expert assistance to reach this goal.[7]

These processes of harmonization, which include the adoption of generally recognized standards of impartial and independent judging, are well under way in those countries which intend to become EU members.

- The European Convention on Human Rights and the Canadian Charter of Rights and Freedoms share numerous similarities not only in the substantive provisions but also in the way Canadian and European judges interpret these provisions. In many cases, the reasoning and contextual analyses employed by Canadian judges are strikingly similar to those that have been so effectively used by the European Court of Human Rights in Strasbourg.[8] This signifies another form of judicial convergence.

- Globalization and continental economic integration created new legal regimes such as the World Trade Organization (WTO) and the North American Free Trade Agreement (NAFTA), establishing new mechanisms and procedures for dispute resolution which impose universal or continental rules and standards to be respected and applied by the arbitration tribunals and by the national courts of the member-states.[9]

- International courses and seminars on judgment-writing standards, alternative dispute resolution (ADR), international trade dispute resolution, and so forth, are increasingly attracting Canadian judges, including those from Quebec, both as teachers and students.[10] These professional training activities are based on the assumption that good judging practices and standards are universal and that an increased convergence of judicial behaviour across national boundaries makes good common sense.

The Interviews

The Quebec Court of Appeal is one of the busiest appellate courts in Canada. It maintains two official venues, one in Quebec City with eight or nine judges, and one in Montreal with at least fifteen judges.[11] In 1995 the court heard over 1,300 civil and criminal appeals and rendered over 1,200 judgments.[12]

All twenty-one interviews were conducted in Montreal and Quebec City in June of 1991. The interviews lasted far longer than initially anticipated, ranging from one to three hours, with most of them taking close to two hours. When scheduling appointments, many judges expressed concern about the length of the interview, but these concerns were abandoned once the judges became involved in the interview process.

On the whole, the interviews were highly successful, with most respondents giving full and candid answers to over twenty-five multifaceted questions in a ten-page questionnaire. Undoubtedly, the positive attitude of Chief Justice Bisson played a very significant role. It is, perhaps, instructive to quote from the letter of one of a small number of judges who refused to participate in the project: "Because governments show so little consideration for judges, I must limit my activities.... Given this attitude of indifference on the part of the state, I have firmly decided to protest in my own way, because otherwise we would be sending the wrong message: that all is for the best in the best of all worlds."[13]

The Appellate Decision-making Process

It is important to keep in mind the fundamental characteristics of the appeal process as distinct from the trial which, normally, took place some two or three years earlier. In appeal, the dossier becomes of paramount importance. It consists of two factums (*mémoires*), one prepared by the appellant's lawyer and the other by the respondent's lawyer. Typically, a factum is an adversarial document. It is intended to present the best possible case on behalf of a party. It normally includes:

1. A summary of the facts established by the trial judge, which should be presented fairly but is all too often tilted in favour of the party in question;
2. Selections of the evidence given at trial that are favourable to the party in question;
3. A copy of the judgment rendered by the trial judge;
4. A legal argument presented in favour of the party in question supported by selected case law (authorities), by an interpretation of the relevant articles of the Civil Code and other relevant statutory provisions or regulations, if necessary, and by an interpretation of the relevant constitutional and Charter (Canadian and Quebec) provisions, if necessary.

Assuming there are no intervenors, the judges sitting on appeal receive two opposing factums, which become their only sources of information about the case. Normally, the factums are drafted and filed with the court at least two to three years prior to the hearing. The full transcript of the trial is rarely, if ever, examined in appeal. As a general rule, no witnesses are called and no new evidence presented, although permission to hear new evidence may be granted in exceptional cases.

During the hearing the lawyers are not permitted to raise issues that are not dealt with in their factums. The judges are free to intervene at any time to ask questions and to direct the lawyers to address, or not to address, specific issues that they want, or do not want, to hear about. The duration of the hearing is limited, depending upon the complexity of the case and of the issues to be addressed, and each lawyer is given a specific time to speak and then to respond to the argument of his or her opponent. The judgment of the court of appeal can be rendered orally from the bench immediately after the conclusion of the hearing or it can be reserved (taken *en délibéré*) and given to the parties (their lawyers) in writing at a later date.

The Quebec Court of Appeal nearly always sits in panels of three judges. To the extent possible, each panel consists of a mixture of Quebec City and Montreal judges. In an extremely rare situation, the chief justice may decide to strike a panel of five judges. The most senior judge on the panel automatically assumes the role of chair, but he or she is not the lead judge in every appeal that the panel hears.

The court roll (a daily or weekly list of appeals to be heard) is prepared by the clerk at least two months in advance. The most junior judge on the panel assumes the role of the designated lead judge for the first case; the judge with the middle seniority on the panel becomes the lead judge for the second case on the roll, and the most senior judge (the panel's chair) takes on that role for the third case, and so on. The main task of the lead judge is to prepare the first opinion for the panel. The remaining two judges may then simply agree with that opinion or write their own opinions, either concurring or dissenting.

The main task of the chair is to preside over each hearing. The dossiers are distributed to the members of the panels some two months before the scheduled hearings. On a given day, there may be as many as three or four panels hearing appeals, one in Quebec City and two or three in Montreal.

The key steps in the court's decision-making process are as follows:

1. Study and analysis of the dossier by each of the judges on the panel individually;
2. Pre-hearing meeting of the panel at 9:30 a.m. to discuss briefly each appeal scheduled for the day;
3. The hearing;
4. Meeting of the panel at the end of the day to discuss the likely disposition of each appeal;
5. Preparation of the lead (first) opinion and, in response, the concurring or dissenting opinions by panel members and their distribution to all members of the court;
6. Consultation among panel members including comments received from the other members of the court;
7. Judgment of the court.

On the whole, the judges appear to be satisfied with the amount of time they have to study and analyse each dossier. At any given time a judge may have in his or her chambers as many as twenty bulky dossiers at various stages of study and analysis.

Most of our respondents admit that they formulate an initial opinion about the appeal on the basis of the dossier and come to the hearing with a predisposition in favour of one party. Some judges insist that they make every effort to keep an open mind, but in over 80 per cent of appeals the panel members do not change their initial opinions after the hearing. In the past, the practice was not to study the dossier before the hearing at all. It was assumed that ignorance of the case was the best guarantee of impartiality. This practice has been discontinued, and now most judges take the view that a thorough study of the dossier in advance of the hearing is essential. A poorly drafted factum with a weak argument will produce disastrous consequences for a party. Only a truly exceptional salvage performance during the hearing may turn things around. Some judges complain that in large law firms the task of drafting the factums is often allocated to junior associates or even to articling students. Then, two years later, the firm's senior litigation counsel appears at the hearing without having fully read the factum and unable to respond to specific questions about it.

Normally, the pre-hearing meeting of the panel lasts less than thirty minutes. It presents the first opportunity for the judges on a panel to compare notes and exchange their predispositions formed on the basis of the written dossiers. If there are two appeals scheduled for the day, the judges may agree that one of them is frivolous and,

		Table	
	Workload of Quebec		
	1993		
	Quebec	**Montreal**	**Total**
Civil			
Inititated	806	2,322	3,128
Heard	245	458	703
Judgments	252	456	708
Petitions presented before:			
Court	320	1,323	1,643
Judge	715	2,650	3,365
Criminal			
Initiated	210	438	648
Heard	151	206	357
Judgments	149	248	397
Petitions presented before:			
Court	129	180	309
Judge	277	808	1,085

Source: Prepared by clerks of the Quebec Court of Appeal in Montreal and Quebec City.

depending on the hearing, may be dismissed from the bench. With respect to the remaining one, the panel will narrow down the issues they want discussed during the hearing and identify the key questions they want to put to the lawyers. Since time is of the essence, the main objective of the meeting is to make sure that the counsel of both parties address the issues that the judges want to hear.

During the hearing the chair of the panel will monitor the time allocated to each counsel. In Quebec less time is allowed for an average hearing than in Ontario, for example. The reason for this is clear. The Quebec court panels hear a significantly larger number of appeals per week than do the Ontario court panels.

5.1

Court of Appeal

	1994			1995		
	Quebec	**Montreal**	**Total**	**Quebec**	**Montreal**	**Total**
	735	1,984	2,719	656	1,900	2,556
	319	619	938	335	606	941
	306	537	879	334	580	914
	318	1,057	1,375	347	1,125	1,472
	573	1,745	2,318	458	2,108	2,566
	227	376	603	205	462	667
	125	245	378	108	163	271
	106	245	351	87	240	327
	162	188	350	96	163	259
	353	695	1,048	329	920	1,249

Judges' opinions on the quality of the counsel's preparation and oral submission vary considerably. Almost 20 per cent of the respondents rate it poor, and about 15 per cent rate it excellent, while most of the respondents prefer to settle safely in the middle of the scale. Many judges share the view that if the factum is strong, then so is the oral submission, except when the factum was not written by the lawyer who participates in the hearing.

The judges assign a much greater importance to the written dossier than to the oral hearing. They make their initial evaluation of the appeal on the basis of the materials they read and are rarely persuaded to change it by the oral arguments. This undisputed finding may be disturbing to many people. The tradition of *audi alteram partem* (hear both sides before deciding) is believed to be the foundation of the adversarial system of justice. Is it becoming passé in the appellate process?

If there is nothing solid in the appellant's factum, why bother with a hearing at all? Some judges feel strongly that it is too easy for a losing party to lodge an appeal, often wasting the judges' time on frivolous or unnecessary proceedings. This happens frequently in appeals as of right under the Divorce Act dealing with interim alimentary allowances.

If both factums present powerful and persuasive arguments, is an open court hearing the best forum to resolve the conflict? Our respondents say that, sometimes, they resort to additional individual research of fine points of law because they do not trust the research done by the lawyers, or because the authorities cited in a factum are not up to date. In most instances, however, they rely on a well-established internal consultation process, which has become an essential feature of appellate decision-making in Quebec.

Until relatively recently the practice in the Quebec Court of Appeal was to avoid judgments from the bench and to take nearly all cases under advisement (*en délibéré*). This practice was viewed to be a matter of courtroom culture or professional etiquette, which required that lawyers must not be embarrassed in front of their clients in an open court. One court of appeal judge determined to change this practice was approached by an official of the law society (Barreau du Québec) who strongly protested this breach of traditional etiquette.

Today, only about half of the appeals are reserved after the hearing, but some younger judges would like to see this percentage drop considerably. They argue that judgments from the bench should be the norm, except when there is no consensus among the members of the panel or when the issues in appeal are complex or novel. In reality, however, many appeals are taken *en délibéré* because either all or some members of the panel are not ready to decide, have not done their homework prior to the hearing, or are unwilling to commit themselves without further consultation. In consequence, reserved appeals still produce a fair number of unanimous judgments.

The three members of the panel are supposed to meet at the end of the day of hearings to sort out the possible dispositions of the appeals. According to most respondents, this practice does not work as expected because of lack of time dictated by the desire to leave the courthouse at the end of the day. Consequently, each designated lead judge is left with the responsibility of preparing the first opinion and beginning the process of internal consultation. The draft first opinion is circulated to all members of the court, not only to those who sat on the panel, and both written and verbal comments are welcomed and expected. Technically, members of the panel are not bound by any comments made by the other members of the court.

The objective of the consultation process is not only to iron out the existing wrinkles among the members of the panel. It is also to make sure that the proposed judgment is acceptable to the court as a whole and that it is consistent with the past judgments of the court on the issues in question and in keeping with the broad policy of the court in relation to these issues.

The members of the panel may meet to discuss the comments received, but more likely they will exchange views by way of telephone conferences or personal memoranda. When individual judges on the panel take strong opposing positions on specific issues, memos may be flying for some time before an agreement is reached. If a dissent becomes inevitable, the dissenting judge will write his or her own opinion, while the designated lead judge will write the judgment of the court, which may include points and observations made during the consultation process.

This process does not really explain how an individual judge makes up his or her mind, especially when the issues in appeal are difficult, complex, and strongly contentious. Two different respondents have described their own personal experiences in those words:

> You take a cocktail-shaker, a Manhattan shaker. You put in all the facts and then the law and then you put in a little bit of common sense and a drop or two of equity and a drop or two of discretion and you shake it all up. That gives you your decision. But you mustn't put in too much discretion because then the Supreme Court will say it's all wet. That's the way I do it.[14]

> I discuss with my colleagues. I listen. I try to keep an open mind. I think about it when I'm driving my car. I weigh it in my mind all the time, and then I put it aside. It's a bit like cooking. You taste it, and you taste it again until you like it. If you spoil it, if you oversalt it, you must throw it away, and you have to start again and continue until the taste is right.[15]

These examples could just as well have described the decision-making process of any of the judges in the common law appellate courts.

The Doctrine of Precedent: Its Value and Application in Quebec

The respondents' opinions on the value and application of the doctrine of precedent in Quebec present a strangely diversified mosaic. We have selected eight excerpts which speak for themselves.

1. We are used to the British model. When I was a superior court judge, I was subject to the supervisory control of the courts of appeal. In a way, this gave me a sense of security because one should never pretend to have the monopoly on truth. It's the same now when I am on the court of appeal. It's good that there is the Supreme Court above us.[16]

2. I could not care less what a higher court decided five years ago. I will abide by the principle set out in the Quebec Civil Code and use my knowledge.[17]

3. A judge trained in the civil law tradition will start with the analysis of the text, while a common law judge will provide a synthesis of the relevant case law. At the end, both will reach the same result. The difference between these two traditions is significant only in the methodology, not in substance.[18]

4. I do not think that what we do here in Quebec is very different from what the courts do elsewhere in Canada. We are trained to utilize both the common law and the civil law approaches. It is normal for us to analyse the text as well as to examine the relevant case law.[19]

5. The concept of precedent is important, but not because it is a principle of law, as some common law jurists claim. Very simply, it is a rule of natural justice: the same cases should receive the same treatment. The citizens have a right to expect that the courts will give the same rulings for the same problems. But if a decision causes an injustice, there is no sense in repeating the injustice in the name of the precedent. That's all.[20]

6. In Quebec the situation is complicated. In general, precedent must be followed in the field of federal law, public law, administrative law, etc. But the same rule does not apply in the field of civil law of Quebec. Recently, a majority of us decided that the Quebec Court of Appeal is not bound by its past decisions.[21]

7. I had to face this situation once. In an appeal before us a leading decision of the Supreme Court on a question of labour law was cited as a precedent. In my view, the cited decision was badly flawed. I decided to examine very closely both sets of facts, and I discovered at least two material differences. Had the Supreme Court been aware of them, would it still have rendered the same judgment? If the answer is yes, I would tend to follow it even if I disagreed with it. But I could not ignore my conscience.[22]

8. If you want to distinguish a leading decision, a precedent, you will distinguish it. If you want it to be binding, you will make it binding. It's as simple as that.[23]

As is noted in Chapter 4, we received the same spectrum of responses when we asked the judges on Canada's other two appellate courts that combine civil and common law — the Federal Court of Appeal and the Supreme Court of Canada — whether judges with civil law training tend to approach decision-making differently. It would appear that those civil law judges who do approach decision-making differently do so not necessarily because of their different legal training, but also because of a personal belief that the civil law approach produces results that are more just.

A Potpourri of Judicial Attitudes and Opinions

Quebec judges are known for writing long judgments. One respondent recalls a story attributed to Victor Hugo who once wrote a very long letter to one of his friends. At the end he felt obliged to apologize, explaining that he had no time to be brief. Similarly, a judge who prepares a thirty-page opinion knows that he should be more concise, but he has no time (and inclination) to shorten it.

The judgment of the court affects the parties and should be primarily directed to them: the appellant and the respondent. Some judges find it appropriate to address a wider audience. The lawyers who represent the parties should be informed why one lost and the other won. If the appeal is allowed, an explanation is due to the trial judge so that he or she fully understands what went wrong. Then there is the legal community, especially professors of law, editors of law reports, journalists, the other judges of the Court of Appeal, and of course the Supreme Court of Canada. One respondent stated bluntly that he writes only for himself.

All respondents admit that they, as judges, make new law, but they insist that this is not their primary, most frequent, or desired activity.

Some say that they are forced to be lawmakers by the Canadian (and Quebec) Charter, especially Section 1 which permits justification of rights' violations in accordance with reasonable limits prescribed by law, and invites the courts to balance government policy objectives against the severity of the infringement. Individual judges assess the frequency of their lawmaking activity very differently: from a low of 2 per cent to a high of 25 per cent. What they mean is that their lawmaking is not confined to criminal law and Charter cases. One judge stated candidly: "There has never been any doubt in my mind that we are lawmakers and there is nothing illegitimate about it."[24] Another judge expressed a very different view: "Theoretically, we are supposed to interpret existing laws, not to make new ones.... The functions of a lawmaker and law-interpreter should be made clear and kept distinct. A judge who regularly assumes the role of a lawmaker is a bad judge, in my view.... On the other hand, I do not exclude the possibility that, on occasion, we must exercise our discretion and render a decision which will resemble a legislative act.... If we want to be independent as judges, we must also respect the independence of others. We are not elected."[25]

We knew from our preliminary research that, for several years prior to our study, there was fear among some judges that the Charter might lead to what was commonly termed a "crisis of legitimacy" for the courts by appearing to transfer to them powers that more legitimately belonged to the legislative branch. So our interview schedule included a question about whether the interviewee agreed that the Charter had, in fact, created a "crisis of legitimacy."

A majority of the Quebec judges did not agree that the Canadian Charter creates such a crisis for the courts. Several judges claimed that they were opposed to the Charter from the beginning because it gave political power to the judiciary which owes no responsibility to the electorate. "I consider this anti-democratic and illegitimate," said one respondent.[26] One judge pointed out that the volume of Charter issues before the court is not very large (less than 15 per cent) and thus without significant impact on its basic routine work.[27]

Most judges do not perceive any philosophical or political divisions or groups among themselves. They stress professional solidarity and collegiality as the key characteristics of the court. What they really mean is that the differences that do exist do not matter and do not interfere with their collective activities as appellate judges, even though they are reflected in individual judges' approaches to specific legal issues. One respondent put it this way: "We have the left field, centre field, and right field. We have some very conservative people, some liberal people, and some in the middle. These differences reflect themselves in all types of cases, not only in Charter appeals.... Personally, I am a conservative. I always abide by what Parliament has enacted. I am a very humble man. I am only a technician, an arbitrator...."[28]

The Supreme Court represents in the minds of the respondents a fundamental benchmark in relation to their practice of judging, and especially in relation to their exercise of discretion in specific appeals. Yet, many respondents cite circumstances when they would be prepared not to follow a Supreme Court decision, such as an appeal in the field of private law exclusively within the domain of the Civil Code. In this area of litigation, the Quebec Court of Appeal has become the court of last resort for all practical purposes.

Our respondents remain divided on the question of the use of the courts by social and public interest groups to achieve social change. Those who see nothing inappropriate in those pursuits point out that standing can always be denied to groups without a real and direct interest. Those who frown upon such activity usually make a distinction between private and public litigation. In the latter, where parties are governments or governmental institutions, public or social interest groups should be free to intervene provided they demonstrate direct interest. Private litigation (defined to include the corporate and commercial sector), however, should be protected against intervenors whose participation only inflates the cost and the duration of litigation.

Some of our respondents have issued a warning about judicial independence. According to them, the potential threat to judicial independence in Canada (and in Quebec) comes from senior government officials who increasingly perceive and treat judges as if they were a part of the civil service or public administration personnel. "These people have forgotten the concept of the judicial function in a democratic state. The fundamental requirement of the judicial function is intellectual independence from everyone, especially from government and government officials. We are not *les fonctionnaires* (civil servants)."[29]

Concluding Remarks

It appears from our interviews that the decision-making process in the Quebec Court of Appeal is really not all that different from what happens in the common law provinces. The major procedural differences, such as the system of lead judges, are a result of innovations invented by the judges themselves, rather than a result of a different legal training.

There is an important current issue that also indicates that the Quebec Court of Appeal is not all that different from the other large appellate courts in Canada. Because of its heavy case load, some of the judges have put forth the proposition that in order for the court to fulfil the expectation of judicial leadership in the province, the court ought to be divided in two. There would be an intermediate appellate court to hear appeal cases that do not involve the clarification of the law, and a supreme appeal court to hear cases of great legal importance. The very same idea has become prominent in Ontario, and to a lesser extent in British Columbia and Alberta.

Peter McCormick argued that provincial appellate courts perform two functions: the supervisory function of correcting errors committed by trial judges, and the leadership function of building the jurisprudence in major areas of law which give rise to litigation.[30] He suggested that the supervisory function is largely an illusion — first, because "there is a statistically small chance of review"[31] and, second, because the only sanction that the error-prone trial judge can experience is professional embarrassment. The clear implication is that trial judges can relax because the great majority of their mistakes will never come to light before their alleged supervisors, the courts of appeal.

To perform the leadership function adequately, the Quebec Court of Appeal would have to decrease significantly its present case load, concentrate on appeals that raise legal issues of great importance, and significantly increase the per case research and deliberation cost and time.[32] In addition, the number of judges would have to be decreased "to maximize collegiality and consistency." In other words, the Court of Appeal would have to become very much like the Supreme Court of Canada, which has fashioned for itself a clear juridical leadership role in key areas of law of general public importance. The routine supervisory function of correcting trial courts' errors would have to be performed by an intermediate court of appeal, which currently does not exist in any provincial jurisdiction in Canada. Those who favour the creation of such courts base their arguments largely on the U.S. experience with intermediate courts of appeal.[33]

The question whether such an intermediate court of appeal should be created in Quebec has been addressed by the Gilbert Committee.[34]

Its proposal to establish such a court was rejected by a joint commmittee of the Bar and the Court of Appeal, and by the General Council of the Bar of Quebec[35] The joint committee presented two strong arguments against the proposal:

1. Because it is practically impossible to identify the two types of cases[36] in advance and prior to the hearing, the theoretical distinction between the two appellate functions cannot serve as a basis for any court's jurisdiction.
2. The proposal to create an intermediate court of appeal will only introduce another level of appeal, it will not improve the quality of the judgments, nor reduce the delays in appeal; as an intended structural reform of the appellate process, it is both misguided and dysfunctional.[37]

Although the joint committee's conclusions may not be the last word on intermediate courts of appeal, it appears unlikely that this proposal will see the light of the day in Quebec in the near future. The proposal for an intermediate court of appeal in Ontario received a similar negative evaluation from a committee appointed to consider the issue.[38]

In chapters 4 and 5, we have discussed the process of collegial decision-making in the provincial courts of appeal. The highest court of appeal, the Supreme Court of Canada, presents a very different case. It merits a special treatment for a number of reasons, but one clearly stands out. The Supreme Court is the only court that controls its docket and fashions its unique national case load.

The Supreme Court of Canada

The Supreme Court is a unique institution. It is as different from the provincial courts of appeal as the appeal courts are from the trial courts. This is not only because of the kinds of cases the Supreme Court hears, but also because the decision-making procedures are in a class of their own. They have evolved to make the Supreme Court of Canada unique compared with other appellate courts derived from the English model, such as the English Court of Appeal and House of Lords, where judges specialize more and rely more on oral argument, and the U.S. Supreme Court, where a number of institutional procedures are quite different. As we show below, the evolution of decision-making procedures is a result of discretionary decisions by the judges in an effort to continually adjust to the expanding decision-making pressures on this institution that is so key to Canada's democracy.

The Supreme Court spends most of its time deciding cases of its own choosing. Of the 105 to 140 cases that the court has disposed of annually in recent years, sixty to ninety get there because they have been hand-picked by subcommittees of three Supreme Court judges because they deal with legal issues of general importance. The rest are mainly serious criminal cases that either the accused person or the Crown has a right to bring to the Supreme Court. This is because there was a dissent on the case at the provincial court of appeal level on a question of law, or because the court of appeal had overturned a trial court acquittal. (All six Supreme Court judges who were asked how the decision-making process could be improved said that the as-of-right appeals should be reduced or eliminated.) As well, there may be a few reference cases each year, questions sent directly to the Supreme Court from the federal cabinet, and some rehearings.

The proportion of appeals allowed has varied from a third to a half, and the proportion of oral judgments has varied from about 20 per cent to 45 per cent. In 1997, 72 per cent of the applications for leave to appeal originated in Ontario, Quebec, British Columbia or the appellate division of the Federal Court, and 67 per cent of appeals heard originated in these four jurisdictions. The average time between filing a leave to appeal application and the rendering of the final judgment has dropped from about three years in 1987, to about a year and a half in 1997.[1]

The Judges

In mid-1996 the average age of the judges of the Supreme Court of Canada was sixty-five, and their average age at appointment was fifty-six. The judges ranged in age from fifty-three to seventy-one. Age-wise, the 1996 court is typical. (In 1989, for example, a Supreme Court judge's average age was sixty-three, while the average age at appointment was fifty-eight.) As we would expect for the country's top court, the judges are six years older, on average, than their federally appointed colleagues in the courts below, and twelve years older than provincially appointed judges. The average member of the court had served in that capacity for about nine years, up from the average of five years in 1989 but well below the long-term averages for the Supreme Court and for other appeal courts. Indeed, the Supreme Court of the early 1990s was more a "court of juniors" than it has been at any time since the Fitzpatrick Court early in the century, this being the result of the rapid turnover in the 1980s. Only a single member of the current court had served for longer than a dozen years, a comment that could not be made about any other set of Supreme Court judges since the First World War.

In 1996 all of the judges except Mr. Justice John Sopinka had served on other courts prior to their appointment to the top court. They came to the Supreme Court with an average of eight years prior judicial experience. Seven had served on a provincial court of appeal, and Mr. Justice Iacobucci had been chief justice of the Federal Court of Canada. (The pattern of appointments over the last quarter of a century suggests that this ratio of seven from the provincial appeal courts, one from the Federal Court, and one without prior judicial experience can be taken as intentional and persisting.) On average, the eight judges with prior judicial experience had served for four years on these lower appellate courts. In addition, four of the judges had served an average of eight years on a provincial trial court.

According to the Supreme Court Act, three Supreme Court judges must be appointed from Quebec. From 1994 to 1996, when our interviews with Supreme Court judges were conducted, the Quebec judges were Chief Justice Antonio Lamer, Claire L'Heureux-Dubé, and Charles Gonthier. By convention, three are from Ontario; these were Peter Cory, John Sopinka, and Frank Iacobucci. There was one representative of the Atlantic provinces — Gérard La Forest from New Brunswick — and there were two western judges, Beverley McLachlin, former chief justice of the B.C. Supreme Court, and John Major from Alberta.[2]

Just two of the judges are women, down from an all-time high of three women prior to Madam Justice Wilson's retirement in 1991.

Seven judges were asked why they had accepted a judicial appointment in the first instance, and for six, there was a combination of "push" and "pull," which were about equal. The push was caused either by boredom in the previous job (two judges) or the realization that while boredom had not yet set in, the time had come to seek a new challenge (five judges). The "pull" was a result of the enticement of the honour of being a judge (four judges) or the sense that they had a public duty to accept the appointment when offered (two judges).

For seven judges interviewed who were elevated from a lower appellate court, three accepted the Supreme Court appointment because they viewed it as a logical progression of their career. Two said they wanted a new challenge. Three stressed an interest in the law development kind of work in the Supreme Court, and two saw it as a duty to accept when asked. None of the judges said that they had considered retiring early to return to the practice of law.

Six judges were asked what qualities they respected in other judges. Four stressed a sense of even judgment and fairness, and three mentioned the ability to write decisions concisely and promptly. Two underlined the need for strict impartiality, while two alluded to politeness and consideration. There were single references to honesty, collegiality, the quality of the written decision, and self-confidence. Perhaps surprisingly, only two judges mentioned the importance of a knowledge of the law. While this factor is obviously a prerequisite to a Supreme Court appointment, there are other qualities, related more to the individual's sense of justice and personal working style, which determine judicial excellence from the perspective of the current bench. To put the point a little differently: assuming a certain threshold level of knowledge of the law, individuals gain pre-eminence in the eyes of their colleagues less by demonstrating more such knowledge than by exhibiting other personal qualities.

The six judges questioned about the appointment process all stressed that partisan politics no longer plays a role. None felt they could comment on what factors now play a role in appointments to the Supreme Court. However, they said that the factors that ought to be considered are fairness and judgment (two judges), demonstrated legal ability (two judges), being representative of Canadian society in general (two judges), good interpersonal skills (one judge), and good work habits (one judge).

The judges acknowledged that a judicial appointment has a tendency to lead to a certain amount of isolation, although two judges thought that isolation could be brought within reasonable limits through a conscious effort to stay in touch with old friends and through keeping track of current affairs. The most popular sources of news were newspapers, both national and local, and television.

Seven judges were asked what judicial independence means to them, and they all stressed the freedom to make decisions without interference from anyone. Only one of these judges considered that there were no threats to judicial independence at the present time. Three judges thought that the attempt by some interest groups to put pressure on the judges outside the courtroom, such as through the media or through demonstrations, represented an important threat. Other threats included the danger posed by interpreting judicial independence too broadly, judges who have difficulty understanding social change, lack of understanding of judicial independence on the part of the public, and inappropriate procedures for determining judicial salaries. Two judges were worried about the possibility that this new discipline procedures for judges might become threats to independence, although three judges stated that in certain situations, public hearings into judicial misconduct might be appropriate. There was a somewhat higher level of concern about threats to judicial independence among Supreme Court judges, as compared with the judges on the penultimate appeal court, as we show in chapter 9.

With regard to the role of the chief justice, four judges of the six who responded to this question saw the chief justice as primarily an administrator who attended to the scheduling of cases, the composition of panels, and budgetary issues. Two saw the ceremonial aspect, including the chief's role as deputy governor general, as an important part of the job. Two thought that an important function of any chief justice was to promote collegiality, while one saw him or her as the court's intellectual leader. One thought of the chief justice as the chief spokesperson for all Canadian judges to the general public. But all thought of the chief justice as an equal, not a superior, in the decision-making process. None felt accountable to him or her except when it comes to attending hearings and writing judgments in an expeditious manner.

The chief justice spends a great deal of time on administrative and official matters not related to adjudication: up to 40 per cent of his or her working time (most of it over and above a forty-hour work week). The puisne judges, on average, spend about 10 per cent of their working time doing administrative work, such as committee work or a task for one of the judges' associations.

Of seven judges questioned, none said it was desirable to special-ize after appointment, although one conceded that a "focus" is ac-ceptable. Four judges out of five said that some judges are recognized as specialists in a particular field because of previous experience, although they noted that cases with that particular specialty do not often arise. We might note in this context that expertise in a particular area of law does not seem to have been a factor in the appointment of Supreme Court judges. As the most obvious case in point, criminal appeals have in the past decade become the largest component of the Supreme Court case load, although only one member of the current court has a predominantly criminal law background.

Only one judge thought that judges with a civil law training had a different approach to decision-making and, in particular, to the use of precedents than common law judges. Four judges, including two from Quebec, thought that the approach of the judges with a civil law training was not significantly different from that of the common law judges. (The same general pattern was true in the Federal Court of Appeal, where only one judge felt that judges with a civil law training did, in fact, approach their work differently, and in Quebec's court of appeal, most judges did not think that their approach to decision-making was significantly different from that of their com-mon law colleagues in the appellate courts of the other provinces.)

Five of the judges who had previous appellate court experience were asked to comment on the major differences between the Su-preme Court of Canada and the intermediate appellate courts. One judge's view was that in the Supreme Court there was somewhat less emphasis on *stare decisis* and more pressure to "get it right." A second judge, while also acknowledging the court's pressure to be right because of its being the final court of appeal, commented on the time limits imposed on arguments by counsel, which had the effect of forcing counsel to focus and therefore argue more effectively. But the time limits also meant that the judges were more reluctant to intervene with questions during the presentations of counsel than they had been in the intermediate appellate courts. Another judge said the major difference was that there was more of a sense of collegiality among judges in the provincial appeal courts, and another that the Supreme Court places less emphasis on *stare decisis* and more on reasonableness.

Three judges noted that consensus is much harder to reach with nine judges than seven, five, or three. One said it depended on the personalities of the judges on the panel, although one judge felt that the size of the panel made no difference.

Some judges described the differences between the Supreme Court and the provincial court of appeal on which they had served:

Judge A:[3] There's a lot more paper here. When you consider there are five to six hundred applications for leave, and more than 120 files that you have got to read for the substantive appeals, that's substantially more to read than in the provincial appeal court. The panel has to be familiar with all of the material. But aside from the leave applications, there is not a lot of difference except that the nature of the appeal process is different. Here, the parties have time limits and because of these and the fact that there are nine judges, you really are restrained from interrupting. There is not as much dialogue between the court and the lawyers as there was in the court of appeal. If a judge is interested in a case in the court of appeal, the judge can take an hour or so to debate the point, although it seldom goes on that long. When I was in practice, I preferred an active court because if you are arguing and the judges aren't doing anything but blinking, you do not know whether you have made your point.

Another difference is that three people can come to an opinion or an agreement to disagree a lot faster than nine can, because with nine points of view — and there's something to all of them — it is a little slower getting a judgment.

A third difference is that you have to be a little more careful when you are part of the court of last resort. Even though 90 per cent of the cases that go to the provincial court of appeal die there, nonetheless you can say, "Well this is my view, and if I am wrong there is another court that can correct it," so you don't have to hang on to the appeal indefinitely until you reach moral certitude.

Judge D: The major difference is that panels are usually composed of nine judges rather than three and, second, you use clerks more in the Supreme Court. Those are the main distinctions, but there are many minor distinctions in the nature of the work. On the provincial appeal court, 80 per cent or more of the work is correction of errors, for example, a trial judge's misstatement in the charge to the jury, a wrong application of a principle to the facts, errors in sentencing, and so on. There's a small percentage at the top where you really have to look at the law and there's a disagreement as to the principle that should apply, but the provincial appeal court does not have much of a law development function. Here, it's the other way around. Most of our cases concern points of law, or we would not have granted leave. Therefore, the work here is much more difficult, but also more interesting. We are really challenged to work through how the law should develop and to set out our positions clearly.

Judge F: In the Supreme Court, the main difference is sitting with colleagues with a different legal education. This is a real privilege. But there is sometimes a tendency for the Supreme Court to become nine individual law firms in the same building.

Judge H: This is a very stressful place. There are nine judges, each with their own personalities and egos, and you have to work with them for many years. It is not possible to spend as much time as I would like discussing issues and drafts with my colleagues, or just socializing with them. To be efficient, we must communicate through memoranda. It would be possible to go for a couple of weeks without talking to another judge here, unless you make the effort to do it.

Interviewer: How does the court handle the pressure and workload?

Judge D: We're very well organized. We decide 130 cases a year and I sit on 100 of them; that's two decisions per week, not taking off time for holidays, and not considering the leave applications, which are very time consuming. To keep up with those two decisions per week is difficult. I have to read the materials, and in some cases write, and in any event I have to read what the other judges have drafted, so I'm always amazed that we do it. And that's just a small portion of what we do —

there are the leave applications, administrative work, and many other things. We have a well-organized staff and machine behind us. There are the case summaries written by the legal staff. Factums are brief because of the rule on limitations. The hearing time is circumscribed because of the time limits. There is careful control of the whole process. Before I came to the court, there was a big backlog, and the process was tightened up. We're now feeling the positive effects of those changes. Even with all machinery in place, keeping up requires concentration and a lot of hard work.

There is no doubt that the members of the Supreme Court of Canada work extremely hard, putting in long days and working most weekends. The resulting stress showed in the faces of most of the judges. Even in the busiest of the provincial courts of appeal, the atmosphere was more relaxed in comparison.

Supreme Court of Canada judges are top-notch legal practitioners who aspire to the toughest challenges the law has to offer. Most could be described as "workaholics," although they realize the importance of, and make an effort to keep abreast of current affairs and social change. Although they place a high premium on knowledge of the law, they feel that a good Supreme Court judge must be both personable and well organized and must possess excellent writing skills. Most importantly, a Supreme Court judge needs a highly developed personal sense of judgment and fairness.

Leave to Appeal Applications

Most cases heard by the Supreme Court must be granted "leave to appeal." The 550 to 650 leave applications received each year by the court are considered by three-judge panels. The three-judge panels are set by the chief justice on an annual basis. However, because of innovations introduced by Chief Justice Lamer after discussion with all the judges on the court, every judge now potentially has some say over whether leave should be granted in each case.

Under the new system, all applications for leave to appeal are put on a list called the "A List" and circulated to all members of the court. Those cases that the panels have tentatively decided to grant leave to are put on a "B List," which is then circulated. Those judges who object to the granting of leave must give notice of their objection within six days of receiving the list, and the result is that this application is discussed by the full court at a subsequent meeting. The decision is still the panel's to make, but usually the panel will defer to the judgment of the majority on the court.

Those cases tentatively denied leave by the panels are listed and circulated, and any judges who object to a particular case not being granted leave must give notice within six days. Such cases are put on a "D List," and the judge who raised the objection has the right to try to persuade the panel, at a subsequent meeting of the plenary court, that leave ought to be granted. According to the chief justice, about thirty to forty leave to appeal cases end up on the "D List" each year.

Finally, there is a "C List," or list of cases that are related to other applications for leave, other pending cases, or cases recently decided. As a result of discussion of the C List in the plenary court, a panel might decide to remand one of these cases to the court below to reconsider in the light of a recent Supreme Court decision, or the panel may decide that the issue raised by the case is premature. Occasionally, the court may decide that a C List case should be heard with another similar case if the other case is granted leave or has already been granted leave. According to Chief Justice Lamer, the C List is always "very short."

Since the late 1980s the Supreme Court has been able to consider leave applications without oral argument. Today oral arguments rarely occur in leave applications, but when they do there is a fifteen-minute time limit imposed on lawyers for each side. For the past decade, lawyers have had the option of arguing leave applications through closed-circuit television.

Leave applications contain records from the courts below, copies or citations of relevant legal and academic authorities, and most importantly, a factum in which the applicant tries to show why the issue in the case is one of national or general importance. These factums are now limited in length to twenty pages, but even so the total package could be several hundred pages in length.

In a year in which the court considered 550 leave applications, each panel of three would consider about 180 of these applications. The court alternates between "sitting" weeks and "judgment-writing" weeks, so to keep up with the volume of leave applications each panel would have to dispose of seven or eight leave applications per sitting week. If each judge were to spend three or four hours on each leave application file, then considering leave applications could easily occupy nearly all of the judges' sitting weeks. The court obviously needs to devote most of its sitting time to the appeals which make it past the leave threshold, so the leave applications must be dealt with in another way. Not surprisingly, therefore, at the time we conducted our interviews, the three clerks who are assigned to each judge spent a considerable amount of their time working on the leave application files.

Lorne Sossin, who clerked in the Supreme Court of Canada in 1992–93, has described the clerks' role in reviewing leave applications as follows: "The law clerks are ... divided into three groups [to parallel the three panels of judges that consider leave applications]. Each panel is then designated a number of appeals seeking leave, and the clerks assigned to that panel divide the applications among themselves with a view to interest and a rough equality of workload. The clerk reviews the materials, and prepares a generally short memorandum [averaging fifteen pages] for the panel of justices, which concludes by recommending whether or not the case should be granted leave. Thus the work of one clerk typically will be used by all the justices deciding on an application for leave."[4]

Sossin's assessment is that the clerks tend to recommend considerably more cases for acceptance than are actually accepted. Conversely, if a clerk recommends that leave not be granted, this recommendation is rarely reversed by the three-judge panel. He notes that the criteria for granting leave to appeal to the Supreme Court are "extremely vague and largely subjective.... Some factors that have been taken to indicate an issue of 'national importance' include splits in appellate courts on the issue, the impact of the uncertainty in the law, and whether the appeal in question presents 'the right case' to use as a vehicle to clarify or interpret the relevant law."[5]

Here is how the judges described their procedures for determining whether leave should be granted.

Judge A: The court receives an application for leave. It is vetted through four or five [staff] lawyers, who gather the material and summarize it. It is an objective summary of what the application is about. There is no comment made on the strengths or weaknesses of the argument. In a paragraph, it tells us what the trial judge said. And then there is a summary of what the respondent and the appellant said. You get that and you get the factums, and generally you have one of the clerks look at the material and they will do a memorandum of law and almost always express opinion as to whether they think leave should be granted. (As an aside, when the clerks first arrive, they are more generous in what they see as cases that deserve leave than they are by the time they leave.)

By the time I get the clerk's memo, I have read the material. I seldom read the evidence; I rely on the summary and the factum unless there is some particular point I need to check. But I have read the factums and almost always I have made up my mind before I see the clerk's memo. Probably 5, 10 per cent of the time — not a lot of the time — but sometimes when you read the clerk's memo you can change your mind; you can get a different appreciation of the case. What it does with me is not change my mind as much as bring me from thinking leave should not be granted to where I do not know. I have not been moved all the way over, but I have come to where I am not as sure that what I thought was the important point really is the point.

There are three-member panels to consider leave applications and the make-up of the panels changes from time to time. The panel decides whether leave will be granted. If the panel is unanimous then leave is either rejected or allowed. If they're not unanimous, then it goes to a conference of all the members of the court, but it is still the panel's responsibility to make the decision. You frequently will make your mind up at the conference. If you have been pushed off your original position by the clerk's memo or another judge's opinion, in the conference you generally get refocused again. Sometimes you are back to where you started, and at other times you see that you missed the point before. It is a little different from hearing the appeal itself because with the leave applications you are just determining whether the case should be heard. You are not determining much more.

Judge C: We grant leave only in cases we think are of general importance. An issue might be of importance to a large number of persons in a province, but the question is whether it is of general importance in the whole country. But of the 140 or so cases we hear in a year, about fifty of them we do not select — they come to us as-of-right. And while some of these cases do raise issues of general national importance, many of them don't. Added to that are many cases in which we granted leave because we felt that they were of general national importance, and with the passage of time or with changes in legislation, or some other event, they have lost their national general importance.

The chief justice does not strike panels of nine unless he feels that there is an issue of general national importance where the judges might have differing views.

Judge D: I use my clerks, first of all, in applications for leave. They do a bench memo which is a memo of about ten pages which identifies the issues, how the issues were dealt with by the courts below, and what is the matter of public importance. However, even in matters of public importance, if a court of appeal, for whatever reason, has not had the opportunity to express an opinion on an issue, we will often decline to grant leave because we want cases where we have the opinion of a court of appeal or preferably several courts of appeal.

Interviewer: Is there a tradition that if one judge thinks that leave should be granted, then it is granted?

Judge A: I think there is a generosity in that regard. If one judge really believed a matter to be important, I think the other two members on the panel would accommodate. What is the harm in that? I think the cooperative nature of the court during my time here is that if one wants it heard, I think he or she could probably prevail and have it.

Interviewer: Would it ever happen that a judge would want a case heard and the panel would turn it down?

Judge B: Yes. A judge may want a particular case heard, and so it goes on what's called a "D List," and then at the meeting of the entire court you can put forward your position as to why it should be heard, why it is a matter of public importance, etc. Sometimes there's a majority that agrees with you, and the case goes on the list.

Interviewer: Are there ever any cases heard by the court that you think should not have been granted leave? If so, why was leave granted?

Judge A: Yes. This does not happen often, but it happens often enough that your breath is not taken away when it does. It just happens with some cases that they do not live up to the expectations that were created for it.

I think that the lawyers may represent in good faith that there is an important point, and when you get into the case the point isn't there at all because, for example, it was not raised at the trial level.

Judge B: You don't get the full picture in a leave application. Then it comes before you with the complete transcript, and you find you cannot even get to a big issue of law: it is determined on the basis of the facts presented.

Judge D: Sometimes, once counsel have fully submitted their factums, a case takes on a different complexion than it had when you first looked at the application for leave. Counsel are often very skilful in presenting their argument in writing on a leave application as if the case is of public importance. When it comes to the actual appeal, it sometimes turns out that the case can be decided by reason of a finding of fact, and an important issue of law really does not arise.

The interviews indicate that the cases most likely to be granted leave are not only those that raise issues of general legal importance, but also those in which the lawyers submitting the applications are able to describe the central issue clearly and succinctly. There is no sense in overwhelming the judges with massive files; they have no time to read them. If the lawyers want the judges actually to read carefully the materials they submit, rather than summaries of them prepared by the legal staff or the clerks, then these materials must be brief.

There are undoubtedly applications for leave that have raised issues of general importance, but that were denied because the important issue was so hidden in a mass of documents that it was never noticed, just as there are cases inadvertently granted leave because counsel were skilled at feigning an issue of general importance.

More recently, partly because of the steep rise in the number of applications for leave (there were 637 filed in 1997), the task of summarizing leave applications has been transferred from the clerks to staff lawyers who report to the court's registrar. In 1987, there were two staff lawyers in the Supreme Court; in 1998 there were thirteen. These staff lawyers are hired through the Public Service Commission. The clerks now focus more on assisting the judges with the research needed to prepare for appeal hearings, and to support the writing of opinions, although the judges still discuss the potential merit of the leave applications with them. Thus, the method of selection of clerks is an important variable.

Selection of Clerks

Each judge has three clerks, selected from among the "best and brightest" law school graduates. They assist the judges with the leave applications, research, and a variety of other activities.

Sossin described the clerks as "a relatively homogeneous group.... Women ... now commonly comprise a majority of clerks, indeed, 17 of the 27 clerks for the 1992–93 term. Law clerks at the Supreme Court are overwhelmingly white and affluent, reflecting the homogeneity of the 'feeder' law schools on which they rely."[6]

Here is how the judges described the clerk selection process:

Judge A: This is how the selection process works. Law students who are about to graduate send in their application to the Office of the Chief Justice for a clerk's position. Sometimes, if they don't know the process, they might write to separate judges, but these letters are forwarded to the chief justice. The staff in the chief justice's chambers compiles and organizes the applications. If a student wants a chance to be interviewed, he or she will need a recommendation from the dean. Each law school dean will probably recommend one or two students, depending on the size of the graduating class.[7]

There are twenty-seven spots for clerks, and the judges can interview as many on the short list as they have time to.[8] Last year I probably interviewed twenty applicants. The chief justice gets first pick, and then the judges get their pick in order of seniority. It is like a draft selection in a hockey league; often the first draft choice is gone!

So if all the judges had exactly the same point of view about all the applicants, then the newest judge on the court would always get assigned clerks who are his or her last choice. Now, human nature being what it is, we all make mistakes in the selection process, and sometimes the applicant who ranked twenty-seventh will turn out to be the best clerk of the bunch. Frankly, given the work that the law schools do to recommend their best students, I could almost choose my three clerks by throwing three stones on the twenty-seven files to see where they landed, and I would come up with three clerks that are very competent. It is really very hard to select them.

One of the things I tell law students is that it is worth applying and that if you are picked it is probably worth doing, but if you are not picked don't lose any sleep over it. If you apply for something and you do not get it, you are disappointed, but you have to get over the disappointment. You might find that you use your time a lot more usefully in practice. A year of practice, as compared with clerking in the Supreme Court, might not look quite as good on your CV for the first couple of years, but by the fifth year in practice nobody cares whether you articled at the Supreme Court.

Because of the selection process, there is a great deal of emphasis on scholarship. There is more scholarship here than there would be in a law office. On the other hand, you do not learn how to be a lawyer here.

Judge H: I choose law clerks that have a social conscience, who are mature, thoughtful. Law clerks have to be able to think creatively and meticulously; they have to be able to do research thoroughly. It is not a case of just reciting information, but providing critical interpretations of the information and the significance of the information. They have to be able to write elegantly. The human side is very important.

The clerks represent the "cream of the crop" of the annual law school graduates. But of hundreds of top-quality graduates each year, only twenty-seven can be chosen to work in the Supreme Court of Canada. The final selection is a result of the views of the law school deans, the views of the judges about the relative importance of various academic and non-academic factors, and the views of the current clerks about the suitability of the new applicants.[9] Undoubtedly, the "critical interpretations" provided by the clerks constitute one significant factor in the court's decisions about whether to grant leave.

It is interesting that two judges mentioned that they would like to have additional clerks assigned to them to assist with research, while two others felt that additional clerks would be counterproductive because of the increased time that it would take to supervise their work.

Striking Panels

The ideal in the Supreme Court is for all nine judges to hear every case. For a variety of reasons, this ideal situation is not always possible or desirable. In cases where nine judges cannot sit on a case, or where this is not appropriate, the chief justice determines who will sit, provided always that a judge who is not chosen for a panel has the right to sit anyway. The number of judges on a panel is odd rather than even to avoid a situation where the panel is split into two even camps, one for allowing the appeal and the other for dismissing it. Occasionally, an even-numbered panel of judges will develop because one member has had to leave because of illness; in these cases, if the panel is evenly split, the appeal fails and the lower court ruling prevails.

The composition of the panels has been criticized by some academics in recent years because there have been several 4–3 splits on critical cases. From this perspective, the make-up of the seven-judge panel is crucial to the outcome of the case, because if nine judges had served on the panel, the court's decision might have been a 5–4 split with the opposite outcome.

Between 1 April 1990 and 31 March 1996 an average of 45 per cent of the appeal corams consisted of seven-judge panels, while 28 per cent were nine-judge panels, and 27 per cent were five-judge panels. The nine-judge panels ranged from a low of 8 per cent in 1991–92, to a high of 46 per cent in 1995–96. Conversely, the seven-judge panels ranged from a high of 57 per cent in 1991–92 to a low of 28 per cent in 1995–96.[10] This is consistent with the long-term trend towards larger panel sizes on the Supreme Court of Canada.[11]

Here is how Chief Justice Lamer described his method of striking panels (he is quoted on this issue with permission):

If there is a possibility that the outcome of a case might be different with fewer than nine judges, I'll do my best to strike a panel of nine judges. How do I know if there will be a division? First, my executive legal officer helps me to flag these cases. Also, I know my colleagues and I have a fairly good idea about what they are thinking on particular issues. I might ask what the other judges think about a particular issue, even if it is not of national general importance. I wouldn't like to see a minority in the court impose its views on the court, and even for the cases that are not of general importance I will strike the bench of nine if necessary. But I will go down to five if it is an as-of-right case that we would not have granted leave to, and where it appears that we are practically unanimous. So you don't see many 3–2 split decisions in recent years.

Academics must be careful when they analyse the data because in previous years we had illness on the court and we had a death. This might cause us to start off with a seven-judge panel but hand down a judgment with four. So you have got to look at the initial composition of the bench. If, for some reason, judges are dropped from that initial panel, then in most of these cases we ask the parties whether they will consent to proceeding or if they would rather have a rehearing.

If I see that a case is strictly common law, I am inclined to take two of the Quebec judges off. I would not like to see the swing vote to be in the hands of a civilian judge. Similarly, if a case is strictly on the Civil Code with no issue of general importance, I would of course include the Quebec judges, but I would not use all nine judges. I have the impression that in cases where there is a possibility of changing the common law and if a civilian judge ends up having the swing vote for the change, the judge probably would prefer the status quo. Now that is not a rule, but I think that it is the proper thing to do.

Setting aside those cases that have lost their importance or didn't have it initially because they came here as of right, the rule is that we try to sit nine. However, we sometimes cannot sit nine because of the illness of a judge. Several years ago, there was a judge who was sick a great deal, and so we were down to seven whether we wanted it or not. Then, when a judge resigns or retires, it sometimes takes several months for the government to appoint a replacement. Added to that is that occasionally the newly appointed judges from the courts of appeal below may run into cases here where they have a conflict of interest. This is because they were part of the appeal court panel which decided the case prior to the appeal to the Supreme Court of Canada, or they may have had discussions with their former colleagues about the case, and the judge would feel uncomfortable sitting on the panel here.

Then, unusual cases come to us such as the David Milgaard case. [The cabinet sent a reference question to the Supreme Court in 1991, asking whether the conviction of David Milgaard for murder in 1970 constituted a miscarriage of justice, and if so, what remedial action would be appropriate.] We sat eighteen days on the Milgaard case. I did not feel I could assign nine judges to one case for that length of time, given our regular workload, so I assigned a bench of five. We did not postpone any other cases due to the Milgaard case, but it would have been too much to ask all five judges on the Milgaard panel to continue with all of the other cases they had already been assigned. So I had to reduce some of the other panels from nine to lighten the load a little for the judges on the Milgaard panel. I would take the judges on the Milgaard panel three at a time and rotate them with the other four judges on the court. That is why for practically a whole term the court sat in benches of seven. It might have been possible to have spread these eighteen days over a longer period of time, but we were dealing with a prisoner who said he was innocent, and I felt that we were duty-bound to deal with this matter on an urgent basis.

As I mentioned earlier, I try to avoid setting up panels of seven where there might be a four to three split, but during the term when we heard the Milgaard case, there were these kinds of splits. However, I am confident that the end results reflected the views of all nine judges. In a couple of instances I think we ordered a rehearing when it was not all that clear that the majority of the court would share the views of the majority of the panel.

Decades ago, as Ian Bushnell noted, the choice of the chief justice as to who would sit on a particular panel might have had an impact on the outcome of cases. Because of the court's current policy, it would appear that this factor is now less relevant, even when the court sits with fewer than nine judges and there is a 4–3 or 3–2 split.[12]

Decision-making

Once a case has been granted leave and the panel for it established, then the central part of the decision-making process begins. The judges receive the relevant documents for each case about a month in advance of the scheduled hearing. These include the factums (lawyers' arguments and summaries of facts) for each side (limited to forty pages in length, although in important legal cases the parties can apply for, and often receive, permission to present longer factums), the book of authorities (copies of precedent decisions and academic articles that the lawyers think are relevant), and the transcripts of the decisions of the courts which previously considered the case. Except for reference cases, every case coming to the Supreme Court has already been considered at least by a trial court and the provincial or federal court of appeal; occasionally additional courts might have been involved.

The judges do not have the time to read thoroughly all of the documents provided to them. During our interviews, cartloads of documents were sometimes wheeled into a judge's office; these often represented the relevant materials for a single case. The judges do read carefully the parts of the documents which they consider essential to understanding each case, and they have their clerks examine the rest and summarize them. Three of the judges told us that they spent four to eight hours preparing for an "average" case, although the preparation time might be shorter for an as-of-right case and longer for a complex constitutional law case. Five judges were asked in what proportion of cases they felt they had enough time to prepare. Two judges said that more time would be useful for most cases, while two said that enough time was available for all cases. One said that it was simply a case of fitting the work into the limited time available. Most judges have a sense of how they think the case will be decided after reading these materials, although they all remain open to changing their minds during oral argument.

During sitting weeks[13] the court normally hears two cases per day starting at 9:45 a.m. and ending around 4:00 p.m. A practice direction of the court stipulates that the oral arguments of the appellant and respondent are limited to one hour. (The time limits are enforced through a system of small lights, akin to signal lights, on the lecterns used by counsel.) Therefore, the judges will often finish with the first case, and get into the second and sometimes even complete it, before lunch, which is normally scheduled from 12:30 p.m. to 2:00 p.m. Fridays see more as-of-right appeals than other days. It is more common for the court to decline to call on the lawyer for the respondent in as-of-right appeals than appeals that have been granted leave, and therefore the as-of-right appeals tend to move along somewhat more quickly. Thus, it is rare for the court to sit on a Friday afternoon. (In as-of-right appeals, the court will not call on the lawyer for the respondent if the court feels that the respondent has the much stronger argument.)

The judges gather in an antechamber before going into court, and occasionally they will have an informal discussion about procedural questions. For example, if it appears that the appellant has an overwhelmingly strong case, they may decide to call on the respondent's lawyer first. (Normally, the appellant is called upon first, but if the judges are already convinced by the appellant's position, then the appellant's oral argument may be redundant.)

As in other appeal courts, the judges will sometimes interrupt counsel with questions, but the time limits make the Supreme Court judges somewhat more restrained than their counterparts in the lower appeal courts. The hearings in the Supreme Court are now broadcast regularly on Saturday evenings on the Canadian Parliamentary Channel (CPAC). The video feed is taken from the small, unobtrusive cameras mounted along the walls of the main courtroom in the Supreme Court building, and so the views of the court are not terribly inspiring. However, the broadcasts provide viewers with a sense of how the Supreme Court conducts its business.

After most hearings the judges go immediately into the conference room. They are seated around a large round table in order of seniority. The chief justice calls on each judge, beginning with the most junior and working in order to the most senior, for a brief summary of his or her views about how they think the case should be decided. The reason why the junior judges speak first is to encourage them to speak freely, without worrying about the views of the more senior judges. By the time the chief justice has spoken, it is usually clear what the outcome of the case will be (although the judges may yet change their minds prior to "signing on" to a decision), and there is a sense of which judge best represents the majority thinking. That person often volunteers to write the first draft of the majority decision, although someone else may volunteer who feels that, from the perspective of workload, it is his or her "turn." Occasionally, a case will revolve around an issue of law that was a particular judge's specialty prior to judicial appointment, and in these situations that judge is the most likely to volunteer to write the draft. If more than one judge offers to write the draft, then the most senior judge is considered to have priority. If there are dissenters, someone on the dissenting side usually volunteers to write the first draft of the dissenting judgment. If there is a lack of volunteers either for the majority or dissenting judgment, the chief justice will ask a judge to write, and that request is invariably honoured.

The rationale for having the most junior judges speak first in conference deliberations is to encourage their full participation and to reduce the likelihood of undue reticence or deference. However, we wonder whether it does not have a further unforeseen implication, stemming from the logical proposition that the earlier a judge speaks in the deliberations, the less likely it is that his or her contribution will provide the definitive or clinching moment, that is, any comments after the first will either build on what has gone before, or differ from it, or attempt a synthesis. To draw a metaphor from contract bridge: if you lead, you never get to trump an ace, although you constantly expose yourself to the risk of being trumped. By way of empirical verification of this hypothesis, it should be noted that on the Supreme Court of Canada, junior judges deliver less, and senior judges more, than their "share" of the decisions of the court.[14]

Some of the judges interviewed suggested that it is only normal for newly appointed members to take some time to come up to speed, but this is demonstrably not the case for the U.S. Supreme Court, where junior members deliver more, not less, than their proportionate share of decisions.[15] On the U.S. Supreme Court, it might be noted, judges make their contributions to conference deliberations in the reverse order, junior members speaking last.

As a general rule, the judges spend about the same amount of time drafting judgments during their judgment weeks as they do preparing for hearings. Each judge uses his or her clerks in different ways. The clerks often draft the first part of the judgment, which summarizes the facts of the case. Two of the judges said they asked their clerks to do a first draft of the body of the judgment, but specific instructions are first given about the content of the draft. Other judges do the first draft of the body of the judgment themselves, but the clerks are asked to comment and criticize. Still other judges have the clerks concentrate more on researching specific points in the judgment. Sossin's view of the impact of the clerks on Canadian Supreme Court decision-making is that the clerks do not "have significant and direct influence *on* the decisions of the Supreme Court, but ... in a variety of subtle and indirect ways, clerks affect the Court's decision-making process, and the policy-making that results."[16] For example, certain issues might receive more attention in a written decision than otherwise, and on the whole, decisions may be more lengthy than they otherwise might be.

Supreme Court judges do a great deal of research about the issues that come before them. This includes reviewing precedents and scholarly articles and books in the law, the social sciences, and other relevant disciplines. Two of the judges clearly had no qualms about working until the wee hours of the morning on a fairly regular basis because they enjoyed the research aspect so much. The clerks do much of the legwork for the judges' research activities and summarize what they have found, but all the judges do at least some of the research themselves. One judge said that once or twice they had asked a law professor about academic sources relevant to an issue before the court (it was emphasized that actual cases were never discussed outside the court), but three judges said they relied entirely on their clerks and court staff. Five judges were asked whether they consulted judges who were not on their panel about issues before the court; three said that they occasionally did, while two said that they never did.

The first draft is circulated, and then the other judges begin to comment on it. Occasionally the judges will discuss the draft in person with each other, but given the workload of the court, these face-to-face discussions are rare because they are considered inefficient. More commonly, comments are in the form of memoranda, sometimes drafted by the clerks according their judge's instructions.

Six judges were asked whether obiter should be avoided in the reasons for judgment. None thought that obiter should be avoided, but three said that judges ought to exercise restraint.

Six judges were asked in what situations the court wrote per curiam decisions. While stressing how rarely this happens, they said that when it does, it is nearly always in a case of great national importance, or one of little importance, but only if all the judges have all made some contribution to the decision. In either case, a *per curiam* decision may help to emphasize how united the judges are on the issue.

It is considered bad form for the dissenting judgment, if there is one, to be drafted prior to the release of the first draft of the majority judgment. A dissenting judgment is circulated not long after the majority judgment, and it is also subject to comment by memorandum. Eight judges were asked whether it is important to try to avoid dissenting opinions. Seven replied that dissenting opinions are healthy, while one felt that the judges should take care to avoid unnecessary or unimportant dissents.[17] Eventually, the majority judgment is finalized, and at that point the others on the majority side have to decide whether to concur in full, or to write separate concurring judgments.

The Supreme Court has been criticized in recent years for producing too many separate concurring decisions. These multifarious judgments do not help to clarify the law in the minds of lawyers and judges in the courts below.[18] There is a variety of thought among the judges about this issue, but a slight majority of judges does not see the number of separate concurring decisions as a major problem. From their perspective, the law is always in a state of flux, and too much rigidity mitigates against fairness and justice. On the other hand, three judges felt that one way to improve the decision-making process in the Supreme Court would be for the judges to find a way to reduce the number of separate concurring decisions.[19]

After the circulation of the draft judgments some judges "switch sides," and occasionally this means that what was the dissenting opinion becomes the majority judgment. Finally, all the judges on the panel "sign off," and the judgment is released to the litigants and to the public. The judgments are eventually printed in the *Supreme Court Reports* and other law reports, but they are also available immediately after release through various electronic reporting services, and free of charge through the Internet.

Five judges were asked whether they had an individual thought process that helps them reach a conclusion about a case, as opposed to the institutional or collegial process described above. Three judges described a general individual strategy, while two said that each case was so different that an overall strategy was not useful. One of the individual strategies was to come to a tentative conclusion after reading the case materials, and then test this conclusion most importantly during oral argument, but also in the post-hearing conference. A second strategy was to continually weigh the individual litigant's interests against the community's interest. The third approach involved focusing on "the three p's": principle, precedent, and policy.

The judges' comments about decision-making help this process to come alive:

> Judge A: Once a case has been granted leave, then you get factums for these cases about a month in advance of the hearing. You get the substantive arguments on the relevant issues, as opposed to the arguments on national importance which were in the leave application. Otherwise, much the same process applies as in the leave application, except that the objective summary from the legal staff that you had initially does not come again because you already have it.
>
> But then you get a "bench memo" from your clerks on the case, and different judges have different ways of doing that. They will sometimes discuss the case with their clerks before they write a bench memo. At other times the bench memo comes in quite unexpectedly because in the process nothing works the way it should — you may not get the books and the clerk has them and does a bench memo without thinking much about it. Sometimes you are quite content to let the clerk do the bench memo before you discuss the case with him or her, unless you have focused on something that you want looked at more carefully. In some cases you are ahead of the clerk in that you have read the factums, so they can save themselves work by talking to you before they do the bench memo. But it probably comes out about the same whether they talk to you or not; they

express an opinion on what they think that this position should be — appeal allowed or appeal dismissed.

I do not think the clerk's recommendation is of any consequence. I mean you are curious, but you read the material without regard to the clerk's recommendation because you know that ultimately you are going to have to make up your own mind. I find that more frequently than I would have thought, more frequently than I thought as a lawyer, judges change their mind during the course of the appeal, once they hear the argument. I was dubious about that in practice. I thought their minds were made up after reading the material. But it is surprising the number of times that counsel raises something that gets you thinking in a different direction.

Six judges were asked how often they changed their minds during oral argument, and five answered in the 20 to 25 per cent range. (Answers to this question from the intermediate appellate judges were similar.) One judge, however, simply said that it was best to keep an open mind until the end of the hearing.

Judge A: After the argument, almost always the case is reserved, probably over 90 per cent of the time. Then you go to conference, and the conference is not lengthy but everybody speaks on their view of how the case should be disposed of. If everyone agrees — nine all one way — then somebody will either volunteer or be asked to write reasons. These reasons are circulated, and usually if there is unanimity at the conference then it stays that way. Frequently, there are cases where there is something to be said on both sides, so you will get five in favour and four against at the conference. Somebody in the majority will write the first draft which is circulated.

Interviewer: How is the decision made about who will write the first draft?

Judge A: With only nine people, you get a pretty good sense of who got stuck, for example, on Monday to write an opinion. And if for some reason or another he picked up something on Wednesday, then by Thursday it becomes pretty clear that you have not, so you either volunteer, or the chief justice will say, "Would you mind?" and it is all very genteel. But if the chief justice would like a particular judge to write, I just cannot imagine any judge who wouldn't. It seems that there is a pretty good sense of fairness. I think the chief justice over a period of time would reach conclusions that some people know more about, say, criminal law, so he'd be inclined to ask them to do a draft in a criminal case. Or some have a better knowledge of Section 1 of the Charter. But generally it seems that after taking on the writing for a particular judgment, then the ninth case that comes along after that is your case to write again. There are exceptions, but generally that's the way it goes.

Judge B: Right after the oral argument, we retire to our conference room which is right behind the courtroom and starting with the most junior judge, each judge in turn expresses his or her views briefly as to how he or she would dispose of the case and when that process is completed we either have unanimity, or we have a majority and a minority view. Either somebody in the majority volunteers to write the majority reasons, or the chief justice may suggest that somebody draft them. We have a lot of judges here that are hard workers and very eager, and it is usually not a problem to get somebody to write the reasons. Sometimes there is competition over who will write, very politely done, of course.

Interviewer: Does it make a difference that the junior judge speaks first?

Judge A: It's a very healthy tradition, very salutary. It's just a very sound idea.

Judge B: I think it makes a difference when the junior judge speaks first. The junior judges are generally more prepared, they don't rely on the older ones, and they are fresher. It's a healthy exercise. But it's very frightening when you are a junior judge. I wasn't aware of the tradition; no one had told me. So on my first case, I was surprised to be asked first what I thought. I was also surprised that we didn't have a general discussion. But sometimes now, this general discussion does occur, and I think it helps us to make up our minds. The chief justice of the United States seems to think that a general discussion is a waste of time because the judges have already made up their minds. But at least here in Canada, that is not the case.

Judge D: I do not think so. I guess the reason for it is that the junior judge will be more likely to express his or her opinion because he has not been intimidated by hearing the opinions of those who have been around longer. But the Supreme Court of the United States is just the opposite. When you consider that most judges that come here either have been on courts of appeal, or have done enough counsel work that they are not reluctant to express their opinion, and they are all used to being disagreed with, then it probably doesn't make any difference.

Judge E: I think that is an excellent process but I feel that it makes the junior judge a full participant right off the mark when he or she is appointed, and it avoids the tendency, should there be any, to defer to the senior judges. I do not think we have ever experienced that problem, but perhaps this is because we have insisted on the junior judge speaking first.

Judge H: I think it makes a difference. But it puts a lot of pressure on the junior judge. I remember my first case here, and it was not an easy case. Suddenly, I was expected to tell my colleagues, whom I had regarded as being next to divinity, how to decide the case! But I eventually liked this tradition, because once I had gotten over the initial fright, I felt that it gave the junior judge a lot of influence.

Interviewer: What happens after the draft judgment is circulated?

Judge A: The draft reasons for judgment are eventually circulated, and there is usually a period of time for the other judges to start signing on. The other judges will comment, perhaps suggesting that if the judge writing the majority judgment will make some changes, they will concur. Or they may say, "I am going to concur anyway, but I suggest you make this particular change." There is some discussion, usually by memorandum. If there is a dissent, the same process may happen with respect to the dissenting reasons. Sometimes, the dissent eventually attracts a majority. It is a process of persuasion. Generally speaking, the result is the same as at the conference, but sometimes it changes.

The key to a written decision is its persuasive value. If a set of reasons is persuasive to the bar and the judiciary, then it may have precedent value for decades; sometimes today's persuasive dissent becomes tomorrow's law.[20] Three of seven judges questioned had attended a judgment-writing course while serving on an intermediate appellate court, and all three were very positive about how these courses had helped them to write clearer, briefer, and more persuasive decisions. Four, however, had never attended a judgment-writing course.[21]

In thinking about the audience for the written decision, three judges had the litigants primarily in mind when writing decisions, two thought primarily of the judges below, and one wrote principally for the bar.

Two factors were important in the judges' decisions about what cases to cite: relevance and persuasive value. Four out of five judges who answered this question said they would cite the leading recent cases relevant to the issue at hand. In addition, they were concerned about persuading their colleagues, in the short run, and their readers in the long run, and so would choose citations for their persuasive value. When being innovative, the persuasive value of certain precedents was particularly important.

Five judges were asked whether they cite authorities not mentioned by counsel. They all answered in the affirmative, with the proportion varying from 5 to 20 per cent, and the average being 10 per cent. Three judges said they sometimes cited authorities not mentioned by counsel because the court's library was so extensive that they had access to recent precedents and relevant scholarly articles that counsel could not have been expected to have found.[22] One judge mentioned that most counsel were not yet familiar with the decisions of the European courts, and these decisions were sometimes relevant in Charter cases.

While in the intermediate appeal courts, most judges considered it wrong to cite cases not mentioned by counsel unless counsel had had an opportunity to comment on them, in the Supreme Court the judges had a different perspective: cases not mentioned by counsel were often useful to cite to make their opinions more persuasive.

The Supreme Court's Lawmaking Role

Seven judges were asked whether they saw their role as that of lawmaker or law interpreter, or both. We used a 5-point scale, where 1 represented "lawmaker," and 5, "law interpreter." All of the judges saw themselves as having a dual role, and four of the judges responded with a "3," meaning that the two roles were evenly split. Two judges placed themselves at "4," meaning that they were a little closer to the law interpreter side, while one judge was at "2," or slightly closer to the lawmaking side.

Four out of five judges felt that the Charter of Rights had changed the role of the court, bringing it closer to a lawmaking function. One judge ventured that about 60 per cent of the court's cases now involved lawmaking to some extent. But of five judges questioned, all disagreed with the proposition that the Charter had created a crisis of legitimacy for the court, and one strongly disagreed. The consensus was that through the political process, the Supreme Court had been handed a lawmaking role by the people of Canada, and that this new role was generally accepted.

Four judges were asked whether it is appropriate for social and public interest groups to use the court to achieve social change. On a 1 to 5 scale, 5 being "extremely appropriate" and 1 being "not at all appropriate," the average response was 3.5. Two judges mentioned that public interest groups can present very useful briefs as intervenors, and one judge saw the courts as a part of the democratic process. One judge, however, saw a danger to the courts being used as political tools.

Three judges were asked when they would not follow a precedent of the Supreme Court of Canada, and all three said they would not hesitate to overrule a "bad" precedent. For one judge, a bad precedent would include even a recent precedent in a new area of law (such as the Charter), where the judges had not been able to consider all the implications of the situation because of the newness of the issue.

Five judges were asked how they choose between conflicting lines of precedents. Only one responded with a standard legal answer: recent precedents are more persuasive, as well as those from the highest-ranking authorities. Four judges, however, simply said that they would choose the most compelling, fair, or just line of precedents (and one of these said that the position of the authority on the judicial hierarchy should also be considered). This kind of response was typical of many intermediate appellate court judges as well, which is why the judges' individual sense of justice is so important in understanding the decision-making process.

One of the ways in which judges can be creative in a law-development role is to take a less strict approach towards applying precedents through distinguishing. Five judges were asked how they decide whether a particular precedent is binding, or whether it should be distinguished. Two of the judges described a strict legal approach: a precedent simply could not be distinguished unless the facts of the precedent cases were significantly different from those in the instant case. The other three judges, however, stressed the need for following precedents that are both fair and helpful; those that were not could likely be distinguished in some way.

Four judges were asked whether they took judicial notice of social or political facts not mentioned by counsel. One judge said that this was not done, while the other three said that it happens occasionally, in from 5 to 50 per cent of cases (depending on how broadly the term is defined). In general, the judges did not regard the taking of judicial notice as an important part of their role.[23]

Six judges were asked whether the judges of the Supreme Court could be divided philosophically into discernible groups. None of these judges answered "no," although one did not know. Four said that the philosophical groups are different for each kind of case, and so there was no overall way that the judges could be classified, while one judge mentioned that there were "hawks" and "doves" on the issue of mens rea. One judge mentioned that life experience is what causes all human beings, judges included, to fall into different philosophical groupings.

Decision-making in the Supreme Court

To the extent that legal culture influences Canadian appellate judging, the responses of individual judges about how they decide may be similar — regardless of whether they sit on penultimate appeal courts that handle many routine cases and can refuse hearings to very few, or whether the judges sit on the Supreme Court, where most appellants must first convince them to hear the case at all. Canadian appellate courts resemble one another in ways that become apparent after a comparison with their counterparts in England or the United States. For example, Supreme Court judges and the judges in the appellate courts below them value both detailed factums that they consider carefully in advance of the hearing, and oral arguments, and they say they have changed their minds as a result of oral arguments in about the same proportion of cases. On the other hand, there are some important differences between the Supreme Court and the lower appellate courts. The legal culture of the Supreme Court of Canada, for example, emphasizes a tolerance of separate concurring decisions, extensive conference deliberations led off by the most junior members, and the occasional use of the *per curiam* device for particularly important (or particularly unimportant) cases. As the previous chapters show, these features are only sometimes replicated in the provincial courts of appeal. The fact that most Supreme Court judges got there after serving on provincial appeal benches suggests one explanation for the continuity that does exist.

Conversely, judicial performance may reflect and reinforce institutional processes and practices that vary from court to court. The expectations of lawyers preparing to argue before the various courts are likely to reflect differences in time pressures and judges' perceived personalities from one court to another. For example, the recent practices of the Supreme Court of Canada emphasize large panels, an enhanced role for law clerks and staff lawyers, and strictly limited time allocations for oral argument (which in turn inhibits intervention and questioning by the judges). It is to be expected that quite different institutional dynamics would surround the deliberations of the provincial courts of appeal, especially in the smaller provinces.

The importance of the judges' personal sense of justice is demonstrated by the fact that a sense of even judgement and fairness is the single most important factor in the qualities which the judges respect in their colleagues, and it is high on the list of traits which they say ought to be considered in judicial appointments. When faced with conflicting lines of precedents, most judges choose the line that appears to them to be the most just or fair, and they are open to overruling precedents that seem unjust. Because there is less emphasis on *stare decisis* in the Supreme Court, and a fair amount of latitude on distinguishing precedents that seem unfair, the judges have opportunities to implement some of their thinking about justice and fairness. In one of his more famous dicta, U.S. Chief Justice John Marshall once said, "We must never forget that it is a constitution that we are expounding." Similarly, we as citizens in a democracy must never forget that it is individual judges who are doing the expounding, individuals who are accountable for explaining their decisions and the values that guide them. Legal culture and institutional processes constrain but do not determine outcome.

The Judicial Decision: Reasons and Citations

It is important to consider not just what judicial decisions do or how appeal courts organize themselves to make them, but also — at an even more basic and obvious level — what those decisions look like: how they are written and why they are written that way. This chapter will begin by looking at the decisions of the provincial courts of appeal and conclude by applying the same criteria of analysis to the decisions of the Supreme Court. Decisions about how to write decisions, what to include in them and what to leave out, what precedents to cite and which to ignore are all discretionary matters that comprise part of the notion of judicial power.

What is a Judicial "Decision"?

As all legal professionals know, but as many laypersons do not realize until they stop to think about it, when judges make a decision they do not simply declare an outcome; they also give reasons. That is to say, although they will conclude by saying that an appeal is allowed (or dismissed), they typically get there only after a discursive explanation which is intended to give compelling logical reasons why the appeal deserved to be allowed (or dismissed). This process of explanation normally involves making explicit the general rule or doctrine on which the immediate decision is based, usually by linking it to the decisions of other judges in the same or other courts. As a general formula, then, decision = outcome + reasons; and for everyone except the immediate parties (and sometimes even for them) these reasons may well be more important than the outcome itself. This statement may be slightly dubious for trial decisions, but much more compelling for appeal decisions.

It has frequently been observed that the "giving reasons" requirement constitutes a significant check upon the "power" of judges.[1] First, there are some outcomes that an individual decision-maker might personally prefer but that cannot be linked to the kind of "reasons" that other actors will accept. Second, the giving of reasons exposes a logical trail that invites further examination and subsequent review by a "higher" court, a review that would be far more difficult if a decision were simply a flat one-line outcome. Third, the giving of reasons constitutes a promise of similar treatment to similar actors in the future, a way in which they can make undesirable outcomes less likely and desirable outcomes more likely simply by shaping their actions so as to conform with the standards that the immediate case declares. This is why the reasons may be more important than the outcome: the outcome affects the immediate participants in a direct way, but the reasons can ripple very wide indeed. For example, when the Supreme Court of Canada handed down the *Daviault* decision[2] in 1995, it did not just send the case of a single specific individual back for retrial. In the process of giving its reasoned explanation for that outcome, it also dramatically publicized the "extreme drunkenness" defence that lawyers, lower court judges, and politicians have been wrestling with ever since.

More epigrammatically, we should not think of the reasons as a disposable wrapping around the inner core that is the outcome itself. Rather, we should think of the outcome as the gritty sand around which the judicial oyster builds a doctrinal pearl, some of greater lustre and value than others. An appeal decision is not normally a one-line outcome, although on occasion it can be, as when an appeal is curtly "dismissed for the reasons given in the court below." The reasons given are usually, although not always, more extensive than the rather minimalist and therefore uninformative syllogism of French appeal decisions, which are often along the form: "X being against the law, and Y having done X, the appeal is therefore dismissed."[3] Instead, we should think of it as a short legal essay focused on the specific issue or more rarely, issues, raised in the appeal, giving reasons for dealing with that issue in a particular way.

Attributes of Appeal Court Decisions

The emphasis is very much on the word "short." In 1992 the average reported provincial appeal court decision in Canada was just under six pages long, that is, reported in one or more of the standard national, regional, provincial, or topical law reports in this country, and counting only one language version in those jurisdictions which publish bilingual reports. It surprises many of our students to find that the average appeal court decision is so short — much shorter than the trial court decision from which it arises — and that the average appeal consumes very little time for the process of argument and deliberation.⁴ However, this simply follows from the nature of an appeal, which requires the appellant to focus on that part of the trial process or decision that is alleged to be in error. The appeal therefore only needs to deal with the point or points that have been raised in this way and not the uncontested issues. Some appeal court decisions can be very long — more than ten times the average length — but these are unusual. The length of this atypical decisions can sometimes be explained by the critical importance of the issues raised by the case and by the desire of the court to deal with these issues thoroughly and completely. However, sometimes it is a consequence of the extremely technical nature of the issues regardless of their intrinsic importance to the legal system as a whole; insurance cases in particular are notoriously longer than most other types of appeal case. As shown in Table 7.1, the average length of a reported decision of a provincial court of appeal has not changed very much during this century, and can best be thought of as rising slowly to an all-century high in the 1960s, falling gradually but not dramatically in the decades since.

The judicial decision in the 1990s, especially in the penultimate appeal courts, is usually a single argument written by a single judge who is usually identified. Since appeal court decisions are panel decisions, that is, decisions reached by three or more judges who sit together and confer together before rendering a decision, it is always possible that they may not be able to agree on a single set of "outcome plus reasons." This may mean that one or more of the judges writes a dissent (essentially voting for the opposite outcome from that reached by a majority of the court, and issuing a set of reasons for that dissenting vote) or a separate concurring opinion (voting for the same outcome as the majority but writing substantially different, or sometimes just minor, additional reasons for the appropriateness of that outcome). Such lack of agreement usually reduces the impact of the decision on the evolution of legal doctrine. If there are three or four different sets of reasons delivered by a single panel, and if no set of "outcome plus reasons" draws the signatures of even a majority of the panel, then it becomes much more difficult to read the case as delivering a clear message to other judges and other courts. (A prominent example is *R.* v. *Morgentaler*,⁵ in which a panel of seven judges delivered four different sets of reasons, none signed by more than a pair of judges. It is somewhat ironic that public opinion generally accepts the decision as having firmly and clearly settled the abortion issue in Canada.)

In the past a substantial number of provincial appeal court decisions consisted of multiple sets of opinions. Table 7.2 tracks the frequency of dissents in reported appeal court decisions for every fifth year since 1922; separate concurrences were comparably frequent. The trend is clearly away from dissents, which before the Second World War tended to occur in fully one-quarter of reported decisions, but in recent decades are only one-third that frequent. In the 1990s the panel of a Canadian provincial court of appeal typically speaks with a single and united voice. However, despite this increasing practice of unanimity about two-thirds of the judges that we interviewed said that unanimity was not important, and only 5 per cent said that it was important for a panel to avoid dissent. The more important value was that judges speak with independence and candour on legal issues and that such disagreements are openly indicated in public.

In part this higher degree of unanimity has come about because appeal court panels are now smaller. In the 1920s and 1930s a majority of all provincial appeal court decisions were rendered by a panel of more than three judges — usually odd numbers (five or seven and very rarely as high as nine), but sometimes even numbers as well, in which case tie votes resulted in the appeal "failing on equal division." Since that time larger panels have become more infrequent, and since the mid-1960s they have become very rare indeed. In recent decades, 98 per cent or more of all reported decisions have been made by three-judge panels. This has an obvious impact on the frequency of minority opinions — the more judges there are on a panel, the more likely one of them will be offside from the majority — but since the decline in dissent frequency is both steadier and less precipitous than the decline in panel size, there is clearly something else working here as well. One appeal court judge suggested to us that it was the product of an evolution in the conception of the judicial role. Appeal court judges in recent years see themselves as fulfilling a judicial leadership role, and this is facilitated by the delivery of a single set of reasons on behalf of a unanimous panel, not precluding dissents or separate concurrences but certainly discouraging them except where the disagreement reflects significant issues. This leadership role is more easily attained by a judge who has only two other judges to convince about a possible consensual approach. Two-thirds of the judges we questioned said

Table 7.1

Attributes of Reported Decisions of the Provincial Courts of Appeal, 1922–1992

Year	Average length in pages	# Academic cites/case	# Judicial cites/case	Average age of judicial cite
1922	5.2	0.60	4.6	31.3
1927	4.7	0.55	4.4	33.9
1932	5.4	0.52	5.8	33.5
1937	6.5	0.53	5.6	33.4
1942	6.0	0.54	6.0	34.8
1947	6.8	0.65	6.8	38.9
1952	6.3	0.61	6.3	38.8
1957	6.6	0.48	6.0	39.3
1962	7.7	0.57	7.2	33.8
1967	7.7	0.52	6.1	35.4
1972	7.1	0.25	4.3	29.2
1977	7.3	0.49	4.9	29.5
1982	5.9	0.38	3.7	24.6
1987	4.1	0.45	4.2	20.6
1992	6.1	0.26	4.3	17.2
All:	5.9	0.45	4.9	

that consensus was more easily reached on three-member panels than on larger ones.

How Do Judges Support Their Decisions?

Judicial decisions do not simply make reasoned logical arguments about why the actual outcome is the most appropriate outcome; they also support that argument by making reference to authority. It is an important feature of our judicial system, and of similar systems like those of the United States and Britain, that the most important and the most frequently used authorities are the decisions of other judges in earlier cases that raised similar or related issues. This book, being written by academics, tends to support its ideas by referring to other academic books and journal articles; that is the mode of explanation that academics themselves use and expect to find in the writings of other academics. If this were a judicial decision, however, then you would expect to find references not to books and articles, but rather to judicial decisions (like the *Daviault* case mentioned above). Just as our quotations from books and articles will tend to be drawn from the best known and most highly regarded experts in the field, so the citation of earlier decisions will tend to emphasize the courts, the judges, and the cases carrying the most weight and stature on the kind of issue before the court — the highest courts, the most respected judges, the clearest and most direct decision.

To be sure, the academic and judicial comparison should not be pushed too far. Academics have no "higher" panel of academic experts to which their assertions can be appealed, no hierarchy of merit even vaguely comparable to the hierarchy of the courts. Our respect for other academics falls far short of the judicial doctrine of *stare decisis*, which in its extreme form implies that a prior decision should be followed whether or not the current judge is completely persuaded of the merits of the argument it encapsulates.[6] According to the doctrine of precedent, "each and every case decided by the court becomes a part of the law itself, not merely an explanation which later judges may adopt or reject."[7] Although there is some indication that the rigour of *stare decisis* is fading, and that this extreme statement no longer accurately describes what most judges are doing, it remains the case that the weight of precedent — of the statements of principle and doctrine that have gone before — counts for much more in a judicial decision than in an academic setting.[8]

As Table 7.3 shows, some provinces tend to write longer decisions than others, and some tend to use more judicial citations in the average decision than others, but the variation is not so great that we would not describe them all as doing the same kind of thing in the same general way. And as Table 7.1 shows, the use of judicial citations, like the average length of the decision itself, has not changed very much over the past seventy years. The average decision is half a dozen pages long (give or take a page or two), and it uses about five judicial citations (give or take a citation or two). This is not a very high citation density — a normal publication in an academic journal might use between two and five citations on the aver-

Table 7.2

Large Panel Frequency, and Dissent Frequency
Reported Decisions of Provincial Appeal Courts, 1922–1992

Year	% Large Panels	% Dissent
1922	73.5	23.4
1927	84.7	28.3
1932	57.6	25.8
1937	42.8	28.1
1942	41.6	27.4
1947	31.7	21.2
1952	38.5	24.2
1957	22.8	14.6
1962	19.6	18.8
1967	3.1	17.4
1972	2.1	8.7
1977	4.2	8.2
1982	2.0	8.7
1987	1.6	9.4
1992	1.0	10.4

age page — but neither is it so low that a citationless judicial decision would fail to astonish us.

It is probably true that when most people think of judicial opinions and judicial citations, they assume an emphasis on impenetrable Latin phrasing studded with references to and quotations from court decisions from previous centuries. This impression is very wide of the mark in several ways. For one thing, judicial decisions in the past ten or twenty years are written in a much less technical and opaque way, and are far more accessible to an informed general audience (although probably not as much so as many of the judges who write them would like to think!). The judicial decisions around which they build their own reasons for judgment tend increasingly to be very recent — most of them are less than ten years old, and many are less than five years old. The modern practice of citation and precedent is much less antiquarian than most would assume.

Do Judges Cite Professors?

Appeal court judges also refer to academic books and articles, although much less frequently, and they do so more often in some provinces, such as Quebec and Ontario, than in others, such as British Columbia and Alberta. The density of these references is very low — less than one on every dozen pages — and most appeal court decisions include no such references at all. The pattern that displays itself over time, as shown in Table 7.1, is intriguing, even counterintuitive. Even assuming that the preferred weapon in the judicial arsenal is judicial citations rather than references to books or articles, it would seem logical to think of this preference becoming less pronounced in recent years. For one thing, the ban that existed until surprisingly recently on citing a living academic writer as an authority in arguments before the courts has been lifted — dented by Queen's University law professor William Lederman, and completely smashed by Osgoode Hall law dean Peter Hogg, who now is quoted more often and more approvingly than many sitting judges.[9] This change opens the door for the consideration of recent scholarship, at the same time that the number of judges with academic credentials (that is, who served as law professors at universities as well as, and sometimes instead of, as legal practitioners) is going up. For another, the major issues raised by the Canadian Charter of Rights and Freedoms are often thoroughly aired in the academic literature before they arrive in the appeal courts linked to concrete cases, and one would have expected judges to draw on (although not necessarily to follow) these lines of analysis.

In fact, however, the reverse is true in the reported decisions of the provincial courts of appeal. The relative frequency of academic citations has declined in recent decades. In the 1990s, as in the 1920s, judges explained their decisions by linking them to the earlier decisions of other judges, rather than by explicitly drawing on the thoughts of legal and other academics. Quebec is the modest exception to this robust generalization; in the court of appeal of that province, academic citations are about one-fifth as frequent as non-academic citations. This can perhaps be seen as a by-product of Quebec's civil code system, which is different from the common law system used in the other nine provinces.[10] Judicial decision-making in the code-driven systems of continental Europe leans heavily on

Table 7.3					
Attributes of Reported Decisions of the Provincial Courts of Appeal 1992					
Province	**Average length in pages**	**# Judicial cites/case**	**# Academic cites/case**	**Dissent %**	**% of panels with three+ judges**
B.C.	10.4	4.9	0.0	10.7	1.8
Alta.	4.8	3.0	0.1	8.5	0.0
Sask.	5.0	4.0	0.4	5.8	0.0
Man.	3.2	3.3	0.2	13.0	2.2
Ont.	7.9	6.3	0.8	13.0	1.9
Que.	9.3	11.4	2.2	22.8	2.0
N.B.	3.1	2.4	0.2	20.2	0.0
N.S.	4.4	4.2	0.2	6.6	0.0
Nfld.	8.7	5.2	0.6	10.7	3.6
P.E.I.	4.4	3.7	0.0	0.0	0.0
All:	6.1	4.3	0.3	10.3	1.1

academic texts to explain the legislated code, and it very seldom uses the case citation that Anglo-American judges take for granted. However, the Quebec difference should not be overstated; its practices are more like those of its Canadian common law neighbours than they are like those of France or Belgium, to such an extent that Quebec clearly represents a minor variant on the all-province theme, rather than a new theme of its own.

What Courts Do Judges Cite?

When we asked them what courts or judges they tended to cite, most judges were somewhat at a loss to answer. They said they cited the most appropriate decision, the most relevant decision, the one that they needed to make the point. For them, citation is a practical process rather than a theoretical one, and one that they had trouble discussing in such general terms. They stressed fidelity to the decisions of higher courts and their own court, but a small number

Table 7.4

Provincial Appeal Court Citations of Judicial Authority, by Source, Reported Appeal Court Decisions, 1992

Province	% JCPC	% SCC	% UK	% Own Appeal Court	% Other Appeal Court	% Trial Court in same prov.	% All Other Citations
Ont.	0.6	39.0	5.9	27.4	10.5	9.05	7.47
Que.	1.5	36.7	2.9	33.4	10.7	11.43	3.39
B.C.	0.4	25.4	15.9	29.7	8.7	12.18	7.76
Alta.	0.5	32.9	9.8	21.1	17.2	6.17	13.34
N.S.	0.7	31.3	6.1	35.9	16.3	4.51	5.21
Man.	0.0	34.9	8.7	17.9	25.6	2.84	10.05
Sask.	1.3	28.4	8.1	31.0	13.7	9.34	8.24
N.B.	0.0	34.3	8.0	31.8	16.9	3.48	5.48
Nfld.	4.8	36.6	8.3	13.8	20.0	6.21	10.35
P.E.I.	2.3	26.7	3.5	16.3	24.4	8.14	18.60
All Appellate Courts	0.9	32.9	8.0	28.9	13.5	8.63	7.2

suggested that they would under some circumstances ignore or evade a Supreme Court decision — which implies that the process is not mechanical, that it does not run on "auto pilot," and that it reflects judgment and consideration. When pressed, they agreed that appropriateness and relevance implied a selection from the enormous diversity of available precedents, and therefore some kind of evaluation of judges and courts, but not one that they could articulate in any definitive way. What follows, then, is our attempt to penetrate the judicial citation process by collecting the relevant statistics, grouping them in a logical and defensible way, and using these groupings to make explicit the priorities and values that are implicit in the less than formally structured citation practices of individual judges. We hope that the judges will recognize in our descriptions a more intellectualized version of what they do every day, but we do want to stress that the categories and the implicit rankings emerge from the statistics, not directly from the interviews.

It seems to us that the study of the citation of judicial authorities might usefully be organized around the basic values served by the process of judicial citation and by the linkages between specific sets of courts that the practice creates. We would suggest six basic values: hierarchy, consistency, deference, coordination, leadership, and diversity. Each of these is explained in turn and related to the citation practices (current and historical) of the provincial courts of appeal.

Hierarchy

The first principle recognized through the practice of judicial citation is *hierarchy*. The Canadian court system can be diagrammed as a pyramid with the "purely provincial" trial courts at the base and the Supreme Court of Canada at the apex. This diagram would identify the "higher" courts to which the immediate case could theoretically be appealed. Such appeals are statistically infrequent. Only about 1 per cent of the decisions of any court are actually appealed to the court or courts above it, and sometimes the figure is much lower. However, the possibility of such appeal and the hierarchical deference that it generates constitute an important dimension of the judicial process. It is a valued and central principle of the judicial decision-making of any court that it shape its own decisions around an acceptance of the prior decisions of "higher" courts. Nevertheless, this statement should not be understood in such a way as to deny the intellectual challenges and the creative responses of the lower courts.

This being the case, it is hardly surprising that the Supreme Court of Canada, the only court to which decisions of the provincial courts of appeal can themselves be appealed, supplies more of the citations to judicial authority made by the provincial courts of appeal than does any other single source as Table 7.4 shows. Just under one-third of all citations to judicial authority are Supreme Court decisions, this figure being the highest for Ontario (39 per cent) and Quebec (36.7 per cent), and somewhat surprisingly, the lowest for British Columbia (25.4 per cent). This proportion has tracked steadily upward through the century, from about 10 per cent up until the 1950s, rising to more than 20 per cent in the late 1960s, to more than 25 per cent in the 1980s, and over 30 per cent in the 1990s.

For the first half of this century the highest court of appeal for Canada, as for other political entities that had not shed their connection with the British Empire, was the Judicial Committee of the Privy

Council in London. Not only could decisions of the Supreme Court of Canada be appealed to the Judicial Committee, which happened 253 times, but decisions of the provincial courts of appeal could, with the agreement of both parties, be appealed *per saltum* directly from the province to London, and this happened a total of 414 times. Only in 1949, with an amendment to the Supreme Court Act, did the Supreme Court become truly supreme with the severing of this connection to the Judicial Committee — although that "court" continued (and continues) to exist.[11] These Judicial Committee decisions were for a long time the major terms of reference for the interpretation of the Canadian constitution, but by the 1990s they had largely been supplanted by more recent Supreme Court decisions. They now account for less than 1 per cent of all provincial appeal court citations (down from about 10 per cent in the 1920s), even though this figure includes both Judicial Committee decisions on appeals from countries other than Canada and decisions delivered since 1949.

Although the Judicial Committee element has almost vanished in recent years, the citation patterns of the provincial courts of appeal over much of this century show a strong emphasis on the decisions of the courts to which the appeal courts themselves could be appealed. In recent years, this has meant the Supreme Court of Canada. Some of the judges we spoke with grumbled about the length and the complexity of Supreme Court decisions, and also about the readiness of its members to muddy the waters by writing dissenting and (increasingly in recent years) separate concurring judgments. They nevertheless accepted a responsibility for fitting their own decisions in with Supreme Court doctrine. The statistical record of their citation patterns shows that they follow through in practice.

Consistency

The second value promoted by judicial citations is *consistency*. Viewed functionally, one of the purposes of judicial decisions is to promote predictability in order to create a regime in which most people most of the time know how their situation will be resolved should a legal dispute arise. This is promoted by a situation in which past decisions of the immediate court have become a normative background into which any specific decision is integrated, which means that a decision (or string of decisions) is valued for its predictive capacity. Reinterpreting, fine-tuning, or expanding upon (or sometimes retreating from) the explanations contained in the court's own past decisions is an important part of what the process of judicial decision-making is about.

In Canada there is considerable confusion about the extent to which an appellate court is bound by its own past decisions. It has been suggested that the practices of the ten provincial courts of appeal on this point show such diversity as to defy generalized description.[12] Whether a court feels more or less bound by precedent, it will still cite earlier decisions, either to tell lawyers and lower court judges which prior decisions no longer carry weight within the court or, more frequently, to show how the current decision fits in with, amplifies or modifies the patterns established in earlier cases.

Among the provincial courts of appeal, citations to their own prior decisions make up one of the largest elements of citation to judicial authority, just fractionally behind the largest category, which is comprised of citations to the Supreme Court itself.[13] Slightly more than one decision in four falls into the category of self-citation, the proportion being the highest (one-third or more) in Quebec and Nova Scotia and the lowest (near or below one-sixth) in Manitoba, Prince Edward Island, and Newfoundland. For much of the century, the frequency of self-citation was rather lower, at about one citation in five, but in the past decade it has risen significantly. This strongly supports the notion that establishing consistency with its own prior decisions is an important element of appeal court decisions in Canada, one that is becoming more important and more pronounced over time.

The "outliers" for the frequency of self-citation are partly self-explanatory and partly intriguing. It is not surprising that the Quebec Court of Appeal should cite its own prior decision more often than similar courts in other provinces; the uniqueness of the Quebec Civil Code, and the fact that much of the jurisprudence of Quebec but of few other provinces is available in French, combine to make this pattern entirely predictable. However, it is curious that the Court of Appeal of Nova Scotia, to which neither consideration applies, should cite itself even more often. At the other end of the scale, it is not surprising that the courts of appeal of Newfoundland and Prince Edward Island should cite themselves less often than the parallel courts in other provinces. These are after all the newest of the courts of appeal, established in 1975 and 1987 respectively, and therefore the ones that have had the shortest time to build up a broad range of precedents.[14] (Prior to the establishment of separate provincial courts of appeal, the appeal function was handled by panels selected from the provincial superior courts. The panel court not include the trial judge whose decision was being appealed.) However, it is anomalous that Manitoba, which is the third most senior of the specialized provincial courts of appeal, should be the third on this list. Manitoba's situation can be partly attributed to the personal preferences of the judges. One Manitoba appellate judge told us that given a choice, he would prefer to cite U.K. decisions rather than those of many other courts (including his own) because he found them "better-written." Indeed, the Manitoba court has the second-highest rate of citing U.K. precedents.

Deference

A third value promoted through judicial citation is *deference*, referring in this case to the practice of citing English decisions (particularly decisions of English courts other than the Judicial Committee, although both are included in the U.K. figures for the sake of simplicity). English law and English judicial authorities have long been highly regarded and extensively followed in Canada, whether this be regarded as the product of membership in a larger common law community or a persisting (and possibly unwelcome) residue of Canada's previous colonial and imperial status.

Before 1949 the Judicial Committee of the Privy Council was the final court of appeal for Canada, and the House of Lords was in a position comparable in a roundabout way. For one thing, it was from the ranks of the Law Lords that the panel of the Judicial Committee was struck (supplemented from time to time with judges drawn from the highest courts of the Empire and Commonwealth, including the Supreme Court of Canada itself). For another, the Judicial Committee itself described the House of Lords as the final authority on questions of English law, which (given Canada's adoption of the English common law) made the Lords an authority for Canadian courts as well.[15] To this extent, the citation of English authorities is therefore a special example of hierarchical authority. However, even leaving these two rather special cases aside, the citation of the decisions of a wide range of English courts is an important and enduring dimension of the citation practices of the provincial courts of appeal, even when those English courts are in no way hierarchical authorities, such as the English Court of Appeal, or the Court of Queen's or King's Bench, or when the cases post-date the patriation of judicial authority (Judicial Committee and House of Lords decisions since 1949).

References to English cases account for just under 10 per cent of all citations of judicial authority, about one-tenth of these being citations of the Judicial Committee; this is very close to the frequency with which the Supreme Court itself cites English sources, as discussed below. The extent to which this is a characteristic of the Canadian judiciary, rather than of the common law itself, is shown by comparison with the practices of U.S. courts, where citations to English authority are extremely rare.[16]

The decline in the relative frequency of English citations has been steady. In the 1920s English courts, including the Judicial Committee, were supplying a majority of all citations to judicial authority made by the provincial courts of appeal. In the 1960s they still accounted for one-third of all citations, and only in the 1980s were the English courts collectively cited less often than the Supreme Court of Canada. British Columbia very much leads the way; citations of English authorities still account for almost one citation in every six, half again the frequency of the Alberta Court of Appeal which ranks second in this regard. Unsurprisingly, the Quebec Court of Appeal is the least likely to cite English authorities, doing so less than 3 per cent of the time.

Coordination

A fourth function of judicial citation is *coordination*, using this term to pick up on what Ross Flowers has called "co-ordinate citation," that is, references to the decisions of courts that are neither above nor below the citing court but which occupy a similar position within the judicial hierarchy.[17] This type of citation is all the more interesting because it represents persuasive rather than binding precedent. Because they are courts of coordinate jurisdiction occupying parallel positions within the Canadian judicial hierarchy, any provincial court of appeal is free to follow or to disagree with or simply to ignore the law as stated by another provincial court of appeal, something which they are much less free to do to a prior decision of their own court or, for quite different reasons, to a decision of the Supreme Court. Flowers cited no less an authority than the Supreme Court of Canada for the proposition that "[a] provincial appellate court is not obliged as a matter either of law or of practice, to follow a decision of the appellate court of another province, unless it is persuaded that it should do so on its merits or for other independent reasons."[18] Indeed, Bora Laskin, speaking for the court, concluded even more bluntly that "[t]he only required uniformity among provincial appellate courts is that which is the result of the decisions of this court."[19]

However, because they tend to deal with a similar range of problems at a similar level, courts of coordinate jurisdiction provide an obvious source of ideas for dealing with new or difficult legal questions. Interprovincial cites do not loom overwhelmingly large in the citation lists. In the explanatory and precedential arsenal of appeal court judges, the decisions of fellow judges in other provinces rank lower than Supreme Court citations, or references to earlier decisions of their own court, or (for many of the courts over much of the period considered) citations to such English courts as the House of Lords or the Court of Appeal. However, the frequency of these citations has climbed steadily through the century, and they now account for about one citation of judicial authority in every seven. The voluntary and optional nature of the relationship, and the mutual respect between coordinate actors it implies, make it an indicator of the changing attitudes of appeal court judges, even while it illuminates an increasingly important dimension of the influence the judges acknowledge in their written reasons.

The same phenomenon has been observed in the United States, and considerable literature examines the communication of precedent and the patterns of influence between the U.S. state supreme courts, although the different scale involved (fifty actors in paired relationships in the United States, six in Canada for the period in question) as well as the different scope of the phenomenon (interprovincial citations are much more frequent in Canada than interstate citations in the United States) makes their methodology of limited applicability.[20]

Several patterns can be identified regarding the tendency of provincial appeal courts to draw on each other's decisions as a source of judicial authority.[21] The first is the growing frequency of interprovincial citations, rising steadily from just under 7 per cent in the 1920s to about 15 per cent in the 1980s and 1990s. This is not a question of the "younger" appeal courts importing precedents from the "older" ones, because the interprovincial citation rates of the two oldest appeal courts (Ontario and Quebec) show the steadiest rise, and have crossed the 10 per cent threshold only within the past two decades. To a significant and persistent extent, provincial appeal court judges show an interest in what their fellow judges in the other provinces are doing, and their citation patterns reflect this interest.

A second and equally obvious finding is the predominant, even overwhelming, role of the Ontario Court of Appeal, which accounts for about 40 per cent of all interprovincial citations over the entire span from the 1920s to the 1990s. Friedman poetically suggested that "state supreme courts regard themselves as siblings of a single family, speaking dialects of a common legal language." By contrast, the Canadian provincial appeal courts constitute an uneven chorus, with Ontario booming the antiphon and everyone else whispering the response.[22] The impact of Ontario is so pronounced that it simply washes everything else out. All the courts of appeal show a much stronger relationship with Ontario than with the court of any other province. But this relationship tends to be one-sided. Ontario provides, but does not receive, significant precedential leadership in the relationship that it enjoys with each and every one of the other courts. The single rather intriguing exception is the British Columbia Court of Appeal since 1970, which cited Ontario only half again as often as it was cited by Ontario. In all, the Ontario court was cited by its coordinate counterparts almost five times as often as it cited them, reflecting a very favourable "balance of precedential trade."

The predominance of Ontario is hardly unexpected. Of the established appeal courts in the 1920s, Ontario's was pre-eminently the one with a lengthy accumulation of English-language precedents and with a long-standing reputation as a powerful court drawn from a very strong bar. Indeed, for the early decades of the century its prestige rivalled, and for some periods may have exceeded, that of the Supreme Court itself.[23] However, the enduring extent of this predominance may be surprising once it is put in such specific statistical terms. No state supreme court, indeed no half dozen state supreme courts, dominate interstate citation in the United States the way the Ontario Court of Appeal dominates interprovincial citation in Canada. No other comparably situated court in either country makes the phrase "first among equals" such a misleading understatement of its influence. To the extent that citation patterns imply doctrinal leadership, it would almost be more to the point to think of the Ontario Court of Appeal as a "junior Supreme Court."

The third finding is the "double isolation" of Quebec. It seldom cites other provincial appeal courts and is cited by them even less often. If the former feature is changing since 1970 (largely because of the Quebec court's greater readiness to cite the Ontario Court of Appeal), the second persists. Given the impediment to the transmission of judicial authority posed by Quebec's double uniqueness as the only majority Francophone province and the only Civil Code province, this is hardly surprising.

Fourth, it appears that the British Columbia Court of Appeal has emerged as the second most frequently cited provincial court, replacing the Alberta Court of Appeal, which filled this role before the Second World War. Given that the interprovincial citation patterns also point to a Western bloc characterized by a significant degree of mutual influence, the British Columbia court can also be thought of as the "lead court" for the area, cited by each of the other three Western courts more often than it cites them or they cite each other.

Fifth, and finally, there is the situation of the four Atlantic provinces, whose specialized appeal courts are the most recently established. Nova Scotia's position within this region is something of a faint echo of British Columbia's role in the West. It is the only one of the Atlantic courts with any significant degree of visibility outside the region, and it is cited by the other Atlantic courts more often than it cites them or they cite each other. But both of these patterns are much less pronounced than they are for British Columbia. Also striking is the relatively high proportion of interprovincial citations on the younger courts, although this is of necessity based on a smaller number of reported cases and therefore a smaller number of total citations.

Leadership

The fifth value served by the practice of citation is that of judicial *leadership*, exemplified by the citation of decisions of the lower courts. By making such citations, the court is arguably less concerned to fit its own decision in with the practices of these courts than to accomplish the reverse — to show the lower courts which statements of law and doctrine do, and which set of decisions do not, mesh with their own views. To some extent this is done directly by upholding or reversing or altering the immediate case under appeal. This study, however, has explicitly excluded the immediate case under appeal from the citation data base. The count is therefore of other decisions of lower courts within the province. In the process of commenting on these cases, the court of appeal may endorse, reject, modify, or distinguish the statements of law and doctrine enunciated by these lower courts, singling out those decisions that constitute particularly good (or, more rarely, particularly bad) examples of how to handle specific issues or situations. Indeed, an important part of the function of a general court of appeal lies in its capacity to take advantage of its one-further-step removal from the immediacy of the trial situation, as well as the diversity of context and fact situations that may have emerged in a broad range of trial courts and been considered by several appeal courts to present a running synthesis of legal doctrine on new or maturing legal issues.

In the 1990s about one-twelfth of all provincial appeal court citations to judicial authority have been to the decisions of lower courts within their own province, a proportion that has remained fairly constant through the century. The practice is the most pronounced in Quebec and in British Columbia, least frequent in Manitoba and New Brunswick.

The heading for this section is convenient, but it is also misleading in a double sense. First, and least critically, the "higher" courts are exerting leadership over the decisions and processes of lower courts all the time, and not only when they cite lower court decisions. But, second, and more critically, there is a sense in which the logic of the common law is not hierarchical but collegial. If one logic of the common law system is that of hierarchies and appeals and binding precedent, another parallel logic is of a grand conversation in which all judges take part.[24] This is reflected in the tone with which "higher" courts frequently cite "lower" courts. More often than not, they treat them less as well-meaning juniors in need of gentle correction, than as competent and reputable finders of law whose formulations often deserve serious attention and direct attribution. Finding the balance between hierarchy and collegiality, between remonstrance and conversation, is an important part of understanding the process of appeal court decision-making and citation.

Diversity

The sixth value that is served by judicial citations is *diversity*. If the underlying principle of the common law is that law is discovered not made, then it can be discovered not just within the courts of the immediate judicial hierarchy but literally anywhere. The range of sources theoretically available to the Canadian judge is overwhelming. Not just in the decisions of Canadian courts and English courts, but also in the case law of the courts of the Anglo-American judicial systems inside and outside the Commonwealth, judges apply the logical processes of the common law to a wide range of modern social and legal problems. The Quebec courts also draw, to a limited but nonetheless significant extent, on the Civil Code systems of France and other countries.

In the 1990s only about one citation to judicial authority in every fourteen falls into this category. Most of these (5.1 per cent out of the total of 7.2 per cent) are to the decisions of the trial courts of other provinces (almost invariably the provincial superior trial courts). Less than 1 per cent of all citations were to U.S. authorities at all levels. Contrary to expectations that the age of the Charter of Rights and Freedoms would drive our judges to a greater reliance on American jurisprudence, this number is lower than it has been for any previous decade, although the jump to more than 2 per cent of all citations in the 1980s may be a better indication of the long-run trend. Ontario and British Columbia are the most likely to use U.S. sources. Only half of 1 per cent of all citations were to decisions of the federal courts, for example, Exchequer Court, Federal Court, Federal Court of Appeal, and about half that many were to decisions of various tribunals — mostly labour review boards and human rights commissions. This leaves only half of 1 per cent to draw on judicial decisions from the rest of the world, primarily Australia (for the provinces other than Quebec) and France (for Quebec). The Ontario and Quebec courts of appeal are the heaviest users of these international citations, but in the case of Quebec this was much more pronounced before the Second World War than it is today.

What Are the Practices of the Supreme Court of Canada?

Like the provincial courts of appeal, the Supreme Court of Canada sits in multijudge panels to hear appeals from the decisions of lower courts. Indeed, most (about 85 per cent) of the cases decided by the Supreme Court are decisions from the provincial appeal courts. Further to emphasize the continuity, most of the personnel on the Supreme Court are promoted (legal professionals tend to say "elevated") from the provincial appeal courts as well. The normal practice in recent years is for seven of the nine judges on the Supreme Court of Canada to be former provincial appeal court judges, one to be from the Federal Court of Appeal, and one to have had no prior judicial experience prior to appointment to the highest court in the land. (Sopinka and Binnie are the two most recent examples of such appointments.)

There are important differences as well. The Supreme Court has much more control over its own case load. Most of the time appeals will only be heard after an application for leave, and most such applications are refused.[25] It sits in larger panels; under the Lamer

Court, this has averaged seven judges per panel, with a general practice of assigning the more important cases to full nine-judge panels and more routine cases to smaller, five-judge panels. The Supreme Court tends to write much longer decisions than the provincial courts of appeal (averaging just under thirty pages), and to make more citations to academic authority (almost twenty per case). It also differs from the provincial courts in having a much higher rate of visible disagreement on the court, only 55 per cent of its decisions being rendered by unanimous panels, although as previously noted this is in part simply a function of a larger panel.

Does the Supreme Court Use Academic Citations?

Until fairly recently the Supreme Court of Canada did not have a practice of citing academic sources or of encouraging the lawyers appearing before them to present such authorities as part of their arguments. Just after the Second World War, there was a brief but spirited controversy over the fact that Chief Justice Rinfret reacted very negatively when counsel tried to use a *Canadian Bar Review* article as an authority. Despite vigorous arguments defending the practice,[26] the Supreme Court was unmoved, and by the end of the 1960s there were still barely a dozen references a year to academic texts, and virtually none to legal journals.

By the 1990s, however, things were rather different, and the Supreme Court of Canada now cites academic books and articles hundreds of times every year.[27] Many of these are citations to living authors, an overlapping argument that much engaged the profession forty years ago, but has now become completely routine. Most of the references are to Canadian texts and Canadian legal periodicals, although there is an American influence as well. U.S. academics are referred to about half as often as Canadian. The heaviest use of academic citations is in Charter cases, family law cases, and tort cases.

It is mildly intriguing that the Supreme Court of Canada's use of academic citations has been increasing steadily over the past two decades,[28] but there is no corresponding increase in the extent to which the provincial courts of appeal use academic authorities. Supreme Court judges have the support of more law clerks than their provincial counterparts, as well as enviable resources for conducting library research. Whatever the reason, this pattern now differentiates Supreme Court practices from provincial appeal court practices.

Table 7.5

Source of Judicial Citations by the Supreme Court of Canada Reported Decisions 1984–1994

Source	#	%
Judicial Committee of the Privy Council	387	2.6
Supreme Court of Canada	5,763	39.3
Other English Courts	1,830	12.5
Coordinate Courts	762	5.2
Lower Canadian Courts	5,217	35.5
Other Courts	719	4.9
Total:	14,678	

What Courts Does the Supreme Court Cite?

Just as the statistical count of provincial appeal court citations can be penetrated in terms of the six suggested values, the same process can help us understand the way the Supreme Court of Canada uses judicial authority in its own decisions. Table 7.5 presents this material, accumulated for reported decisions of the Supreme Court for the eleven years from 1984 to 1994.

Hierarchy

For the first seventy-five years of its existence, the Supreme Court of Canada was subject to appeal to the Judicial Committee of the Privy Council in London. Only about 250 Supreme Court decisions were ever actually carried to London on appeal, along with a further 400 or so *per saltum* appeals. The Judicial Committee's decisions on these cases long constituted binding precedent for the Supreme Court of Canada in the same way that its own decisions bound all other Canadian courts. Only in 1978 in *Re Agricultural Products Marketing Act*[29] did the Supreme Court under Chief Justice Laskin explicitly refuse to follow a Privy Council precedent.

Of the total of 14,000-plus citations to judicial authority made by the Supreme Court of Canada in reported decisions over an eleven-year period, less than four hundred, about one in every forty, were to decisions of the Judicial Committee. This figure includes both

Judicial Committee decisions on appeals from countries other than Canada and decisions delivered since 1949, although these enjoy a less binding status than decisions on appeals from Canada itself. Not surprisingly, these low figures are a rather recent development in Supreme Court decision-making; for the Rinfret and Kerwin courts, references to the Privy Council were about six times as frequent. The waning influence of the Supreme Court's one-time hierarchical superior demonstrates the extent to which the "truly Supreme Court" of the period since 1949 is taking its own independence very seriously.

Consistency

The second value promoted by judicial citations is *consistency*. Viewed functionally, one of the purposes of judicial decisions is to promote predictability. At one time the Supreme Court of Canada held that it was very much bound to follow its own prior decisions — the critical case was *Stuart* v *Bank of Montreal*.[30] More recently, however, "the Court has gradually come to accept that, while it should normally adhere to its prior decisions, it was not absolutely bound to do so; and the Court has explicitly refused to follow a prior decision in several cases."[31] It was a hallmark of the early Charter decisions in particular that the Supreme Court began by declaring that pre-Charter decisions even on very similar points were not necessarily binding in the new judicial world of the Charter. For example, on the issue of Sunday observance *R.* v *Big M Drug Mart*[32] charted a very different course from that set by *Robertson & Rosetanni* v *R.*[33] The case of *R.* v *Therens*[34] similarly overturned *Chromiak.* v *R.*[35] on the issue of roadside Breathalyzer testing.

References to its own prior decisions similarly loom large within the practices of the Supreme Court of Canada, constituting the largest single bloc among its citations to judicial authority. More than 5,700 citations, just under two-fifths of the total, fall into this category. There are useful clues to the evolution of the way that judicial influence is transmitted and operates in the Supreme Court in such questions as which specific Supreme Court cases are cited most often,[36] and which individual Supreme Court judges are cited (and named) most often;[37] for present purposes, what is significant is the large but not overwhelming proportion of total citations that they constitute. These figures have been rising over time. For the Rinfret court in the late 1940s, citations to its own earlier decisions made up barely one-fifth of all citations, and for the subsequent Kerwin court, although not after this period, the total number of Supreme Court citations was less than the total number of English citations.

Deference

References to English cases other than those of the Judicial Committee account for almost two thousand cases over the eleven-year period, about one-eighth of the total, which is far more than the numbers for the decisions of the Judicial Committee itself, but less frequent than either citations of prior decisions of the Supreme Court or (perhaps surprisingly) citations to lower Canadian courts. As already noted, the provincial courts of appeal cite British sources (and the Judicial Committee) comparably often. In U.S. appellate courts, citations to English authority are extremely rare.[38]

The decline in the relative frequency of English citations has been steady. In the 1940s English courts accounted for almost six of every ten citations to judicial authority by the Supreme Court of Canada (just over four out of ten if the Judicial Committee is excluded). Half a century later, their proportion had fallen to about one-tenth of this level. The English courts remain a significant source of precedent for Supreme Court decisions — for example, in the area of criminal law — but they are now a supplemental source rather than the dominant one. To this extent, the "captive court" of which (then Professor) Bora Laskin complained so long ago, writing critically of a time when the Supreme Court so completely subordinated itself to the English authorities, has come to an end, and the hopes of those who saw the termination of appeals beyond the Supreme Court as a new and important starting point have been fulfilled.[39]

Coordination

Strictly speaking, "coordinate authority" refers to courts that occupy a similar position in the sense of both being subject to appeal to the same higher authority. In this restricted sense, the only citations that would qualify would be pre-1949 references to the courts of other countries that were similarly subject to appeal to the Judicial Committee, that is, the highest courts of other countries within the Empire or Commonwealth such as Australia or New Zealand. Such citations are, and always have been, extremely rare.

However, the term can be used in a more expanded sense. The Supreme Court of Canada is the final court of appeal in a federal system. This implies that parallel authorities would be those similarly located at the top of a pyramid of judicial review within a federal or quasi-federal setting — the Supreme Court of the United States, or the Australian High Court, or (more recently and perhaps a little more dubiously) the European Court of Justice or the European Court of Human Rights. Only the first named is cited at all frequently. The coordinate citations in Table 7.5 include 625 references to the Supreme Court of the United States, ninety-two to the Australian High Court, and forty-five references to the highest European Court (almost all to the European Court of Human Rights, rather than the European Court of Justice). Together, these account for barely one in every twenty of the Supreme Court's citations of judicial authority. Right up until the late 1980s, the Supreme Court of Canada was more likely to cite the Judicial Committee of the Privy Council than the U.S. Supreme Court and the Australian High Court combined, even though these constitute the two federal common law systems in the world most similar to Canada's.

It should be noted that these patterns are changing somewhat in recent years. Citations of U.S. authority have been increasingly frequent, by all members of the court and in all areas of law.[40] However, even for the whole period of the Lamer court they account for barely 7 per cent of all citations and only half of these are to the U.S. Supreme Court. Some may have worried that the entrenchment of the Charter was opening the door to a flood of American jurisprudential influence. So far, there has been less a flood than a trickle, much of it directed to other than Charter issues, for example, insurance law. American authorities are cited more often than they ever have been, but they are still not cited very often, for example, not as often as the English courts. Canadian judges may be peeking over the border for doctrinal ideas more than they ever have, but they are still peeking rather than staring.

This is perhaps the most interesting contrast between the citation practices of the Supreme Court and those of the provincial courts of appeal, where the "conversation of equals" in coordinate citation is well established. As against its provincial counterparts, the Supreme Court draws from a precedential pool that is less diversified and more concentrated on a relatively small number of sources, including primarily its own prior citations. On the other hand, given that the provincial appeal courts, with the sporadic exception of the Ontario Court of Appeal, do not make much use of U.S. case law, the limited extent to which the Supreme Court uses U.S. citations currently constitutes the Canadian judiciary's major access point for American influences and ideas.

Leadership

With 5,763 citations, just over one-third of the total, references to the decisions of the lower courts rank second in Supreme Court citation patterns only to the prior decisions of the Supreme Court itself. This has been a persisting pattern; citations to "lower" Canadian courts accounted for almost one-fifth of the citations of the Rinfret court as well. The Ontario Court of Appeal is (quite predictably) the most frequently cited, but Quebec is cited only half so often. Of the individual judges cited, seven of the top ten are from the Ontario Court of Appeal, with one each from British Columbia, Nova Scotia, and Alberta breaking the monopoly.

Although this component of citation has been characterized as exhibiting judicial leadership, it would be misleading to think of this as entirely a one-way street. Sometimes the Supreme Court lines up two or more different lines of decisions from the lower courts in order to choose one and reject the other(s). But other times they refer to their appeal court counterparts as finders of law and declarers of doctrine in a much more respectful and egalitarian tone. Certainly very strong judges have served on the various courts of appeal, and given the accidents of timing and regional representation that surround the appointment process, it is on the face of it unlikely that the nine judges on the Supreme Court have always been the nine best judges in the country. Justice Learned Hand of the federal circuit court is sometimes referred to as the finest judge never to serve on the U.S. Supreme Court,[41] the implication being that he has made a larger contribution to the law than some of the lesser lights who cleared this last hurdle.[42] Ontario's Justice Martin of the Court of Appeal may well be the leading example of his Canadian counterparts.

Diversity

During the eleven-year period considered, the Supreme Court made just over 700 citations to sources that could not be brought under any of the five categories above. Most of these were citations to U.S. courts other than the Supreme Court, accounting for 539 citations that were divided roughly equally between the federal circuit and appeal courts and a wide range of state courts. It should be noted in passing that this is the first decade for which the number of U.S. Supreme Court cites exceeded the number of U.S. lower court cites. To the extent that the Supreme Court of Canada has in the past drawn on U.S. law, this has been less the law of the Supreme Court than that of the state and federal courts.[43]

There were also more than a hundred citations to the lower courts of various commonwealth countries, mostly Australia and New Zealand, but with scattered references to Ireland, South Africa, India, and Hong Kong. These too have been a continuing source at a comparably modest level for decades. References to European courts (other than the European Court of Justice or the European Court of Human Rights) accounted for a total of sixty-two citations. Although European references have figured sporadically in the earlier jurisprudence of the Supreme Court, it is only recently that there were any significant number of references to any European courts other than those of France. Finally, there were almost a dozen "other" citations — half to Israeli courts, and half to the decisions of the post–Second World War International War Crimes Tribunal.

These diversity citations account for only one citation in twenty by the Supreme Court of Canada, a modest figure that has grown only slightly over earlier decades, although it is more pronounced if "foreign" law is taken to include the category of coordinate citation above. The use of foreign authority is clearly an example of what Glenn has referred to as the "open view of the common law," and he suggests as well that the Supreme Court's openness to a wide range of European civil law sources is one of the reasons why its jurisprudence is so well received in Quebec.[44] The use of this diversity of citations is therefore a significant indication of the evolution of the judicial role in Canada, even if the actual citation frequencies are not high.

Conclusion

Some of our more health-conscious colleagues often try to tell us that "you are what you eat." The intellectual equivalent that we are suggesting here is something along the lines of "you are what you cite." In other words: the citation patterns of any court are the visible indicators of the sources of its ideas, the lasting record of the authorities to which it attaches importance and which it is willing to follow. They therefore constitute an objective measure of the evolution of the judicial role. When we say that the Canadian courts over the past few decades have carved out their own jurisprudence and cast off the overwhelming authority of the English courts, we can demonstrate this by the sharp decline in the frequency of English citations and their replacement by references to the decisions of other Canadian courts. When we say that Canadian courts have, even in the age of the Charter, resisted the siren call of U.S. jurisprudence, we can prove this statement by showing how seldom any courts (and even more so any court other than the Supreme Court itself) cite U.S. judicial decisions. When we say that the Supreme Court now draws on a wider range of sources to make its doctrinal developments more credible and accessible to a more general audience, this is confirmed by the increase in the frequency of academic citations — at one and the same time acknowledging, drawing upon, and reaching out to an intellectual audience that only a few decades ago it disdained and consciously ignored.

In general terms, a statistical study of the citation patterns of the Supreme Court of Canada in recent years shows that of every six of its citations to judicial authority, two are to its own prior decisions, two are to the decisions of other ("lower") Canadian courts, one is to the English courts, and one is to everything else. For the provincial courts of appeal, two of every six citations to judicial authority are to the Supreme Court of Canada, two are to its own prior decisions, one is to the decisions of other provincial courts of appeal, and the sixth includes everything else. On the other hand, the Appeal Division of the Federal Court (not discussed in detail in this chapter because the data base is not yet complete) gives two of every six judicial citations to the Supreme Court of Canada, two to prior decisions of the Federal Court (Court of Appeal, Federal Court Trial Division, or the Exchequer Court that it replaced in 1971), one to the decisions of other Canadian courts, and one to the United Kingdom.

What all three have in common is a focus on the Supreme Court of Canada, a focus that was entirely absent just a few decades ago, and we suggest that this demonstrates the "coming of age" (on the one hand) of a purely Canadian jurisprudence and (on the other) of the Supreme Court itself. This clearly marks the end of what then-professor Bora Laskin once described as the "captivity" of the Canadian judiciary in general and the Supreme Court in particular. Within this country, the Supreme Court itself now holds the judicial predominance once enjoyed by the English courts, especially the English Court of Appeal and the House of Lords.

This commonality aside, the three face rather different directions. The Supreme Court cites mainly Canadian sources, with a dwindling but significant remainder of English citations. The provincial courts of appeal are devoting considerable citation space to an unusual and intriguing conversation of coordinate equals, and the Appeal Division of the Federal Court frequently cites provincial courts of appeal that virtually never return the favour. This combination is, by the way, quite different from what is happening in the apparently parallel court system of the United States, so there is no notion of some kind of structural determinism involved.

What we describe is a present that is rather different from the past, even from the recent past. What we cannot use it to do is to predict the future. Will the purely Canadian focus remain? Will U.S. influence grow? Will the "globalization of judicial power"[45] gradually generate an increasingly cosmopolitan tone to judicial citation?

What is important about all these questions is the implicit assumption that the traditionalism of the legal and judicial professions is largely a facade, and in actual fact the system has been (and continues to be) undergoing rapid change at many levels. This change is not dictated by the law or by legislatures, but by the evolution of thinking among counsel about how to write more persuasive factums, and among the judges themselves about how to write increasingly more persuasive and relevant decisions. The role of counsel in providing judges with grist for their decision-writing mills must never be overlooked. It is counsel who provide appellate judges with most of their ideas for sources of citations. The factums, however, usually contain many more citations than the judges choose to refer to. In the penultimate appellate courts, the judges do not often stray far away from the list of citations presented by counsel, but the judges of the Supreme Court themselves have told us that they think they cite authorities not mentioned by counsel around 10 per cent of the time. There are two important elements of judicial discretion here: the choice of which of the cases cited by counsel to cite in the judicial opinion, and the decision about whether to cite authorities not mentioned by counsel.

The single most important factor that the judges told us that they take into account when deciding what precedents to cite is their relevance to the main issues of a decision. As lawyers and judges become aware of an increasing range of potentially-relevant precedents through technological innovation, citation patterns may change depending on the views of lawyers about the kinds of citations that are most persuasive to judges, and the views of the judges about which citations are the most credible for the audiences they perceive themselves as writing for.[46]

The Performance of Canadian Appellate Courts

We have examined how Canadian appellate judges exercise discretion in the course of hearing and deciding appeals, and in justifying the way they exercised their discretion. It is much more difficult to consider how well that discretion has been exercised.

In terms of the approach we take to the judiciary's role in democratic government, how well it does comes down to how effectively the courts promote mutual respect. This is accomplished not only by whether, on balance, their specific decisions reinforce that principle, or whether the quality and persuasiveness of the justifications that panels present in their written and oral reasons contribute to the democratic dialogue (and the public's support for continuing that dialogue). It is also accomplished by how expeditiously the courts do their work.

Thus, the major emphasis in this chapter is the apparently mundane but fundamentally important question of how promptly the Canadian courts of appeal hear and decide their cases. How much delay exists? In the language of court research, we will look at the pace of litigation. How long do appeals take before they are decided? Are some provincial appellate courts performing more effectively than others, in the sense that their cases are decided more promptly than others? Do some kinds of appeals take longer than others, regardless of what provincial appellate court is making the decision? What is the significance of how promptly appeals are heard?

This chapter will also assess the courts' performance in terms of who the winners and losers are. How often do appeals succeed? Do some parties succeed more frequently than others? When we sort out more successful and less successful groups of litigants, it is essential to remember that the quality and fairness of a court's work cannot be measured with statistical won–lost percentages. For example, if one set of parties appeals more frequently than another, this may signal that it is less selective in bringing appeals, and may therefore lose a higher proportion of appeals than parties that are more selective. However, before it is possible to examine why some parties do better than others, we must first see whether there are in fact any differences, and whether those differences tend to be found in appellate courts across the country, or only in the courts of particular provinces.

The Pace of Litigation

Introduction

Research on court delay has been transformed in the past twenty years into research on the pace of litigation. This reflects the fact that an analysis of "delay" requires making assumptions about how long cases *ought* to take to be decided. How long should it take for a trial or an appeal to be completed, from filing the case in the trial court to the final appeal decision? The answer to this question may vary across countries, cultures, and legal systems. A judge in a country with an authoritarian government where the pace of litigation is typically slow might be convinced that an accused person was railroaded when his trial occurred a year after his arrest, while a Canadian judge might be asked to consider whether a year's delay violates our Charter of Rights.

Furthermore, even if agreement can be reached on how much time constitutes delay, there would be different definitions of the time periods on which to focus. When does the clock start ticking on an appeal: at the end of the trial, or when the appeal is filed, or when the appeal is perfected? Judges are likely to choose the "perfection" date, since the time that elapses prior to the perfection of the appeal is generally viewed as beyond their control, for example, time taken for preparation of the transcript by the court reporter or completion of the factums by the lawyers. But to the litigant waiting for justice or at least for the end of his or her encounter with the legal system, the entire time period is relevant and important.

The Data Base

To avoid these interpretive difficulties, it is essential to start by simply plotting the time it takes a case to move from initiation to completion (disposition). The figures presented here count from the filing of the appeal through to the beginning of the hearing, the end of the hearing, and the decision of the panel. They are more precise than most earlier figures, because they are based not on the participants' estimates, but on data from samples of the courts' case files. Researchers on site examined case files and entered information on a standard form developed for the project. (Only in British Columbia was a computerized data base rich enough that printouts of case information could be used in place of a more time-consuming file search.) The coverage is comprehensive, but with a number of specific limitations:

- Only criminal appeals are analysed. Given the variations between civil and criminal appeals, it would be inappropriate simply to add them up and report them together in a single table. The criminal case data were more complete, so the analysis began there. While criminal appeals are an important part of the appellate courts' work, they make up a smaller percentage of scheduled court time than civil cases: from 25 per cent in Quebec and 30 per cent in New Brunswick to 50 per cent each in Ontario and Prince Edward Island.[1]

- Appeals are analysed from nine provinces. We were unable to obtain data from Alberta in a timely manner, and some earlier baseline data had already been published. Furthermore, the Federal Court of Canada does not hear criminal appeals, and the Supreme Court of Canada only hears appeals from other appellate courts; the nature of its case load and its place at the end of the process limits its comparability with the work of the provincial appellate courts.

- Only cases that went to hearing were used in analysing the pace of litigation. This criterion for selecting cases would, following the analysis in Chapter 3, mean that half the criminal appeals in the nine provinces would be excluded from analysis, since they were filed but never reached a hearing. This limitation was built in for two reasons: first, figures for the time it takes to reach a hearing provide the best snapshot of a court's performance. Cases that appellants have discontinued before a hearing do not provide an accurate view of the pace of fully adjudicated cases. Second, it was often not possible to identify from the court file the exact date on which an appeal was abandoned, since appellants may not have notified the court at the time.

Table 8.1

Mean Number of Days from Filing of Appeal to Decision, Criminal Appeals that Went to Hearing, Provincial Courts of Appeal

Province	Mean Days	Number of Cases
B.C.	263	180
Sask.	126	195
Man.	164	200
Ont.	361	319
Que.	601	174
N.B.	197	53
P.E.I.	186	44
N.S.	175	223
Nfld.	243	52
Total, 9 Provs.	274	1,440

Within these limitations, the data base available to examine the pace of appellate litigation is still substantial. It includes over 1,400 criminal cases in nine provinces sampled from appeals heard from 1988 to 1992.

Findings: Overall Provincial Performance

Table 8.1 provides the simplest overall "report card" on the amount of time criminal appeals take from start to finish in provincial courts of appeal. The single figure is the average time from the filing of an appeal to the decision of the court following an oral hearing. The "average" reported here is the arithmetic mean, so a relatively small number of exceptionally fast or exceptionally protracted cases could skew the figure for a particular province. At the same time, the number of cases in most provinces is large enough to provide a picture of how well the nine provinces are doing in comparison with one another.

Table 8.1 shows the Saskatchewan Court of Appeal as the most expeditious, and the Quebec Court of Appeal as the slowest by far. At the same time, criminal appeals in the three largest provinces —

Table 8.2

Time from Filing of Appeal to Decision by Quartiles, Criminal Appeals that Went to Hearing, Provincial Courts of Appeal

Province	First Quartile	Second Quartile	Third Quartile	Fourth Quartile	Number of Cases
B.C.	51	27	44	58	180
Sask.	93	66	26	10	195
Man.	82	49	45	24	200
Ont.	45	56	77	142	320
Que.	42	20	16	97	175
N.B.	5	25	17	6	53
P.E.I.	3	16	21	4	44
N.S.	28	88	101	6	223
Nfld.	17	10	12	13	52
Total, 9 Provs.	366	357	359	360	1,442

Ontario, Quebec, and British Columbia — all take longer than in the other six provinces. Newfoundland is the only less populous province even to approach the time taken the largest three. Conversely, the three Maritime Provinces cluster with Manitoba and Saskatchewan on the expeditious side of the ledger. If Quebec's delay did not stand at twenty months, the twelve-month delay in Ontario would stand out from all seven other provinces as a figure far slower than a generally acceptable pace of appellate litigation.

Table 8.2 presents the same data in a somewhat different way. Rather than provide one number as an average, it takes the 1,442 cases and divides them into four groups of equal size (or as close to being equal as tie scores allow). The cases in these four groups, or quartiles, are then broken down by provinces, presenting a more complete picture of how the pace of appeals compares. The fastest and slowest courts are still apparent. For example, almost half the Saskatchewan appeals (93 out of 195) were among the first 25 per cent completed nationally, while more than half (97 out of 175) of the Quebec appeals were in the slowest 25 per cent. Newfoundland,

Table 8.3

Mean Number of Days from Filing of Appeal to Beginning of Hearing, Criminal Appeals that Went to Hearing, Provincial Courts of Appeal

Province	Mean Days	Additional Days to Dec'n	Number of Cases
B.C.	256	7	188
Sask.	110	16	195
Man.	149	15	200
Ont.	344	17	322
Que.	586	15	183
N.S.	167	30	56
P.E.I.	164	22	45
N.S.	164	11	223
Nfld.	211	32	52
Total, 9 Provs.	260	14	1,464

which fell in the middle in Table 8.1, has perhaps the most even distribution of its cases in the four quartiles.

At the same time, Table 8.2 shows the different ways in which overall provincial averages are reached. In this respect, the three Maritime Provinces stand out. While they are uniformly more expeditious than four of the other six provinces, a very low percentage of their cases fall in the first quartile, and an equal or smaller percentage fall in the slowest (fourth) quartile. Thus, those three provinces score well not by rushing through a cluster of cases, but by ensuring that all but a handful of their cases are completed within an acceptable time period.

Findings: Provincial Performance at Three Stages

Tables 8.3, 8.4, and 8.5 break down the time that an appeal takes from initiation to disposition into three stages: the time from initiation (filing) to the beginning of the oral hearing, the time from the beginning to the end of the oral hearing, and the time from the end of the oral hearing until the decision has been made (and announced or released).

A comparison of Table 8.3 with Table 8.1 will immediately suggest that all but a small proportion of the time from initiation to disposition elapses before a case ever goes to hearing. The middle column in Table 8.3 summarizes those differences, which are just over two weeks in four provinces, one week in British Columbia, and a month in New Brunswick and Newfoundland. Except for the virtual dead heat between the three Maritime Provinces, court rankings are unchanged.

Given that delays happen largely before the hearing starts rather than after, it would be useful to break this time period down further. In fact, most appellate courts divide pre-hearing time into the periods before and after the appeal is perfected. An appeal is perfected when the lawyers for both parties file their factums and notify the court that they are ready to be scheduled for hearing, that is, to present their arguments orally. The time prior to perfection is likely to be longer, given delays in preparation of the trial transcript by the court reporter, eligibility screening by legal aid, and researching and writing the factums by counsel for the appellant and respondent. Most of the time that elapses after perfection of the appeal reflects the backlog of other appeals waiting to be argued. Thus, appeal courts commonly consider the time prior to perfection to be "lawyer delay" and the time after perfection to be "court delay."

This attribution of delay to the parties or to the court is misleading, in our view. We believe that virtually all time that elapses after a case is filed in a court is properly attributed to that court. A far more important distinction exists between necessary and unnecessary delay. The former includes, for example, the time needed by the parties to consider and articulate their arguments and the court to consider its decision and articulate its reasons. Necessary time is usually reflected in court rules and practices that allow a particular period of time to file factums or present oral argument. Unnecessary time usually occurs when a court does not effectively monitor and ensure compliance with time standards that hold cases within necessary time periods. An increase in unnecessary time, or delay, may be a product of inadequate resources, whether of court reporters to prepare transcripts or judges to hear cases, or antiquated technology, for example, the absence of computer-assisted transcription (CAT) technology for transcript preparation. But the fact that the resources are inadequate before perfection is no different in principle than their inadequacy after perfection. No appellate court can fund its own operation, but it does have an obligation to ensure that its resources are adequate at every stage and that it uses available resources as best it can to avoid delay.

Notwithstanding our concern that elapsed-time data broken down into "time from filing to perfection" and "time from perfection to beginning of hearing" might be misinterpreted, we would have preferred to present those figures, along with this extended caveat. Unfortunately, the number of case files that recorded perfection dates were so few in number — more than half the case files omitted those dates — that was unclear whether the figures available were representative of the work of provincial courts of appeal. Future researchers will have ample work to do measuring the components of pre-hearing.

Table 8.4 shifts the focus to the time that elapses in the hearing itself. As most observers would expect, almost all the appeals were heard in a single day, 96 per cent to be exact. Of the fifty-eight cases in the data base that were heard for more than a day, thirty-seven were completed the following day. In fact, it is unlikely that most of those cases required two days of argument. It is more likely that most had begun late on one afternoon, perhaps because an earlier case before the panel was running late, and were completed the next morning. The fact that twenty-nine of the thirty-seven cases were in the Ontario Court of Appeal, which schedules multiple appeals in a single day to keep up with its heavy case load, reinforces the likelihood that most of those hearings did not take more than a half-day or a full day of argument time.

There are also a handful of cases (eight out of 1,479) in which the hearing ended more than a month after it began. Again, this obviously does not mean that counsel took that much time to present their case, but perhaps that the hearing was adjourned and reconvened at a later date.

The data in Table 8.4 confirm that Canadian appellate practice falls between the normal practice in U.S. courts and the normal practice in English and other common law courts. In American courts, time limits are more strictly established and enforced, and it would not be surprising if over 99 per cent of the cases were completed in a single day. Counsel in California, for example, can expect thirty minutes to present their case, with no extra time when the judges interrupt to ask questions. In England or Australia, where the tradition of oral advocacy has only recently begun to give way to

Table 8.4

Number of Days from Beginning of Hearing to End of Hearing, Criminal Appeals that Went to Hearing, Provincial Courts of Appeal

Province	Zero	One Day	Two Days	3–7 Days	8–30 Days	Over 30 Days	Number of Cases
B.C.	179	4	4	1	0	0	188
Sask.	195	0	0	0	0	0	195
Man.	193	1	1	0	1	4	200
Ont.	297	29	3	2	0	3	334
Que.	181	3	0	0	0	0	184
N.B.	56	0	0	0	0	0	56
P.E.I.	43	0	0	1	0	1	45
N.S.	225	0	0	0	0	0	225
Nfld.	52	0	0	0	0	0	52
Total	1,421	37	8	4	1	8	1,479
% of Total	96.1	2.5	0.5	0.3	0.1	0.5	100

more extensive use of written material, appeals that take two or three days to argue would not be unusual at all.

Our data indicate that the time that elapses from the beginning to the end of the oral hearing does not add significantly to the elapsed time for litigation in provincial courts of appeal. Whether reducing the amount of time allowed for oral argument might increase the number of hearings that could be scheduled in a given day or week, and thus reduce the time that elapses from perfection to hearing, is a separate question that will require additional research. That research might also consider whether greater restrictions in hearing time would increase the amount of time the judges need to reach a decision and craft their reasons for judgment, as well as whether it would affect the quality of the court's judgment.

What about the final stage of appellate litigation: the time from the end of the hearing to the decision? Table 8.5 summarizes the elapsed times. As in Table 8.4 the use of means or quartiles would

Table 8.5

Number of Days from End of Hearing to Decision, Criminal Appeals that Went to Hearing, Provincial Courts of Appeal

Province	Zero	One Day	Two Days	3–7 Days	8–30 Days	Over 30 Days	Number of Cases
B.C.	141	2	2	5	10	20	180
Sask.	149	9	2	13	8	14	195
Man.	170	0	3	2	6	19	200
Ont.	266	9	2	14	12	27	330
Que.	40	11	14	25	35	50	175
N.B.	9	12	2	7	12	11	53
P.E.I.	10	0	0	6	17	11	44
N.S.	151	3	4	5	27	35	225
Nfld.	15	1	3	8	14	11	52
Total	951	47	32	85	141	198	1,454
% of Total	65.4	3.2	2.2	5.8	9.7	13.6	100

not be effective in describing the data because almost two-thirds of the cases come out as zero. No days elapse from the end of the hearing to the decision. Instead, the appellate panel confers immediately after the close of argument and informs the parties orally of its decision. In some provinces panels often meet after hearing only the appellant's argument and inform the respondent that he or she will not be called upon, since the court has decided that the appellant's arguments were not sufficient to overturn the judgment at trial.

However, if 65 per cent of the appeals are decided on the last hearing day, that means over one-third of the criminal appeals required at least one additional day to reach a decision. In fact, close to one-fourth required over a week, and almost one in seven required a month or more.

What makes the figures in Table 8.5 particularly interesting are the sharp differences they show from province to province. In the first four provinces, 75 to 85 per cent of all criminal appeals are decided on the same day the hearing ends. As we move east, the practice is (with the exception of Nova Scotia) totally reversed. Only 23 per cent of Quebec's criminal appeals are decided on the last day of the hearing, compared with 20 per cent in one to four weeks and 29 per cent in a month or more. Similarly in New Brunswick, Prince Edward Island and Newfoundland, only a minority of criminal appeals are decided on the last day of the hearing (17, 23, and 29 per cent respectively).

These are more than differences in degree and suggest that a whole different set of expectations operates in Quebec and most of Atlantic Canada than operates in Ontario and the West. Quebec practice mirrors the expectations in its superior trial court, where the Code of Civil Procedure requires that written reasons be prepared for litigants following a trial. This requirement exists nowhere else in Canada, a doubly ironic situation since judgments in the rest of Canada have the force of common law precedent that judgments under the Civil Code of Quebec do not.

However, unique practices in Quebec do not explain the similarities between the pattern of reserving decisions and preparing written judgments in New Brunswick, Prince Edward Island and Newfoundland as well as Quebec. Our interviews in Atlantic Canada suggest that the absence of case load pressures allows the judges to maintain the tradition of providing written decisions. New Brunswick judges explicitly said they are able to reserve because they have the time. Since the Nova Scotia court is much busier, it is closer to its Western counterparts than its fellow Atlantic provincial courts of appeal. In this sense, Quebec is unusual because it continues to reserve and to prepare written reasons for judgment even as delay expands far beyond that of any other province.

Variations among Case Types

Before attributing interprovincial differences to the effects of legal culture or some other characteristic of particular provinces, it is important to see whether the pace of appellate litigation is related to other variations among the cases.

The most important characteristic of criminal appeals that leads some appeals to be completed with less delay than others is whether the case involves a sentence appeal or a substantive appeal, that is, an appeal from the conviction or acquittal of the accused.[2] Sentence appeals proceed more promptly than substantive appeals. When cases

Table 8.6

Time from Filing of Appeal to Decision by Quartiles, by Type of Criminal Appeal that Went to Hearing, Provincial Courts of Appeal

Type of Appeal	First Quartile	Second Quartile	Third Quartile	Fourth Quartile	Number of Cases
Sentence Only	290	241	144	44	719
	40.3%	33.5%	20.0%	6.1%	
Substantive Only	48	84	150	203	485
	9.9%	17.3%	30.9%	41.9%	
Sentence and Substantive	28	32	65	113	238
	11.8%	13.4%	27.3%	47.5%	
All Cases	366	357	359	360	1,442

combine a sentence appeal with a substantive appeal, they take as long or somewhat longer than substantive appeals alone.

Table 8.6 summarizes these findings. The cases are divided into quartiles as in Table 8.2, with the fastest 25 per cent of the cases in the first quartile and the slowest 25 per cent in the fourth quartile. Sharp differences are visible. For sentence appeals, 73.8 per cent are among the first 50 per cent to be heard, while 72.8 per cent of the substantive appeals are in the slower 50 per cent, as are 74.8 per cent of the appeals that have both a sentence and a substantive component. These differences are also reflected, and dramatically so, in the mean number of days from filing to decision: in sentence appeals, 146 days; in substantive appeals, 399 days; and in substantive plus sentence appeals, 409 days.

Given the sharp difference between the pace of sentence appeals and substantive appeals, it is important to link this finding back to the interprovincial differences shown in Tables 8.1 and 8.2. Thus, for example, it may be that Quebec's slower pace of litigation is a result of having a smaller proportion of sentence appeals in its case mix. Conversely, however, it may be that substantive appeals appear slower than sentence appeals if a disproportionate number come from Quebec.

To get a handle on these two variables — province and type of case — at the same time, averages (means) were calculated for each

Table 8.7

Mean Number of Days from Filing of Appeal to Decision, by Type of Criminal Appeal that Went to Hearing, Provincial Courts of Appeal

Province	Sentence Appeals	Substantive Appeal	Both	Number of Cases
B.C.	133	410	381	92/55/33
Sask.	94	185	175	124/47/24
Man.	108	230	238	109/53/38
Ont.	206	465	511	142/100/77
Que.	159	870	975	69/84/21
N.B.	151	243	267	28/19/6
P.E.I.	153	237	153	24/17/3
N.S.	141	183	246	91/99/33
Nfld.	208	309	467	39/10/3
Total, 9 Provs.	146	399	409	718/484/238

of the three case types (sentence appeal alone, substantive appeal alone, and combined sentence and substantive appeal) in each of the nine provinces. While this resulted in very small numbers of combined appeals in some of the Atlantic Provinces, every province had sufficient sentence-only and substantive-only appeals to see how the two variables interact with one another.

The results are summarized in Table 8.7. In every province, substantive appeals take longer than sentence appeals. If the third column, showing combined appeals separately, is added to the substantive appeal column, the differences would be even sharper. Thus, the type of appeal has an independent effect on the pace of litigation. Sentence appeals, whether in Quebec or Saskatchewan, proceed much more expeditiously than substantive appeals.

Interestingly, sentence appeals are handled so expeditiously in Quebec that they are completed on average one-and-one-half months sooner than in Ontario and Newfoundland. Conversely, however, substantive appeals are so slow in Quebec that they take as long as those in the next two slowest provinces (Ontario and British Columbia) combined. British Columbia's sentence appeals are also comparatively expeditious. While its overall average in Table 8.1 made it third slowest out of nine provinces, its sentence appeals proceed third fastest. This shift reflects the fact that the gap between the pace of sentence appeals and substantive appeals is smaller in all four provinces of Atlantic Canada.

In summary, both interprovincial differences and differences in case type affect the pace of criminal appeals in Canada. If avoiding unnecessary delay is an important priority in Canadian courts, a number of provinces have work to do. At the same time, the extremely slow pace of substantive appeals in some provinces suggests that this may be where to begin.

Delay Reduction in Appellate Courts

The Canadian judiciary has recognized the importance of reducing delay in dealing with cases, whether those cases are criminal or civil, trials, or appeals. In the aftermath of the Supreme Court of Canada's October 1990 judgment in *Regina* v. *Askov*, which established a constitutional guideline for unreasonable delay in criminal trials, over fifty thousand criminal charges were dismissed in the next eighteen months. The Canadian Judicial Council, composed of the chief justices of all superior and appellate courts in Canada, accepted the challenge set forth by Chief Justice of Canada Antonio Lamer, chair of the council, and established a nationwide Delays Project. That project was designed to collect information on the pace of litigation and develop policies to reduce delay in all courts with federally appointed judges.

From the start, the project's committee of appellate court judges was particularly active. Under the leadership of Ontario Associate Chief Justice John Morden, it launched a systematic effort to collect quantitative data on appellate delay. It faced the usual frustrations, as available statistics initially made interprovincial comparisons difficult. But the committee developed baseline data and a set of recommendations that went into the first comprehensive national report on court delay produced by the council.

What made the appellate courts' initiative significant was that the participating judges recognized the value of expeditiously handling appeals even though there were no constitutional or statutory requirements that they take action. The *Askov* case constrained trial courts, not appeal courts, and when the question of whether the same Charter requirement applied to appeals, the Supreme Court of Canada held in *Potvin* that it did not. Section 11(b) required only that an accused receive a "trial within a reasonable time," the court majority reasoned that an appeal was not a trial. While this seems to be an easy call, the dissent in *Potvin* pointed out that the French-language version of Section 11(b) used the word for "hearing" (audition), thus applying to appeals as well as trials — the same construction used by national courts under the European Convention on Human Rights to dismiss criminal charges when appeals have been pending for over eighteen months.

Even if appeal courts do not face the threat of Charter sanctions for excessive delay, principles of fairness and mutual respect call for them to complete their work expeditiously. Fairness entitles accused persons to have questions about their guilt or innocence and their loss of liberty adjudicated without delay, and the public interest also requires that the system of criminal justice move promptly to punish those deemed guilty, and exonerate all others.

Not only did appeal court chief judges take important steps in 1991 to develop a systematic national strategy to address delay, but the appeal court committee has continued to publish an annual statistical report monitoring filings and dispositions and the time intervals those appeals required. In 1995 the statistics showed dispositions running ahead of filings nationally, with 3,596 new cases compared with 4,265 judgments and other dispositions. Ontario was making especially substantial inroads into its criminal appeal backlog.

At the same time, however, the 1995 Judicial Council data on time intervals from notice of appeal to judgment were less encouraging. Times were reported separately for sentence appeals, conviction, or acquittal appeals (what we termed "substantive appeals" in Table 8.7 above), and the combined category of "sentence and conviction appeals," so that the 1995 figures could be compared with our data covering 1988–92. The council's time interval data reported the median time in months, a figure comparable to the mean time in days shown in Table 8.7.[3] Table 8.8 shows the comparative figures.

The figures in Table 8.8 show that delays have increased in British Columbia and Ontario, but decreased in Manitoba and Nova Scotia. The fact that British Columbia and Ontario both reduced their pending criminal appeals during 1995 suggests that the pace of litigation had been slower in the previous year, and had therefore increased even more between 1988–92 and 1994.

But these figures should be interpreted with caution. It is unclear whether the 1995 figures are informed estimates or the product of

Table 8.8

Mean and Median Number of Days from Filing of Appeal to Decision, by Type of Criminal Appeal that Went to Hearing, Provincial Courts of Appeal

Province	Sentence Appeals		Substantive Appeals		Both	
	1988–92	**1995**	**1988–92**	**1995**	**1988–92**	**1995**
B.C.	133	187	410	485	381	462
Alta.	—	150	—	362	—	398
Man.	108	83	230	195	238	210
Ont.	206	225	465	569	511	474
N.S.	141	150	183	150	246	150

Note: Numbers of months in 1995 Judicial Council tables have been converted to days.

statistical analysis. For example, it is unlikely that Nova Scotia appeals are completed in an average of five months regardless of the type of appeal involved. Furthermore, the number of missing provinces is disturbing for an annual report undertaken with the ostensible support of the chief justices in every province. No data were reported for Saskatchewan, Quebec, or Newfoundland, and New Brunswick provided estimates only for the time from hearing to judgment.[4] The conspicuous absence of any figures for the Quebec Court of Appeal raises concern about whether that court, the slowest in Canada a few years before, was giving delay reduction the priority it deserves. While one would hope that the extensive delays found in our 1988–92 sample of substantive criminal appeals would have begun to decline by 1995, no evidence was provided. Given the progress made at the trial level in Montreal a decade before (a waiting time of up to six years for a trial date in a civil case had been reduced to under six months), improved performance should be possible.

Winners and Losers

There is likely to be a consensus around the value of expeditious justice, so that regardless of their political views, Canadians would agree that delays in hearing and deciding appeals should be avoided. Respect for all justice values — the rights of the accused, the needs of the victim, the interests of society, the search for truth — requires that criminal appeals be heard without unnecessary delay.

There is less likely to be a consensus around the specific provisions of the criminal law and how they should be applied in individual cases. Thus Canadians often disagree on the appropriate length of sentences for persons convicted of crimes, on the definition of specific particular crimes, or on the application of particular procedures. Given that these issues are the bases of criminal appeals, we would expect Canadians to differ on what the best outcomes of criminal appeals would be.

Because this chapter focuses on the characteristics of over a thousand criminal appeals from across Canada, it does not attempt to evaluate the outcome of any specific case. But it can present data about the patterns of outcomes of many appeals in the aggregate. These aggregate data can then present an overall picture of who wins and who loses in criminal appeals.

Table 8.9 presents an overall picture of winners and losers in criminal cases. Rather than drawing on all 1,400 or more criminal appeals in our data base, we limited this table to what we have called substantive appeals, appeals that include an issue of whether the accused should have been convicted or acquitted. We have not included appeals about sentence alone in this table, since accused persons might have their sentences reduced, but for a period less than they sought, just as the Crown might have a sentence increased for a period less than it sought. Thus, it seemed more difficult and arbitrary to label an outcome in a sentencing appeal a win or a loss.

Table 8.9 in fact shows an interesting pattern of winners and losers. Overall, the appellants win 33 per cent of the time and lose 62 per cent of the time. Thus, while many appeals succeed (228), almost twice as many (429) are unsuccessful. However, when appeals by accused persons are separated from appeals by the Crown, striking differences emerge. Accused persons win only 26 per cent of their appeals, and lose 69 per cent of the time. In contrast, the Crown wins 64 per cent of its appeals and loses 33 per cent.

Table 8.9

Outcomes of Substantive Criminal Appeals Brought by the Crown or the Accused that Went to Hearing in Provincial Courts of Appeal

Appellant	OUTCOME				
	Appellant Won	Appellant Won Part	Issue Not Decided	Appellant Lost on All	Row Total
Accused	144	21	7	386	558
	25.8%	3.8%	1.3%	69.2%	
Crown	84	1	4	43	132
	63.6%	0.8%	3.0%	32.6%	
Totals	228	22	11	429	690
	33.0%	3.2%	1.6%	62.2%	

Note: Not included are substantive appeals by both Crown and accused (13 cases, 5 won and 8 lost) and by journalists (6 cases, 3 won and 3 lost).

These differences in outcome suggest on their face an advantage to the Crown. But we must be careful not to conclude from this that the appellate process is biased towards the Crown or that appellate judges are biased towards one side or the other in hearing criminal appeals. What we need to do is to use this finding as a starting point for a greater understanding of the nature and dynamics of adjudication.

Previous chapters have focused on the discretion of judges — the extent to which they are free to decide an appeal one way or the other, rather than all being bound to reach the same conclusion. An examination of the flow of cases shifts the focus to the discretion of the parties and their lawyers. To what extent are Crown counsel more selective than defence counsel in choosing cases to appeal? The fate of an individual accused is more important to that person and his or her family than to a prosecutor's office, which may be more concerned with whether any individual appeal will establish a precedent that will help or harm the prosecution of other cases in the future. As a result, the Crown may take more care to choose a winner than an accused person. Even when faced with a more difficult appeal, with a one-in-four chance of success, an accused person who has been convicted and faces a criminal penalty would be acting rationally by filing an appeal.

In criminal appeals, the differences between the two sides, Crown and accused, are often drawn in partisan terms. For those who favour tough law enforcement, one party represents the public interest and the other those who commit crimes and try to get away with them. For those concerned with legal rights, one party represents the overwhelming power of the state against a weak and powerless individual.

However, it is more important to consider differences between the two parties in criminal appeals from an analytical than from a partisan perspective. One of the reasons why the Crown succeeds more frequently than the accused, and one of the factors associated with its greater selectivity in choosing which cases to appeal, may be the different relationship between the lawyers and the parties on each side of the case. On the Crown's side, the lawyers have greater discretion in individual cases, since their client is a symbolic entity (the Crown in Canada or England, the state or the people in the United States) that places general constraints on its legal representatives and rarely participates in an individual decision whether to appeal or not. On the defence side, accused persons typically have an intense personal interest in the outcome of their individual cases, and they are thus likely to play a larger part in their lawyer's decision to appeal or not. Under these conditions, defence counsel may in some cases encourage their clients to appeal and in other cases discourage them. But even conscientious defence counsel who are reluctant to carry forward an appeal when the legal grounds are weak may be persuaded to support their clients' desire to appeal, whereas with a similarly weak case, as the Crown, they would decline to appeal. It may be this built-in structural difference in how Crown and defence counsel exercise their and their clients' discretion that reinforces the differences in outcomes shown in Table 8.9.

The argument developed here has set up two competing hypotheses to explain the Crown's aggregate advantage as revealed in Table 8.9. Outcomes that may initially be seen as a result of the preferences of individual judges or groups of judges may instead be a product of the dynamics of adjudication, for example, the relations between parties and their counsel. While it is not possible to evaluate conclusively these competing hypotheses with the current data, Table 8.10 presents a first cut at this issue. It breaks down the figures in Table 8.9 by province to see whether the differences between the Crown

Table 8.10

Outcomes of Substantive Criminal Appeals Brought by the Crown or the Accused that Went to Hearing, by Province

Province	Appeals by Accused		Appeals by Crown	
	Won	Lost	Won	Lost
B.C.	21	45	4	4
	32%	68%	50%	50%
Sask.	21	44	1	4
	32%	68%	20%	80%
Man.	27	52	3	4
	34%	66%	43%	57%
Ont.	35	109	24	7
	24%	76%	77%	23%
Que.	28	48	12	10
	37%	63%	55%	45%
N.B.	4	15	4	2
	21%	79%	67%	33%
P.E.I.	4	8	2	5
	33%	67%	29%	71%
N.S.	23	62	33	6
	27%	73%	85%	15%
Nfld.	3	3	3	1
	50%	50%	75%	25%
Totals	166	386	86	43

and the accused are uniform across the country, or whether some appellate courts differ in the percentage of cases won by accused appellants and by Crown appellants.

The first two columns show the outcome of appeals by the accused. There is a substantial degree of uniformity. Except for Newfoundland, which had only six cases (too few to reveal a pattern), accused persons succeed between 21 and 37 per cent of the time. Accused are most successful in Quebec, and least successful in New

Brunswick and Ontario. Courts that outside observers normally would regard as quite different (for example, Saskatchewan, Manitoba, and British Columbia) are in the aggregate quite similar. These figures reinforce the "dynamics of adjudication" explanation. They suggest, for example, that it would be worthwhile and interesting to examine whether Quebec's legal aid system, which has a more developed institutional structure than the systems in other provinces, produces somewhat more selectivity in the appeals brought by accused persons.

Now consider the third and fourth columns, showing the outcome of Crown appeals. There a different pattern emerges. Only three provinces (Ontario, Quebec, and Nova Scotia) have enough cases to calculate valid percentages. But by cumulating the data for the other six provinces, we generate a comparison group of thirty-seven cases, in which the Crown won a total of seventeen appeals and lost twenty. Examining the resulting figures, the Crown won 85 per cent of its appeals in Nova Scotia and 77 per cent in Ontario, contrasted with 54 per cent in Quebec and 46 per cent in the remaining provinces combined. Thus, significant differences are visible across provinces.

In terms of our competing hypotheses, is it possible from these figures to attribute interprovincial differences in the success of Crown appeals to differences between judges rather than differences in the way Crown counsel select appeals from province to province? One clue might be to examine the ratio of Crown appeals to accused appeals in our sample. For example, if one in ten appeals in a province is initiated by the Crown, this suggests that Crown counsel are more selective than in a province where one in three appeals are brought by the Crown.

Examining Table 8.10 in these terms accentuates differences between the courts. In the three Western provinces (British Columbia, Saskatchewan, and Manitoba), accused appeals outnumber Crown appeals by over ten to one, 210–20, but the Crown won only eight of its twenty appeals, or 40 per cent. In the Nova Scotia sample, however, accused appeals outnumber Crown appeals by just over two to one, 85–39. Yet even with a higher proportion of Crown appeals, the Crown wins by an overwhelming margin. In fact, in Nova Scotia, the Crown wins a higher proportion of appeals brought by the accused than in any other province.

A full exploration of these differences and why they occur would require that complementary data be obtained on trial court outcomes in the provinces. For example, if accused persons are more frequently acquitted in Nova Scotia than in the three Western provinces, we should not be surprised if Crown appeals constitute a larger proportion of the criminal appeals in that province. But is this in fact the case? We also need to see whether appeal rates vary from province to province. Do accused persons in some provinces appeal a higher proportion of their convictions at trial than the accused in other provinces?

Regardless of which competing explanation accounts for differences between the outcomes of Crown appeals and defence appeals, those differences do exist, and are accentuated in some provinces. At the least, therefore, these differences reinforce the need for individual judges to be careful and conscientious in assessing the merits of the arguments and the strength of the cases brought by the different parties in criminal appeals. If judges come to expect Crown appeals to be more compelling than appeals from accused persons, does that undermine their ability to treat each new case on its merits? And if some provincial courts of appeal tend to decide more favourably to the Crown than others, how is their work perceived by those who appear before them, and by the public?

This chapter suggests that discretion is cumulative. How judges exercise their discretion may be affected by how the lawyers and the parties have exercised theirs. On the other hand, judicial discretion remains separate and independent; it may accentuate differences in outcomes, or may mitigate them. In some respects, appellate judges respond to the dynamics of adjudication in predictable ways, as shown in more uniform outcomes of accused appeals. In other respects, they may privilege the arguments of one side over the other, as suggested by the far greater success of the Crown in Nova Scotia. In either case, the legitimacy of appellate adjudication requires that individual attention be given to individual cases, even as aggregate patterns emerge, because the principle of mutual respect emphasizes the worth and importance of every human being.

The Courts and Democracy[1]

As we noted in Chapter 1, judicial power is not a concept with which Canadian judges have long been comfortable, or one which Canadian social scientists have long studied. In large part, this stems from the way that most lawyers and judges understood the judicial process for most of the country's first century. The mechanical approach to jurisprudence highlights professionalism, objectivity, and technical expertise; and by the same token it severely downplays (if it does not altogether preclude) judicial discretion as an appropriate dimension of the judicial role. If lawyers and judges see decision-making as a purely technical exercise, then there is not much that can be discussed with non-experts; and if social scientists accept that description, then there is not much that can usefully be studied. If courts are considered this way, then they are no threat to democracy, and no part of the process whereby policy is developed.

This is no longer an accurate description of how the Canadian social scientist or the Canadian public thinks about the courts, and several factors have contributed to the change. For one thing, Chief Justice Bora Laskin dramatically transformed the Supreme Court of Canada during the 1970s, a process that included an unmistakable shift in the style of judicial decision-making from the formalist approach of earlier years to an explicitly contextual approach.[2] For another, Canadian political scientists finally began to follow the lead of scholars like the University of Toronto's Peter Russell, who had long argued that there was a politically relevant dimension to what courts did and how they did it — something that U.S. social scientists had known for decades. For a third, the entrenchment of the Canadian Charter of Rights and Freedoms in 1982 gave the Supreme Court of Canada a new high profile as it began to tackle the controversial issues of human rights in a complex modern society. The 1982 amendments gave Canadian judges sweeping powers to strike down offending legislation, and even to take more positive steps on their own initiative, to protect the glowing principles rather vaguely enshrined in the Charter. In the Canada of the 1990s, unlike that of the 1960s, nothing is less controversial than the suggestion that judges have power.

The judges themselves have played very little role in the debate about judges and democracy; to do so would, from the perspective of most of them, draw them into the political arena in violation of the principle of judicial independence. Occasionally, a leading judge will make an after-dinner speech acknowledging the increased policy-making role which Canadians handed to judges through the democratic process,[3] or arguing that thanks to the Charter, judges can and must participate in public debates about fundamental principles more than in the past.[4]

The purpose of this chapter is to consider the views of judges themselves about their role in policy-making and, more generally, about the role of courts in a democracy. Our assumption is that the judicial perspective in this debate cannot be gleaned simply by analysing after-dinner speeches — which are at best indicative only of the views of the more outspoken judges, and at worst a bland rehashing of conventional wisdom. Nor can they be determined simply by studying judicial decisions, which although they serve as useful indicators do not often provide much scope for specific consideration of these topics. It is necessary to talk to the judges themselves.

We argue that courts have become more visible and central actors in the Canadian public policy process at the same time that public expectations have risen for stricter adherence to democratic principles. The result is that courts are more important but also more vulnerable than ever, striving as they do to steer a middle course between the Scylla of their elitist traditions (appointed from the ranks of professionals of high class and status) and the Charybdis of democratic expectations (implying transparency of decision-making, a degree of accountability, and the ability to think critically about the principles driving democracy). A great deal is riding on the success or failure of this delicate balancing act.

We should remind our readers that we consider democracy as government based on the principle of mutual respect. While realizing that definitions of democracy often begin with the principle of majority rule through fair and open elections, we consider this to be only one among several subprinciples of this basic axiom of democracy, as we explained in Chapter 1.

The Views of Appellate Judges

Judicial Independence

The rule of law requires that disputes about the application of the law be settled as impartially as possible. Judicial independence is one of the mechanisms developed in rule-of-law countries to promote judicial impartiality; it refers to procedures that are intended to insulate the outcome of a particular decision or class of decisions from any influence outside of legitimate courtroom activity, including the general public but especially the legislative or executive branches of government. In the *Valente* decision of 1985,[5] the Supreme Court of Canada set out three essential conditions for judicial independence: security of judicial tenure (judges can be removed only for judicial misbehaviour and only after a fair and impartial hearing), financial security for judges (their salaries must be established by general legislation), and the institutional independence of tribunals on all matters directly affecting adjudication.

Of sixty judges who responded to the open-ended question, "What does the principle of judicial independence mean to you?" thirty-nine (65 per cent) understood it to mean that no one may attempt to interfere with impartial adjudication, particularly members of the legislative and executive branches of government. Three other types of responses each received support from about one-eighth of the judges interviewed: no interference from other judges, impartiality, and complete freedom to decide. The idea of autonomy (including administrative autonomy) was mentioned by a tenth of the judges. (Multiple responses were recorded so that the totals to our open-ended questions sometimes exceed 100 per cent.)

The judges were also asked whether they perceived any threats to judicial independence at the present time, and if so, what constituted these threats. Of the eighty judges who responded, more than two-thirds (55) listed one or more threats. This proportion was surprising, especially in comparison to the results of interviews with ninety-one trial court and appellate judges in Alberta and Ontario conducted by McCormick and Greene in the early 1980s. Asked if they could think of any instances when their judicial independence had been tampered with, not a single judge in the earlier study could give any examples of such tampering, although some referred to four well-publicized incidents not involving them personally where a federal cabinet minister had telephoned a judge about a particular case.[6] Although the question in the current study is worded slightly differently, we do not think that the stark contrast between the results of the two studies is merely a result of the difference in wording of the question.

A fifth of the appellate judges who perceived threats to their independence (12 out of 55) were concerned that special interest groups seemed to be attempting to bring pressure to bear on the direction of judicial decisions. Five judges complained about pressure to make decisions which were perceived to be "politically correct," and five complained about the impact of media criticism that they could not respond to without themselves violating judicial independence. As well, a handful of judges were concerned that the inaccurate or sensationalist handling of judicial decisions by the media was in a sense putting pressure on them to make decisions that would result in a "good press."[7] As a result of the Charter of Rights and Freedoms, Canadian appellate courts have made controversial decisions regarding subjects such as abortion, rape shield legislation, drunkenness as a defense in sexual assault cases, compulsory retirement, gay rights, Sunday shopping, the rights of refugee claimants, and the spending of union dues for political purposes. These decisions have resulted in an unprecedented level of commentary in the media about judicial decisions, much of it critical. There have even been demonstrations in front of courthouses following controversial decisions — an absolute novelty for Canadians.

Nor has it been only the judges' decisions which have ignited controversy. In 1990 Madam Justice Bertha Wilson, the first woman appointee to the Supreme Court of Canada, gave an address at Osgoode Hall Law School in which she argued that women judges are likely to have different views from male judges on family law, but not criminal law issues. A right-wing women's organization complained to the Canadian Judicial Council that Wilson — the wife of a United Church of Canada minister who had once written a pro-choice opinion[8] — had violated judicial independence. The council exonerated Wilson.

Some appellate judges were also concerned about what they considered to be unwarranted pressure from the executive branch of government. These pressures included criticism of judicial decisions by politicians (9 judges), lack of appropriate administrative support (8 judges), and inappropriate procedures for determining judicial salaries (6 judges). Some judges were particularly concerned about the propensity of some provincial attorneys general publicly to criticize judges' sentencing practices or to take a judge to task for a particular decision which undercut government statements or ran counter to provincial policy priorities. More than one judge reported an impression that provincial governments had cut back on administrative support services to the appellate courts because they were unhappy about the direction of appellate court decisions. One example was the suggestion that judicial secretarial support was being reduced and the provision of personal computers refused in order to force the judges to write briefer decisions. Concerning judicial salaries, several judges were angry that the federal government rejected the advice of the independent commission established to review judicial salaries. Although the government cited the deficit and debt crisis as the reason, some judges were afraid that the real reason was that the appellate judges were making too many decisions that irritated the government.

Seven judges were worried that the Canadian Judicial Council, a body composed of all of the federally appointed chief justices and associate chief justices, had developed inappropriate procedures for disciplining judges. The Judicial Council is empowered to investigate complaints against federally appointed judges, and its annual reports provide a chronicle of how it handles the 150 or so annual complaints it now receives. Many complaints are about a judicial decision, and in these cases complainants are advised of their rights of appeal. Many others do not provide enough facts to make an investigation possible. The few remaining are referred to an investigation panel, which normally results either in the judge providing a satisfactory explanation of his or her actions, or (more rarely) in a judge deciding to retire prior to the completion of the investigation. In only one case since the council was formed in 1971 has it publicly found fault with a judge prior to the judge's retirement. This was the case of Mr. Justice Thomas Berger, who publicly criticized the 1981 constitutional accord for ignoring the rights of native Canadians and women. The council criticized Berger's actions, but did not recommend that he be removed on the grounds that the degree to which judges could make "political" statements had not been clear.

In general, the seven judges who were critical of the council's investigatory procedures felt that it was improper for chief justices to have disciplinary powers through the council. A better approach, they felt, would be to have federally appointed judges elect a judicial disciplinary tribunal. Their argument was that because the puisne judges know that their chief sits on the body that could investigate complaints against them and would likely be involved in deciding whether a complaint warranted a full investigation, the puisne judges would feel pressured to stay on their chief's good side, for example, by supporting his or her point of view in hard cases where the court was split. As well, the chief justices have the reputations of their respective courts to consider, creating an incentive in borderline situations either to exonerate judges who have been complained against or to seize the opportunity to deal with a good but controversial judge. Disciplinary tribunals elected by the judges themselves would be less intimidating, less likely to have a "chilling effect" on the puisne judges. Mr. Justice David Marshall makes a similar point in his book on judicial independence, which suggests that the these concerns may be even more widespread than our interviews indicated.[9]

It is clear that the Charter of Rights has precipitated most of the concerns of the judges about threats to judicial independence. Pressure group activities towards the courts are frequently the result of a Charter decision. Critical remarks by attorneys general and other cabinet ministers are sometimes prompted by Charter decisions, but in any case the Charter has exposed the judges' policy-making role and therefore has drawn judges into political controversy. The increasing visibility of the judiciary has resulted in an unprecedented level of official complaints about judicial behaviour. For example, the number of complaints received by the Canadian Judicial Council has increased from forty-seven in 1987–88 (the year of the Supreme Court's controversial Charter decision striking down Canada's abortion legislation), to 164 in 1993–94 and 200 in 1995–96. However, the number of complaint files opened dropped to 186 in 1996–97.

The Impact of the Canadian Charter of Rights and Freedoms

Here we consider how appellate judges feel about the expanded lawmaking role they have been assigned because of the Charter of Rights. It should be remembered that this enlarged lawmaking role is both directly and indirectly a result of the Charter. For example, one judge told us that his colleagues had been much more prone to altering the common law since the Charter. "After the Charter gave the judges the right to strike down a statute, altering the common law was a piece of cake." This approach might also explain why Canadian courts have, since the Charter, given more weight to the the provincial bills of rights and the human rights acts — all legislation not forming part of the official constitution — than they ever did before 1982. It was not until 1987 that Justice Duff's doctrine that freedom of speech is protected by the original Canadian constitution inexplicably gained majority support on the Supreme Court — forty-nine years after it was first enunciated.[10]

We asked eighty-nine judges to what extent they perceived themselves to be lawmakers, as opposed to being merely law interpreters. They were asked to answer on a five-point scale, with 1 representing "lawmaker" and 5 representing "law interpreter." The average response was 3.8, closer to the law-interpreter role, although the average response of seven Supreme Court judges was just 3.1. Twenty-six judges (29 per cent) saw themselves fundamentally as law interpreters, while only two placed themselves squarely on the lawmaking side of the continuum. However, in response to a question about whether the lawmaking role was changing, half of the judges thought that the Charter had moved them closer to the lawmaking side of the continuum, while only three-tenths thought that the lawmaking role had not changed significantly. On average, the judges thought they were lawmakers in only about 15 per cent of the cases they heard (but one Supreme Court of Canada judge ventured that as many as 60 per cent of the top court's cases involved lawmaking).

On the other hand, more than one long-serving judge suggested that their court used to make law much more frequently than was the case today. They argued that until recently, the Supreme Court of Canada had not dealt with a wide variety of legal issues, which meant that provincial courts of appeal "made law" by addressing these issues for the first time. Similarly, the first wave of Charter cases confronted the appeal courts with "first time" issues that called for imaginative solutions. By contrast, in recent years the Supreme Court has been much more committed to resolving a broad range of legal issues, and the basic elements of Charter interpretation have been clearly established. Thus, the role of intermediate appellate courts has changed not only in terms of how judges relate to legislative institutions but also how the judges on one court relate to judges on another.

We asked the judges whether they thought the Charter had created a "crisis of legitimacy" for the courts — a phrase which was used by some judges in the mid-1980s to describe their fears about judges becoming involved in lawmaking through high-profile Charter of Rights cases. The judges were evenly split on this issue, with thirty-three of seventy-three thinking that such a crisis existed (45 per cent), and thirty-two saying that there was no crisis; the remainder were neutral. The twenty-two judges who described themselves fundamentally as law interpreters were more likely to think that there was a crisis of legitimacy than those who perceived themselves as having a mixed lawmaking and law-interpreting role.

It was most certainly the case prior to the Charter that nearly all Canadian judges resisted a lawmaking role for the courts, and many denied its possibility altogether. Instead, they espoused the legal positivist school of thought that good judges merely interpret the law. It is striking how quickly and completely this traditional view has faded: all but two appellate court judges now admit to having at least some lawmaking role. However, half were clearly uncomfortable with this newly visible role, as reflected by their responses to the "crisis of legitimacy" question.

Worries about the public perception of the lawmaking role of the courts aside, we were curious as to whether appellate judges thought that it was legitimate for Canadians to try to change the law through the courts rather than through the more overtly political process of Parliament and the legislatures. In response to the question, "How appropriate is it for social and public interest groups to use the courts to achieve social change?" thirty of sixty-five judges (45 per cent) thought that these activities were not appropriate, while only twenty-three (35 per cent) thought they were. On a 1 to 5 scale, 5 being "extremely appropriate" and 1 being "not at all appropriate," the average response of the four Supreme Court judges was 3.5, compared with 2.7 for appellate judges as a whole. Two Supreme Court judges mentioned that interest groups can present very useful briefs as intervenors, and one said that the courts are an important part of the democratic process, open for business to those wanting to promote legitimate democratic change. One Supreme Court judge, however, was worried about the consequences of the courts being used as political tools.

Supreme Court of Canada judges are less concerned about the newly expanded lawmaking role of the judges. Four out of five felt that the Charter of Rights had changed the role of the court, bringing it closer to a lawmaking function. But of five judges questioned, all disagreed with the proposition that the Charter had created a crisis of legitimacy for the court, and one strongly disagreed. The consensus was that through the political process, the Supreme Court had been handed a lawmaking role by the people of Canada, and that this new role was generally accepted. But there was certainly no such consensus among appellate judges as a whole on the question.

Collegial Decision-making on Appellate Courts

One major difference between trial and appellate courts is that trial court decision-making is an individual process, while there is always a collegial process involved in the appellate courts (except when appellate judges act individually to consider matters such as interlocutory motions and motions for intervenor status).

The most common outcome is a unanimous decision. Peter McCormick reports that 60 per cent of reported Supreme Court of Canada decisions on appeals from the lower appellate courts have been unanimous since 1949. The proportion of unanimous decisions in the provincial courts of appeal is much higher, ranging from about 96 per cent in Ontario to 85 per cent in Quebec and Manitoba. Dissenting opinions are more common than separate concurring opinions, which are rare outside of the Supreme Court of Canada.[11]

The issue of how extensive dissenting and separate concurring opinions should be is an important one when considering the role of appellate courts in a democracy, because one of the strengths of democratic government is its ability to respect dissenting voices. As we noted in Chapter 4, we asked the judges whether it was important for a panel to try to avoid dissenting opinions. On the 5-point scale, with 1 representing "not at all important" and 5 representing "extremely important," the average was 2.1, meaning that dissents are considered a perfectly acceptable part of the process. Most judges stressed the importance of dissenting opinions in the development of the law, although a few also talked about the need to try to avoid unnecessary or confusing dissents either for the sake of clarity in the law or to help the losing side to accept its loss. On the other hand, some judges in the provincial appeal courts said they were sometimes tempted to register a dissent just in order to give the appellant an opportunity to appeal to the Supreme Court of Canada, as the Supreme Court must hear appeals in criminal cases where there has been a dissent registered in the provincial appeal court.

Separate concurring decisions were another story. Based on the same scale, the average response was 3.5, but it was only 2.9 for eight Supreme Court of Canada judges. This result means that avoiding separate concurring decisions is an important part of the collegial decision-making process in the penultimate appellate courts, but not as important at the Supreme Court level.

The two most common explanations given to us by the judges for unnecessary separate concurring decisions were that newly appointed judges sometimes consider the finer points of law to be more important than they do later in their careers and that some judges are "prima donnas" whose inability to see the legitimacy of alternative views prevents the kind of collegial give-and-take necessary for a court and for democratic society generally to work effectively.

For some judges the effort to avoid unnecessary separate decisions was so important that they would be willing to invest hours either redrafting their own opinions or suggesting changes to their colleagues' decisions in order to reach an acceptable compromise. Just over half of the judges had taken at least one judgment-writing course, and nearly all of them found the courses helpful; some mentioned how the courses had helped them to write decisions that were more likely to discourage separate opinions from others on a panel. But others were simply willing to let the chips fall where they may and were not concerned at all about multiple opinions.

The Supreme Court has been criticized in recent years for producing too many separate concurring decisions; these multifarious judgments do not help to clarify the law in the minds of lawyers and judges in the courts below. An extreme form of this is the "plurality decision" where no single statement of "outcome plus reasons" is able to draw the signatures of a majority of the panel, and this result usually occurs at least once or twice each year. Not surprisingly, a slight majority of Supreme Court judges do not see the number of separate concurring decisions as a major problem. From their perspective, the law is always in a state of flux, and too much rigidity mitigates against fairness and justice. On the other hand, three Supreme Court judges felt that one way to improve the decision-making process in the Supreme Court would be for the judges to find a way to reduce the number of separate concurring decisions.

There are at least two ways of thinking about attempts to avoid non-unanimous decisions from the perspective of democratic theory, and they roughly parallel the two different views expressed about concurring decisions by Supreme Court judges. One view is that in order to respect the rights of minorities, both dissenting opinions and separate concurring opinions are important to ensure that losing litigants are treated with equal concern and respect and to provide an opportunity for a losing class of litigant to become a winning class in the future — such opinions can become the springboards for the future development of the law. The other view is that dissenting and separate concurring decisions are sometimes the result of "prima donna" judges and that the law is better served by a court whose behaviour is made more predictable by a single clear statement of the law. This is a reflection of a more absolutist approach to the law, and one that is more appropriate to a court that is performing a technical exercise than to one that is engaged in a democratic dialogue with citizens.

The Relation Between Trial and Appellate Courts

The right to at least one appeal is considered to be a fundamental way in which fairness and minority rights are promoted in a democracy. But appeals do not involve retrials, and appellate judges are not supposed to reconsider questions of fact that have been determined by trial judges. Nevertheless, trial court judges not infrequently complain that appellate judges have a tendency to retry the facts of cases.[12]

We asked the appellate judges to what extent they felt free to look into questions of fact. On a 5-point scale with 1 representing "not free at all" and 5 representing "completely free," the average response of sixty-two judges was 2.5, a little closer to the constrained side of the continuum. What is surprising about the responses to this question is that they tend to "bunch up" at either end of the continuum rather than in the middle; twenty-one judges felt that they were not free at all to look into factual issues, while twelve felt completely free, and only six placed themselves at the "3" (neutral) position.

A closer analysis helps to explain this particular set of responses. Appellate judges with previous experience as trial judges were less likely than appellate judges appointed "from the street" to feel free to look into questions of fact. We also asked fifty-nine judges how concerned they were about appellate courts usurping the function of trial courts, with 1 representing "extremely concerned" and 5 representing "not at all concerned." The average response was 2.7, closer to the "not at all concerned" end of the continuum. Again, the appellate judges with previous trial judge experience were the ones who tended to be more concerned about appellate courts trying to become trial courts.

Thirty-nine (83 per cent) of forty-seven judges thought that, in areas where the law is not settled, the provincial and federal courts of appeal should put more effort into their written decisions in order to assist the Supreme Court in finally settling the issue. One Supreme Court judge mentioned that one reason for denying leave to appeal in an otherwise important case would be if the lower appellate courts had not canvassed an issue thoroughly.

From the perspective of democratic theory, is it best for appellate judges to become involved in reviewing a trial judge's findings of fact or to concentrate on the proper application of the law to the facts? The answer depends, of course, on how skilled trial judges are at determining the facts, and how successful appellate court judges can be at second-guessing a trial judge's decision when all they have to go on is the transcript — witnesses' words divorced from witnesses' demeanour. Justice is best served by whichever approach leads to the greatest accuracy, and appellate judges with trial judge experience generally feel that reopening issues of fact can often lead to less satisfactory judgments. But technology may change all this. Some appellate courts are experimenting with audio and video transcripts. Will this technology provide appellate courts with the tools they need to review the fact-finding decisions of trial judges? What will be the effects on democratic government of a technology that could encourage appellate judges to substitute their conclusions for those of the trial judge or even the jury? The possibility of enhanced accuracy of factual judgment would need to be weighed carefully against an increased concentration of decision-making power.

Fair Procedures and their Abuse

Because of its promise of mutual respect, democracy is inevitably and necessarily somewhat inefficient. But democracies can face situations where fair procedures are abused enough to cause undue hardship to legitimate users of the system. With regard to the appellate courts, the right of appeal is abused when litigants appeal not because they are convinced that a trial decision should be overturned or modified, but to delay an appropriate penalty, to frustrate the winning side, or to provide counsel with additional remunerative opportunities.

As noted in Chapter 4, we asked appellate judges the proportion of cases they heard where the result was so obvious that the case should not have come before the court. The average response of seventy-nine judges was 21 per cent, and the range was from 1 to 85 per cent, with the modal response being 10 per cent (18 judges). The most common reasons given for these cases coming to appeal were lawyers' abuse of the legal aid system, the refusal of some litigants to take their counsel's advice and insisting on proceeding with a hopeless appeal (the "hope springs eternal" appeal), inexperienced lawyers who could not recognize an empty appeal, and the fact that some less scrupulous litigants were wealthy enough to frustrate the winning side with endless manoeuvres.

This question was less relevant to Supreme Court of Canada judges because most cases that come to the court are granted leave by a panel of three judges, because they raise issues of general legal importance. We asked several of the Supreme Court judges whether some cases slipped through this screening process and turned out not to be of much importance. As we noted in Chapter 6, the court grants leave to cases that the judges later regret having granted more frequently than we might expect. This is partly because of the skill of some lawyers in masking a run-of-the-mill case as having important dimensions and partly because of the reluctance of new law clerks to close off the possibility of an appeal in cases that interest them.

All institutions in a democracy are, by their nature, open to abuse. Clearly, some of the "hopeless" appeals that end up in the provincial or federal appellate courts or even at the Supreme Court of Canada arrive there in spite of the best intentions of those involved. Others are there for reasons that reflect less favourably on the motives and integrity of some lawyers and litigants. If democracy is government based on mutual respect, it is a system that by its nature is based on mutual trust. To the extent that trust is abrogated by those manipulating the system for purely self-interested purposes, democratic institutions are weakened.

Canada's Appellate Courts and Canadian Democracy

We have suggested that the heightened role of Canada's appellate courts in the policy-making arena is not necessarily and inherently anti-democratic, but rather constitutes a mechanism that can help to promote several of the subprinciples of the basic democratic principle of mutual respect. The subprinciples particularly relevant to the judicial lawmaking function are the upholding of the rule of law and the protection of the principles of minority rights, social equality, procedural fairness, and freedom of expression. Our interviews indicate that Canadian appellate judges are more willing than ever before to take on a limited lawmaking role, although about half of them worry that this new role has not yet attained legitimacy in the eyes of the public.

The courts can serve as important supports for democracy only if judges take the impartiality expectation seriously and if they have the necessary independence to practice it. The fact that two-thirds of

Canadian appellate judges perceive threats to their independence is cause for concern. The threats are often attributed to those who do not appear to appreciate the importance of judicial neutrality: some interest groups, overzealous politicians and administrators, and journalists more interested in a sensational story than an accurate one. (We hasten to add that these are the judges' characterizations: the fact that these actors might well put a different description on their own actions and motives is in itself part of the challenge of accommodating judicial professionalism and democratic will.)

Furthermore, the appeal judges may not have emphasized their own responsibilities and opportunities. While judicial neutrality can be undermined by a lack of public or media understanding of the courts' role, the courts need not be passive in response. They can develop capabilities to explain their decisions to the media, via a press officer or (as happened in one province) through the appointment of a retired superior court judge to explain procedural complexities to enquiring journalists. Courts can take the additional time and effort to ensure that controversial appeals are heard by panels that include the appropriate mix of judges, for example, a high-profile sexual abuse case in one province was reviewed by a panel that included the court's most respected authority in criminal law and a particularly able woman judge. They can also ensure that sensitive judgments are more fully elaborated and justified. They can maintain internal standards of timely performance that militate against undue delay in reaching judgment.

Rainer Knopff defined the democratic character as one that emphasizes "moderation, willingness to compromise, and mutual respect among opposing partisans."[13] He argued that the increased policy-making role of judges tends to erode democratic character among the population in general by encouraging combativeness instead of compromise, "all or nothing" court battles instead of political accommodation. While this may be true in some cases, we think that courts can also promote democratic character by setting standards for fairness, social equality, and respect for minorities.

In an interview with David Vienneau of the *Toronto Star*, Chief Justice Antonio Lamer suggested that one reason why the Supreme Court of Canada has had to deal with so many explosive social policy issues since 1982 is because "too often timid politicians have been afraid to confront them directly."[14] As all policy analysts know, a non-decision is a kind of decision, though often not surrounded by the kind of interpersonal respect integral to democracy. If judges can deal with these tough social issues, they have an opportunity to promote rather than to retard democracy.

We would suggest that the democratizing response to the new reality of judicial power is proceeding down three tracks, each one of which has its own potentials and pitfalls and triggers its own critical reactions.

The first track is a governmental commitment towards a more representative and inclusive judiciary, a rather belated acknowledgment that the ranks of Canada's judges have long been neither. As only one example, when Bora Laskin was appointed to the Supreme Court of Canada in 1970, he was the first person ever appointed to that court whose ethnic background was neither British nor French. The presence on the court in the 1990s of names like Sopinka and Iacobucci reflects this new accommodation of diversity. The main thrust of this drive to date has been the appointment of women and members of visible minorities, a project that has achieved demonstrable successes. As of the 1990s, for example, the province of Alberta became the first jurisdiction in Canada's history to have a woman serving as provincial chief justice, as well as the first to have a majority female provincial court of appeal; also in the 1990s the Federal Court was the first in Canadian history to have a Canadian of African heritage as chief justice, Chief Justice Julius Isaac, and Ontario, Alberta, and Manitoba have all recently appointed their first provincial judges of Aboriginal descent.

To be sure this is virtual representation rather than effective representation (to say nothing of the problematic issues implied by judges who "represent" constituencies rather than simply articulating a purely objective law through purely technical means), that is, the appearance within the elite of members of previously excluded groups may say as much about how those individuals have changed themselves to be accepted by the elite as it does about how the elite has changed itself to accept them. Virtual representation itself rests on dubious assumptions about the monolithic nature of the groups being represented, clearly refuted when, for example, American black leaders complained about the appointment of U.S. Supreme Court Justice Clarence Thomas or Canadian feminists rejected any notion that Prime Minister Kim Campbell was one of their own. However, virtual representation is an implicit statement about the relationship between the particular institution and the broader society, and its symbolic and practical aspects must not be minimized.

The second track is the participation of members of the general public in the judicial appointment process. Several provinces have established non-partisan judicial selection procedures that maximize the appointment prospects of community-minded lawyers with excellent legal qualifications. The most advanced of these is Ontario's, where applicants for provincial judgeships are screened by a fourteen-person advisory committee, half of whom are women and half of whom are non-lawyers. Compassion and community service are two important values stressed by the committee. Despite the success of this procedure, its future is uncertain under Ontario's neo-conservative government. In 1997 a member of the judicial appointments advisory committee resigned in protest because he claimed that the attorney general was ignoring the recommendations of the committee and reverting to the old-fashioned system of partisan appointments.[15] There are similar procedures for appointing appellate judges, all of whom have federal commissions, although these have never achieved the level of non-partisan sophistication demonstrated by Ontario's current approach.

Lay participation in screening judicial appointments is clearly a significant move, because it represents a formal acknowledgment that the selection of a judge from a pool of lawyer candidates is not pre-emptively a matter of professional judgment on objective technical grounds. To be sure, cynics might wonder how the lay members who screen the appointments are chosen, or how likely it is that a bloc of lay members would stand up to a forceful united front of legal and judicial members, or whether a screening process behind closed doors really satisfies the democratic expectations built around it. However, even if the achievements of these screening committees are more symbolic than substantive, the symbolism is important, and in the long run it may well carry the substance in its wake.

The third track is a new approach to judicial accountability that leaves many professionals rather uneasy. The "judicial council movement" of the past thirty years has created mechanisms in every jurisdiction for the consideration of complaints against judges, one possible outcome being their removal from the bench. (This rather vague wording hides a bewildering diversity in structures and procedures that should not for a moment distract us from the underlying similarity of purpose.[16]) Initially, these procedures generally reflected a careful consideration for the sensitivities and the status of judges; not only were the hearings themselves held in camera and the reports submitted confidentially to the relevant attorney general, but even the fact that a judge's performance was under review because of public complaints was considered too sensitive and confidential to become public knowledge.

Increasingly, this mood has changed. In some jurisdictions, such as British Columbia, hearings on complaints about judges always were public; in others, such as Ontario and the federal Judicial Council, the process has recently become much more open and public. When an Ontario judge was accused of inappropriate behaviour towards women members of the court staff,[17] or when complaints were made about the comments of a Quebec judge on the Holocaust and the potential for depravity of women criminals, these stories were front page news for weeks.[18]

Quite understandably, these developments have left judges uneasy, and we would suggest that this is reflected in the fact (surprising at first glance) that many of the judges we interviewed saw serious threats to their judicial independence, which some identified with the general public and others linked to the Judicial Council itself. A public enquiry process carries with it the danger that judges may effectively be professionally destroyed even if in the end their judicial colleagues rule that they have done nothing wrong, or at least nothing so wrong as to warrant removal. In other words, the criteria on which judicial performance is to be assessed are no longer exclusively, and may not even be primarily, those of technical and professional expertise objectively assessed by fellow professionals.

This is not a small matter. It implies nothing less than an evolving definition of judicial independence, a notion that is absolutely central to our concept of the judiciary and the judges' own conceptions of their role and duties. Historically, the operational definition of this principle (in Canada as in the United States) has centred around the absolute independence of the individual judge in the courtroom at the moment of judicial decision. To some extent, it was modified in Canada in the 1970s when every trial court in the country gained its own internal hierarchy of chief and associate chief judges or justices, although we are still lacking any careful evaluation of how this new hierarchy affects the performance or the consciousness of the puisne judges. It was modified again in the 1980s, when the Supreme Court of Canada ruled in *McKeigan* v. *Hickman*[19] that although judges were not obliged to give any accounting for their procedures or reasoning to any executive-created commission of enquiry (even when that commission was headed by a judge), they were fully accountable to a judge-dominated judicial council. The principle is implicitly modified again when that judge-dominated council is obliged by the pressure of public expectations to open the windows if not the doors of the committee room in which the review is carried on.

Conclusion

At one time, academics, both in the United States and elsewhere, tended to treat the concept of judicial power as if it were a uniquely American phenomenon. This is no longer remotely appropriate; everywhere in the democratic world, and to a surprising extent even in non-democratic regimes, it is being recognized that courts and judges play a large and valuable role in the operationalization of democratic values.[20] For many Canadians, scholars and citizens alike, this is a rather new and startling discovery, which is requiring us to rethink our notion of democracy and to appreciate more explicitly those elements that go beyond simple majority rule. At the same time, however, the new democratic role of the courts requires us to rethink what courts are and what judges do. For many of us, and not least for the judges themselves, this is a rather disquieting process. But it is unavoidable, and the potential benefits —if it is done right — are high.

Concern about the growth of judicial power in Canada has occurred just as Robert Putnam has focused concern on the erosion of social capital in Western democracies with the reduction of community activity and group membership (attributed perhaps most dramatically to the advent of television).[21] Reduced social and political participation by members of the public might be linked to the rise of expert appointive bodies like the courts, so that these two trends may combine to erode democratic politics. What is important today is that judges be sensitive to these changes and ensure that their work encourages rather than inhibits the democratic involvement whose loss Putnam and others have recognized and lamented.

The Human Elements of Judicial Decision-making

The conventional wisdom about appellate court decision-making goes something like this. Judges decide most appeals based on their expert understanding of how the law ought to apply to a particular situation. There is little room for discretion except in a minority of cases where the law is unclear. However, this minority of cases includes many Canadian Charter of Rights and Freedoms cases as well as other cases involving the interpretation of the constitution, and these decisions sometimes have major impacts on federal or provincial government policy.

At this point, the thinking of court analysts is divided between those who think that the Charter has shifted too much power to judges, and those who applaud the new opportunities for the exercise of judicial power. As well, appellate judges appear to be too conservative for critics on the left such as Michael Mandel or too liberal for critics on the right such as Ted Morton and Rainer Knopff.

There are three ways in which our analysis casts doubt on this conventional wisdom. First, the personal values of the individual judges are a more important factor than was previously thought, and not just for Charter cases but for practically all appeals. Second, each appellate court develops an idiosyncratic set of procedures based on the impact of customs or habits over time, and these procedural differences not only differentiate particular courts from each other, but they have an impact on the outcome of particular cases and case flow in general. Third, judicial collegiality in appellate decision-making, and the variations between courts and panels in this context have an impact on the outcomes of cases to an extent not previously realized.

Thus, four critical factors to consider when analysing the outcome of appellate court decisions are the law in the context of the issues to be resolved, the personal values of the judges, the procedures developed by the court in question, and the nature of interpersonal judicial relations in the court in question.[1] Academic lawyers have written volumes about the impact of the law on appellate decisions. Our task here is to highlight the importance of the other three factors.

We want to emphasize that our analysis ought not to be interpreted as a siren call to reduce the impact of personal values of judges on appellate decision-making or to promote a greater uniformity in appellate court procedures or collegial processes. Personal values, procedure, and interpersonal relations among the judges will always affect appellate decision-making, regardless of the precision of the law. The keys to promoting a more democratic appellate judiciary can be found through improving the process of judicial selection and promotion, cultivating more effective and fair court procedures, studying more carefully the factors that impact interpersonal relations in the appellate courts and applying the results of such studies, and providing more opportunities for judges to broaden their knowledge and understanding of society and its problems through appropriate continuing education. Refinements that improve the democratic character of appellate courts need to be continually explored in the light of research and changing social conditions.

Personal Values

In a rule of law regime, the impact of individual judicial values is properly limited by the law. But the law is an imperfect image of the will of elected legislatures, and an even more imperfect reflection of the will of the people. Individual judicial values always have, and always will influence the outcome of cases both because the law can never be a perfect reflection of the people's will, and because there will always be "hard" cases where even a perfectly clear set of laws will have an ambiguous application.

It is not uncommon for opposing counsel to cite precedents supporting their legal arguments that suggest opposite outcomes. One of the fascinating aspects of the study of Canadian constitutional law in the area of federalism is the extent to which there are opposing lines of precedent concerning such important issues as the scope of the federal trade and commerce power or the scope of the federal "peace, order, and good government" power.[2] In order to resolve these dilemmas, judges are supposed to give priority to more recent precedents and those of higher judicial authorities. However, even these rules do not always provide clear answers.

We asked the judges we interviewed how they decided between opposing precedents. We were surprised that only a third of the judges provided us with the technical legal answer that we had expected. The other two-thirds were divided between those who looked for other factors they considered to be critical, such as their admiration or lack of it for the judges writing the opposing decisions or the size of the panel signing on to the precedent, and those who simply said that they chose the precedent that was the most compelling to them, meaning that it came closest to representing "justice."

Another of canon of judicial interpretation in Canada is that precedents established by the Supreme Court of Canada are never to be departed from, except by the Supreme Court itself. Recognizing this rule, we posed the somewhat mischievous question to our interviewees: in what circumstances would you depart from a precedent established by the Supreme Court? Only one judge said that he would never, ever depart from a Supreme Court precedent. The rest said that it is always possible to "distinguish" a bad precedent. To "distinguish" a precedent means to make a decision that the facts in the case before the court are sufficiently different from the facts of the precedent case that to follow the precedent case would be inappropriate. Although most appellate judges said that they would, on occasion, distinguish a Supreme Court precedent to avoid having to apply a precedent that they considered to be "bad" law, about a quarter of the judges openly admitted that they would not follow a Supreme Court precedent that they considered would result in injustice. Several penultimate appellate court judges pointed with pride to decisions they had made that departed perhaps somewhat illegitimately from precedent, but that the Supreme Court itself had later endorsed.

The personal views of judges about what outcomes they consider to be most "just" or "fair" are critically important in a significant number of cases. Therefore, in a democratic society it is imperative that careful attention is paid both to how appellate court judges are selected and the criteria for their selection. It is obvious that we want appellate judges who have an excellent grasp of the law, can write well, and have good work habits. But because of the discretion that judges have not only in hard cases, but also in seemingly run-of-the-mill cases (as we have shown regarding relative strictness or lenience towards the refugee applicants) and over the style of written judicial decisions, the personal values of the judges count.

We argue that the best candidates for judgeships are those who take democracy seriously. They may never have immersed themselves in the academic literature surrounding mutual respect, but it is essential that they place a high value on the principles of democracy that emanate from mutual respect such as social equality, deference to representative bodies, respect for minority rights, integrity, liberty, and procedural fairness. It is important for them to have demonstrated their commitment to these values both through their pre-judicial career accomplishments and through appropriate community service.

The criteria for judicial selection ought to be made clear so that those who aspire to judgeships will realize from the start that having a social conscience counts as much as does legal expertise. Candidates for the judiciary ought to be able to demonstrate compassion through an appropriate record of community service, and they should be able to demonstrate a capacity to think seriously about the principles that drive democracy. As most judges are recruited from the trial courts, it is critical that the selection process for trial judges be an effective one. The same process should be used for all appointments that are not promotions, including direct appointments to the Supreme Court of Canada.

Although the judicial selection process for federal trial court judges and for appellate judges without prior federal trial court experience has improved dramatically since the late 1960s, the process could still stand some improvement. Most importantly, the procedure for selecting members of the federal judicial selection committees needs closer examination. Judicial appointment is so important that the composition of the selection committees cannot be left to the partisan politics of the minister's office. There ought to be an intensive recruitment process for the non-judicial members of these committees that is at arm's length from partisan politics. Although we do not agree that prospective judicial appointees should be scrutinized by public hearings as prospective appointees to U.S. federal courts are, it would not be inappropriate for a parliamentary committee to review the nominations to judicial selection committees.

The judicial promotion process deserves more careful attention, because most appellate court judges are promoted from a trial court. Currently, there is no process outside of the minister's office for reviewing potential candidates for promotion to an appellate court. If the judicial selection committees are reformed along the lines of our recommendations, then we can think of no good reason why these committees should not be involved in scrutinizing judicial promotions. It is not that the committees would necessarily have to wait for trial judges to "apply" for a judicial promotion. The committees could routinely consider every federally-appointed trial judge with three year's experience, for example, for promotion.[3]

Procedure

Appellate court procedures are intended to be mechanisms for maximizing fairness, but there is no such thing as a perfect set of procedures. It is useful, however, to compare the experiments in procedures — for that is surely what they are — in different jurisdictions and to analyse the impact of these procedures, because this evidence will enable chief justices, rules committees, or legislatures, as the case may be, to learn from the experience of other jurisdictions in order to be in the best position for considering improvements. Moreover, court procedures are necessarily affected by changing social conditions and advances in technology, and for these reasons alone they will never be frozen in time.

We have shown how much procedures vary from court to court and how these varying procedures help to explain the variation in the volume and types of appeals in particular courts. For example, more so than in most provinces, the Alberta Court of Appeal has a deliberate policy of ensuring that information about the appeal process is made available to incarcerated prisoners. Thus, Alberta's appeal court, which sits in the fourth most-populated province, has the second-highest criminal case load, nearly as high in volume as the criminal case loads in Quebec and British Columbia put together.[4]

Several years ago, to handle the higher volume of criminal cases, the Alberta court dealt with both the application for leave to appeal, where this application was necessary, and the substantive appeal at the same time.[5] Leave applications therefore involved the full panel rather than a single judge or a special docket panel as is the case in other provinces such as British Columbia. But if the panel decided to grant leave, then the substantive issue could be considered immediately without having to reconvene another panel. More recently, however, the Alberta court decided to institute a leave to appeal process handled by judges sitting alone in an attempt to save panel time for cases that could demonstrate *prima facie* merit.

A unique innovation developed in Alberta to accommodate the heavy criminal case load is the heavy use of ad hoc judges from the trial court.[6] About 8 per cent of the panel assignments on conviction appeals,[7] and fully two-thirds of panel assignments for sentence appeals,[8] are provincial superior trial court judges sitting as ad hoc members of the Court of Appeal. No other province has any similar practice.[9] In addition to case load considerations, the regular use of ad hoc judges increases the communication and thereby presumably decreases the misunderstandings between the trial and appeal benches.[10]

The fact that the chief justices of the provincial appellate courts typically strike panels composed of a minority of members of the court creates a number of problems for the provincial courts of appeal. The first and largest problem is that of coordination. It is logically possible, and obviously undesirable, that two different panels sitting in two different appeals could make differing (and possibly even conflicting) rulings on a legal issue. (This is the major theoretical drawback with the extensive use of small panels, and the reason why so few of the U.S. state supreme courts have adopted such a method of coping with case load.[11]) The various provincial appellate courts tackle the coordination problem in their own ways.

At the informal level, the fact that the different panels are sitting in the same courthouse and casually "talking shop" at coffee and over lunch provides the opportunity for such potential conflicts to be identified early and worked through to a common conclusion. This practice is helpful in the eight provinces where the appellate court's judges are permanently resident in the same city. But even in Quebec, with its split between Montreal and Quebec City, and Alberta, with its split between Calgary and Edmonton, informal "shop talk" is more effective than it would appear at first glance because the judges from one court centre always sit on panels in the other centre. In the past, the Alberta court itself generally sat in only one of those two cities in any given month; the sittings alternated, with half the court travelling for each set of sittings. More recently, the approach has changed, with panels composed of judges from both centres sitting in both centres simultaneously. In both provinces, judges considered their court to be collegial and cooperative with a great deal of informal exchange of views, to such an extent as to allow them to anticipate possible problems.

At the more formal level, all reserved decisions in Quebec and Alberta are circulated around the entire court, and comments are invited. Despite the heavy workload this implies, most judges in these provinces indicated that they regularly received comments, sometimes quite detailed, even from individuals who were not serving on that particular panel. But in other provinces where informal shop talk is relied on, there is less need to circulate all draft decisions to all judges on the court. In fact, some judges outside of Alberta and Quebec were adamantly opposed to circulating draft decisions because, they asked, how could a judge legitimately comment on a decision without having read the materials or been present at the hearing?

The procedure used by the chief justice to strike panels varies from one appellate court to another, and a new chief justice may decide to modify the existing procedures. Except for the Supreme Court and the appeal court in Prince Edward Island, a panel is rarely composed of the full court, and so there is a "luck of the draw" dimension to appellate decision-making. One panel will not always decide the outcome in the same way as other panels, particularly in hard cases, and the style of the written reserved decisions will always vary to some extent. The fact that the composition of the panel can of itself have an influence on the outcome of specific appeals implies a further potential problem, because what can happen accidentally can also happen on purpose. At the extreme, there is the possibility that panels could be stacked and specific appeals deliberately directed to them. In some provinces, particularly in Western Canada, the chief justice has tried to head off this possibility through a deliberate degree of randomness in the selection of panels. On the one hand, panels that are struck through a perfectly random process without any prior knowledge of what kinds of cases will be handled by which panels precludes any attempt to capitalize on the special expertise of specific members of the court. Such a policy is fully consistent with the "a judge is a judge is a judge" attitude that generally prevails on Canadian appellate courts, although sometimes (when, for example, the court has a single member with extensive expertise in a complex field such as insurance law) it can result in suboptimal utilization of judicial skills to an extent that the average layperson might find surprising. Thus, in Ontario the chief justice assigns panels in order to ensure that one of the court's experts usually sits on the complex cases.

The presiding judge on the panel, whatever its size, is the senior judge in every court. But seniority is measured differently in different courts. In Saskatchewan, for example, seniority is measured in terms of the length of service on the appeal bench; in Alberta, it used to be measured in terms of the length of service on the federally appointed bench, including both the trial and appellate court.[12]

The Alberta court has recently experimented with a "paperless appeal." Faced with a very complex regulatory appeal that would have generated enormous volumes of casebooks, documents, and authorities, the court opted instead to put everything in the form of computer diskettes and then to supply each judge on the panel and

the lawyers appearing before them with computers. Instead of referring to a casebook volume, people would instead refer to document
three on diskette F. According to our interviews, this experiment
worked so well (although it depended on the happenstance of finding
all three judges on a panel who were comfortable with computers)
that by 1998 all counsel were encouraged to submit their casebooks
and authorities on computer diskettes. At the time of writing, the
Alberta court is considering electronic factums with hyperlinks to
citations.

Saskatchewan and Quebec are the two provinces that formally
indicate ahead of time which of the judges on the panel will write
the decision of the court. Unless there is some obvious problem (such
as the individual in question dissenting), the "circled judge" will
carry the responsibility of explaining the outcome to the parties,
which includes writing the decision in reserved cases. In the other
provinces, the choice of which member will deliver the decision is
handled more casually. Quite often, it will be the presiding judge
who delivers the decision, although as the panel works its way
through the list there will be some attempt to balance the workload
or to take advantage of special expertise or experience.

The proportion of the total cases that are reserved for written
decisions varies enormously from province to province. On the
criminal side, the variation is from a low of about an eighth of the
cases in British Columbia, Saskatchewan, and Manitoba to a high of
about four-fifths of criminal cases in New Brunswick, with the national average at about 25 per cent.[13] On the civil side, on average
about a third of the cases are reserved, but only a fifth of the Saskatchewan cases are reserved, while practically all in Prince Edward
Island are reserved.[14] Although some of the variation can be explained in the tendency for the less-busy courts to spend more time
writing decisions, the fact that the variation based on "busy-ness"
alone is far from uniform means that the views of the judges on the
different courts about what kinds of cases deserve a written decision
clearly have an important impact on the proportion of reserved decisions in each court.

Although some of the procedural variations among the courts can
be traced to the impact of differences between the provincial judicature acts and rules of procedure,[15] and the differences between Quebec and the common law provinces may be in part a result of
Quebec's unique civil law system in the realm of private law, we
found that the majority of the procedural differences between the

Canadian appellate courts result from the cumulative effect of the appellate judges' decisions[16] about how best to organize case flow. Although the chief justice is "first among equals" in each appellate court, our interviews indicated that in most courts it is the chief justice who takes the lead in formulating procedural reforms. But whether ideas regarding changes in court procedures emanate from the chief justice or a puisne judge, they are usually discussed in a meeting of the entire court before being implemented.

Because of the potential impact of procedural decisions on justice and fairness in the courts, the potential to innovate administratively is yet another factor that ought to be considered in the judicial selection process. Administrative acumen ought to be particularly important in the decision-making process for the selection of the chief justice of each appellate court. However, because the appointment of the chief justices has historically been the prerogative of the Prime Minister, and that process is highly confidential, very little is known about the factors that are taken into account concerning these appointments. Several of the chief justices we spoke to told us about how completely taken by surprise they were when they received the call from the Prime Minister's Office to confirm that the office would accept their impending appointment as chief justice. Given that the administrative impact that a chief justice can have is every bit as important as that of a university dean, another first among equals, it is somewhat surprising that in the late twentieth century the selection process for a chief justice is nowhere near as systematic.

This is not to say that we have been poorly served by our chief justices. However, given the importance of court procedures on the dispensation of justice in a democratic context, and given the increasing complexity of case flow in the Canadian appellate courts, it may be that we can no longer afford to leave such an important decision as the selection of the chief justice to the discretion of the Prime Minister alone.[17]

Interpersonal Judicial Relations

The interpersonal relations among judges on particular panels, as well as in the full appellate court, can play a critical role in determining the outcomes of individual cases. A judge who appears to be coming in on the side of the minority might, through appropriate arguments, persuade his or her colleagues to change their minds. Much depends on the reputation of that judge, the respect that the others have for him or her, the ability to articulate a viewpoint

Table 10.1

Frequency of Vote with Majority and Delivered Decision, by Judge, Reported Supreme Court Decisions, 1990–1997

Judges	Total	All Appearances %		Divided Panels %	
		With Majority	Delivered Decision	With Majority	Delivered Decision
Lamer CJ	470	85	35	69	28
LaForest	602	83	14	65	13
L'Heureux-Dubé	588	71	8	41	8
Sopinka	667	84	21	66	18
Cory	648	90	14	78	20
Gonthier	650	86	8	70	6
McLachlin	640	76	10	47	13
Iacobucci	612	90	12	77	12
Major	422	85	7	68	8
All judges	5,299	83	14	64	14

Note: Judges are listed from top to bottom in order of seniority. The decisions of Madame Justice Wilson and Mr. Justice Stevenson were not included, as Wilson decided only 22 cases, and Stevenson 92 cases during this period.

without coming across as arrogant or one-sided, and the openness of the other judges on the panel to a different perspective.

Although appellate judges do not frown on dissenting opinions per se, they are usually keen to avoid *unnecessary* dissenting opinions. Similarly, most would prefer to avoid separate concurring opinions. Our interviews indicated that some judges are keener than others to see a consensus develop on their panel, and some seem to be more successful than others in promoting a consensus.

To take the Supreme Court of Canada during the period from 1990 to 1997 as an example, we found that on average each judge voted with the majority 83 per cent of the time. However, Madame Justice L'Heureux-Dubé voted with the majority only 71 per cent of the time, while Justices Iacobucci and Cory were with the majority in 90 per cent of the panels they sat with, as Table 10.1 shows.

The first column in Table 10.1 is the total number of panel appearances in the interval between Lamer becoming chief justice and LaForest leaving the court to be replaced by Bastarache. The two strings of numbers in the second column measure, first, the proportion of those total appearances in which the judge in question "signed on" to the decision of the court and, second, the proportion of those total appearances in which the judge in question actually delivered that opinion — allowing us to say, for example, that Iacobucci and Cory almost never dissent or "separately concur," while L'Heureux-Dubé and McLachlin do so relatively frequently. We can also say that only Lamer and Sopinka were significantly more likely than average to deliver the decision of the court. Since these are the first and fourth most senior members of the court for most of the period, seniority apparently has something to do with their tendency to deliver more decisions, but seniority is not the whole story.

"All appearances" means including the unanimous decisions of the court, and some of these are very routine in nature, that is, they are resolved by the briefest of "reasons for judgment" that clearly add nothing of any significance to judicial doctrine. It is an oversimplification to say that unanimous decisions are always routine decisions, but it is quite safe to assume that virtually all routine decisions will be unanimous. The third column shows the proportion of non-unanimous decisions in which each judge voted with the majority and also the proportion of these non-unanimous decisions in which each judge wrote the decision of the majority.

Both when all appearances are considered, and when only the non-unanimous decisions are examined, on average each judge writes about 14 per cent of the decisions. However, Lamer, Sopinka, and Cory authored more than the average number of decisions in one or both situations. Remember that one factor that the chief justice considers when deciding who to ask to write the majority opinion is which judge seems to represent best the consensus of a panel, or at least of the majority of the panel. The decision-writing records of Lamer, Sopinka, and Cory indicate that these judges may have been the most successful in promoting a consensus among their colleagues.

It is undoubtedly true that some judges are more successful than others in "reaching out" to their colleagues to understand their perspectives and in trying to incorporate these perspectives into their own analysis whenever doing so would not result in compromising their fundamental values. Note that Madam Justice McLachlin, although voting with the majority less than half the time, nevertheless wrote an average proportion of majority decisions for the divided panels. One of her predecessors who also dissented more frequently than usual, but who nevertheless shared a high proportion of majority opinions, was former Chief Justice Laskin.[18] Our view is that the ability to reach out to judicial colleagues, understand their perspectives and incorporate them into one's own view of justice when a fit is indeed possible is one of the hallmarks of mutual respect. The ability to integrate into a collegial situation is another factor that ought to be considered in the judicial selection process.

Judicial Activism and Democracy

Judges in any democracy will always have a certain amount of discretion; the clearest set of laws in the world cannot eliminate judicial discretion. Therefore, careful attention needs to be paid to the judicial selection process to ensure that those who become appellate judges have both the personal and professional qualifications that are likely to promote the uses of discretion that are most compatible with the fundamental values of democracy.

There are some cases in which judicial discretion is unavoidable. There are other cases where judges could choose to settle an issue through the use of discretion or they could "decide not to decide" in order to encourage the legislature to settle the issue. For example, in the *Morgentaler* decision, Mr. Justice McIntyre argued for a very narrow interpretation of the Charter so that the court could avoid finding Canada's abortion law unconstitutional. He wrote that "the courts must confine themselves to such democratic values as are clearly found and expressed in the Charter and refrain from imposing or creating other values not so based."[19] Except for La Forest, the other six judges on the panel disagreed. As we showed in Chapter 9, many judges have accepted a lawmaking role for the courts because they have concluded that legislatures are shirking their responsibility to ensure that defects in the law are corrected.

As we pointed out in Chapter 1, Canadians tend to have a great deal more confidence in their judges than in their elected legislatures. One reason for this lack of confidence in elected officials is the perception, too often supported by fact, that elected members do not behave as ethically as they ought to.[20] One of the factors that should be considered by appellate court judges when thinking about whether to second-guess a legislature is how responsible the legislature is in tackling defects in the law that result in clear human rights abuses. The higher the ethical quality of elected members, the more compelled they will feel to take responsibility for lapses in the protection of human rights, and therefore the less will be the need for judicial activism.

We need to think about improvements to our political system to promote the highest quality of elected members just as much as we need to be concerned about ensuring that judicial selection procedures result in the highest quality of judges.

Appendix

Data Collection

The data for this study were collected primarily from three sources: personal interviews with Canada's appellate judges, background questionnaires filled out by the judges we interviewed, and a representative sample of cases filed for appeal in each province and in the Appeal Division of the Federal Court of Canada. This data collection was supported by a major research grant from the Social Sciences and Humanities Research Council of Canada (SSHRC), and by minor research grants from York University. As well, Peter McCormick collected data from the reported decisions of the Supreme Court of Canada and the provincial appellate courts, and Ian Greene collected data from leave to appeal applications by refugee applicants filed in the Federal Court of Canada (Appeal Division) in 1990.

The catalyst for this project was a speech given by Madame Justice Wilson at the Faculty of Law at the University of Toronto in 1986. Ian Greene was in the audience, and heard Madame Justice Wilson gently chastise academics for having done very little research into appellate court decision-making. In 1988, Greene received a small SSHRC research grant through York University to collect data on case-flow in the Ontario Court of Appeal.[1] Building on this project, the authors of this book applied for an SSHRC research grant to carry out the kind of comprehensive research suggested by Justice Wilson. The SSHRC awarded a research grant to the team in 1990.

Ian Greene and Peter McCormick had already collaborated on a study of decision-making primarily in trial courts in Ontario and Alberta that resulted in the publication of *Judges and Judging* in 1990, and so it was natural for them to continue to collaborate on the appellate courts project. Carl Baar, thanks to many years of experience in studying courts administration in Canada and the United States, is a leading expert on issues in case-flow, and so was invited to join the team. George Szablowski was invited to join not only because he is fluently bilingual and could conduct interviews in French in Quebec, but also because he is both a political scientist and a lawyer, and had valuable experience in studying Canada's top public servants.[2] Martin Thomas teaches statistics and quantitative

methods in York University's Pubic Policy and Administration Pro-
gramme, and was invited to join the team in order to assist with our
data collection and analysis.

Personal Interviews

Our goal was to conduct personal interviews with as many as possible of the 125 or so appellate court judges in Canada about the
decision-making process. The twelve courts we studied included the
ten provincial appellate courts, the Federal Court of Canada (Appeal
Division), and the Supreme Court of Canada. The appellate courts in
Yukon and the Northwest Territories are presided over by the chief
justice of British Columbia and Alberta respectively, and the three-
judges panels are composed of one or two appellate judges in British
Columbia or Alberta respectively, and one or two Supreme Court
judges from the territory.[3] Because of the heavy overlap in personnel
between the territorial appellate courts, and the appellate courts of
the two western provinces, and because of the added expense, we did
not conduct interviews with the superior court judges in the territories.

The ten-page interview questionnaire was developed by members
of the team after several meetings in 1990 and 1991 in which research
hypotheses were developed, and then questions were formulated to
test these hypotheses. Some of the questions developed by McCormick
and Greene for their earlier study were repeated in the appeal courts
questionnaire for comparative purposes. The resulting questionnaire
was discussed with two senior appellate court judges, one from
Alberta and one from Ontario, so that we could ensure, as much as
possible, that the questions we posed were both clear and meaning-
ful.

Prior to any personal interviews, we wrote to the chief justice of
each court to explain the project, and to request advice about how
we might contact the judges in that court to request interviews. We
had learned from previous research projects involving interviews
with judges that the chief justice of a court is truly a "first among
equals." No chief justice would think of "approving" or "rejecting"
a research project such as ours. However, the local culture of each
court is unique, and therefore it was important for us to seek the
advice of the chief justice about how to proceed.

As it turned out, every chief justice agreed to be interviewed, and
provided valuable guidance that assisted us in arranging interviews.
Most suggested particular time periods that would be less disruptive

to their court than others for us to request interviews. Some forwarded our request for interviews to the judges in their court, and even scheduled interviews for us with the judges who agreed to be interviewed after we indicated the days when we could visit their court.

Before each interview, we wrote to each puisne judge to explain the project, to request an interview or to confirm an interview time, and to guarantee the anonymity of the interview. We conducted 101 interviews between July, 1991 and October, 1995. Although we would have prefered to conduct the interviews over a more condensed period of time, this was not possible given the heavy teaching loads of all of us on the research team, and the demands of other research projects we were committed to.

The first interviews were conducted by George Szablowski with twenty-four Quebec appellate judges in July, 1991. Ian Greene held interviews with six appellate judges in Newfoundland in August, 1991. There was then a hiatus in interviews because Greene was conducting research for other projects while on sabbatical in England. The interviews resumed in September and October, 1992, when Greene conducted eight interviews in the Court of Appeal of Ontario, and Carl Baar conducted one interview in that province. In December, 1992 Greene conducted four interviews in New Brunswick, three in Prince Edward Island, and five in Nova Scotia. In the spring of 1993, Greene held interviews with eleven Federal Court of Canada (Appeal Division) judges. In March and June of 1994, Greene interviewed eight judges on the Supreme Court of Canada. During the summer of 1994, Carl Baar interviewed sixteen judges on the Court of Appeal of British Columbia, and Peter McCormick interviewed three judges on the Court of Appeal of Saskatchewan. Greene conducted six interviews on the Manitoba Court of Appeal in May, 1995, and Greene and McCormick interviewed six judges on the Court of Appeal of Alberta in October, 1995. A supplementary interview was conducted by Greene with a Supreme Court of Canada judge in March, 1996.

Background Questionnaires

After each interview, we left a four-page questionnaire designed to collect information about the judge's background with the judge, with a request to fill out the questionnaire and return it to us. Fifty-six the judges filled out the questionnaire, and another ten sent us their

Table A.1		
Case-flow Sample		
	Civil	Criminal
B.C.	589	693
Alta.	55	55
Sask.	243	271
Man.	255	266
On.	672	832
Que.	57	485
N.B.	171	94
P.E.I.	41	60
N.S.	207	313
Nfld.	104	129
Federal CA	256	
Total	2, 650	3,198
Grand Total	5,848	

resumes, and this information provided us with a data set on the judges' backgrounds based on sixty-six cases.

Sample of Cases

Our goal was to choose a representative sample of cases that had been filed in the provincial appellate courts and the Federal Court of Canada (Appeal Division) over a period long enough to be able to collect accurate information about the nature of the disposition of cases, and all the steps leading up to that disposition. We wanted to collect data on case-flow over a three-year period, and so in most provinces we collected data from a sample of cases filed between 1988 and 1990. Most of our data collection took place during the summer of 1991 and 1992 because by then, nearly all of the cases filed between 1988 and 1990 would have been disposed of.

The size of the sample of cases in each court was dependent in part on the number of appeals filed. The less appeals filed, the more we attempted to collect close to a complete sample. In the busier courts, we followed the standard rules of survey research for collecting a representative sample that is as accurate as possible. Once the sample size was determined, we selected every second, third, or fourth file, and so on, depending on the size of the sample required. The number of files from which the data were collected is shown in Table A.1.

We collected data pertaining to approximately 200 variables from each file. The variables included the relevant descriptive information about each case, including all the important dates when a significant event took place with regard to each file, and information about the kind of case, who the litigants were, who the judges were, and the outcome. We put a great deal of effort into designing our data collection instrument so as to be able to collect the same information about cases in each court, in spite of the different methods of filing and recording information in each court.

Most of the data were collected by our primary research assistant, Karen Atkin, during personal visits to all of the courts except the courts in British Columbia, Alberta, and Quebec between August, 1991 and August, 1994. The Quebec data were collected by Rosemary Graf during the summers of 1991 and 1992, the British Columbia data were collected from computer print-outs of appellate court cases by Elaine Ross in 1993, and the Alberta data were collected by Tim Nichols, Peter McCormick and Ian Greene. During the early 1990s, the filing system in the Court of Appeal of Alberta was being re-arranged, and so we were not able to collect data in that province until 1995. By that time, our main research budget had expired and so we were only able to collect data from a small sample of cases. Nadine Changfoot assisted with data collection in the Federal Court of Appeal.

Every research project has its mishaps, and ours was no exception. About three hundred of the data sheets on civil cases in Quebec were lost in transit from Montreal to Toronto, which explains the low number of civil cases from Quebec in our sample.

Notes

Introduction

1. Peter Hogg, *Constitutional Law of Canada* (Toronto: Carswell, 1992), 649.
2. Following is the number of judges on the appellate courts in Canada in October of 1998, according to the office of the Commissioner for Federal Judicial Affairs. The number of supernumerary judges (retired judges working part-time) is shown in brackets. Supreme Court of Canada: 9; The Federal Court of Canada (Appeal Division): 9 (4); Court of Appeal of Alberta: 12 (3); Court of Appeal of British Columbia: 15 (5); Court of Appeal of Manitoba: 6 (2); Court of Appeal of New Brunswick: 7 (1); Supreme Court of Newfoundland (Court of Appeal): 6 (2); Court of Appeal of Nova Scotia: 8 (2); Court of Appeal of Ontario: 19 (4); Supreme Court of Prince Edward Island (Appeal Division): 3; Court of Appeal of Quebec: 19 (2); Court of Appeal of Saskatchewan: 8 (1). The total number of full-time judges was then 121, with several vacancies to be filled, and there were 26 supernumerary judges in addition. The *Canadian Legal Directory* 1998 lists 131 full-time judges based on 1997 information, and it appears that several judges have retired or become supernumerary since their list was published.
3. Our research was supported by a grant from the Social Sciences and Humanities Research Council.
4. In addition, there are usually some supernumerary judges attached to each court to ease the workload.
5. Harold Lasswell, *Politics: Who Gets What, When and How?* (New York: World Publishing, 1958).
6. Harold Lasswell, *Power and Personality* (New York: Viking, 1967).
7. David Easton, *A Systems Analysis of Political Life* (New York: Wiley, 1965).
8. *Regina* v. *Morgentaler, Supreme Court Reports* 1 (1988): 30.
9. *Askov* v. *The Queen, Supreme Court Reports* 2 (1990): 1199.
10. *Egan.* v. *Canada, Supreme Court Reports* 2 (1993): 513.
11. *R.* v. *Mara, Supreme Court Reports* 2 (1997): 630.
12. We acknowledge John Hogarth's book, *Sentencing as a Human Process* (Toronto: University of Toronto Press, 1971), as the source of this phrase.

Chapter 1

1. For example, Gilles Duceppe, leader of the Bloc Québécois when this book was written, explained his three-year flirtation with the Communist Workers party as an attempt to find a set of "right answers" to fill a vacuum created by the decline of the church. "For a lot of us it was communism. It was a rational explanation that had answers to all the questions. Like in the church, the answers were all there, written down. It gives you a sense of security." (Edison Stewart, "Tough-as-nails Bloc Leader Eyes Europe-style Union," the *Toronto Star*, March 16, 1997, A10.)
2. Reginald W. Bibby, *Social Trends Canadian Style* (Toronto: Stoddart, 1995).

3. These data were obtained by Maureen Mancuso, Michael Atkinson, André Blais, Ian Greene and Neil Nevitte as part of the Canadian Political Ethics Study, which was supported by a grant from the SSHRC. Some of these data are reported in *A Question of Ethics* (Toronto: Oxford, 1998), by the same authors.

4. An important exception to this generalization is refugee cases, where unsuccessful applicants must apply for "leave" or permission to appeal.

5. John Austin and other positivists.

6. Proponents of the school of legal realism.

7. For example, if federal and provincial egg marketing regulations conflict, which law do egg producers obey when selling eggs across provincial boundaries?

8. It is not clear, for example, to what extent the content of the Internet is governed by the federal criminal code or provincial censorship laws.

9. Because of the practical necessity for political compromise, parts of Section 91 of the Constitution Act of 1867, which outlines the powers of Parliament, contradict each other.

10. Section 8 of the Charter of Rights and Freedoms prohibits "unreasonable" search and seizure. It is up to the judges to define what "unreasonable" means.

11. See, for example, Ronald Dworkin, *Law's Empire* (Cambridge, Mass.: Harvard University Press, 1986) and David Beatty, *Constitutional Law in Theory and Practice* (Toronto: University of Toronto Press: 1995).

12. For example, see the introductions to the cases in *Leading Constitutional Decisions* (Ottawa: Carleon University Press, 1987), and later with R. Knopff and F.L. Morton in *Federalism and the Charter* (Ottawa: Carleton University Press, 1989). See also "Judicial Power in Canada's Political Culture," in M.L. Friedland, ed., *Courts and Trials: A Multi-disciplinary Approach* (Toronto: University of Toronto Press, 1975), *The Judiciary in Canada: The Third Branch of Government* (Toronto: McGraw-Hill Ryerson, 1987), and with Paul Sniderman *et al.* in *The Clash of Rights* (New Haven: Yale University Press, 1996).

13. "The Supreme Court Decision: Bold Statecraft Based on Questionable Jurisprudence," in Keith Banting and Richard Simeon, eds., *And No One Cheered: Federalism, Democracy and The Constitution Act* (Toronto: Methuen, 1983), and *The Judiciary in Canada*.

14. The first edition was published by Wall & Thompson in 1989. Michael Mandel teaches in Osgoode Hall Law School at York University.

15. The best-known of the legalization of politics critics is David Beatty.

16. See Donald V. Smiley, *The Federal Condition in Canada* (Toronto: McGraw-Hill Ryerson, 1987).

17. Nicola Lacey, "Are Rights Best Left Unwritten?" *Political Quarterly* (December 1989), 438.

18. Rainer Knopff and F.L. Morton teach political science at the University of Calgary.

19. Rainer Knopff, *Human Rights and Social Technology: The New War on Discrimination* (Ottawa: Carleton University Press, 1990).

20. Those who argue that judges need not be bound by the intent of the framers of the constitution are known as "non-interpretivists" because they believe that there is nothing solid in the intent of the framers to interpret. Constitution-makers, such as the authors of the U.S. Constitution of 1787, the British North America Act of 1867, or the Charter of Rights and Freedoms of 1982, did not contemplate the situations that future judges would have to deal with. Moreover,

sticking to a rigid deference to a presumed original intent prevents a constitution from adapting to modern times. "Interpretivists," on the other hand, consider that the intent of the framers can be determined well enough to act as a check on judges so that they will refrain from becoming a super-legislature.

21. Section 33 was used twice prior to this. The Parti Québécois government of René Lévesque added a Section 33 override to all its legislation, and also amended all pre-1982 statutes to include the override, as a protest against Quebec's being left out of the 1982 constitutional accord. This practice stopped after the Liberals were elected in the 1985 provincial election. The government of Saskatchewan used the override clause in settling a public service strike in 1986, but as it turned out, the Supreme Court's subsequent interpretation of the Charter made the use of this override unnecessary. See also Ian Greene, *The Charter of Rights* (Toronto: James Lorimer & Co., 1989), 56-57.

22. *Ford* v. *A.-G. Quebec, Supreme Court Reports* 2 (1988): 712, and *Devine* v. *A.-G. Quebec, Supreme Court Reports* 2 (1988): 790.

23. *Askov* v. *The Queen, Supreme Court Reports* 2 (1990): 1199.

24. *Seaboyer* v. *The Queen, Supreme Court Reports* 2 (1991): 577.

25. *Regina* v. *Morgentaler, Supreme Court Reports* 1 (1988): 30.

26. Patrick Monahan, once an assistant to former Ontario Premier David Peterson, now teaches in Osgoode Hall Law School at York University.

27. See also David Beatty's *Talking Heads and the Supremes* (Toronto: Carswell, 1989). David Beatty teaches in the Faculty of Law at the University of Toronto.

28. See also Cairns' *Reconfigurations: Canadian Citizenship and Constitutional Change* (Toronto: McClelland & Stewart, 1995).

29. *Reference re Secession of Quebec*, decision delivered August 20, 1998, paragraphs 63 to 68.

30. This argument was developed in Ian Greene and David Shugarman, *Honest Politics: Seeking Integrity in Canadian Public Life* (Toronto: James Lorimer & Co., 1997). Their approach differs from that of Monahan in that democracy is not thought of merely as participatory democracy, and from that of Beattie in that there is no particular interpretive method held out as being superior to others.

31. Samuel V. LaSelva, "Is Canadian Democracy Special? Mutual Recognition in a Federal System," in *The Moral Foundations of Canadian Federalism* (Kingston: Mc-Gill-Queen's, 1996).

32. *Ibid.*, 124.

33. John Rawls, *A Theory of Justice* (Cambridge, Harvard University Press, 1971).

34. See Greene and Shugarman, *Honest Politics*, ch. 2.

35. Ronald Dworkin, *Taking Rights Seriously* (Cambridge, Harvard University Press, 1977), 180-2.

36. *Reference re Alberta Statutes, Supreme Court Reports* (1938): 100.

37. Aharon Barak puts it this way: "To me, discretion is the power given to a person with authority to choose between two or more alternatives, when each of the alternatives is lawful." *Judicial Discretion* (New Haven and London: Yale University Press, 1989). See also Janet L. Hiebert, *Limiting Rights: The Dilemma of Judicial Review* (Montreal & Kingston: McGill-Queen's, 1996) for an analysis of the alternatives faced by Canadian judges when interpreting the meaning of the "limitations" clause in Section 1 of the Charter of Rights and Freedoms.

38. Legal pluralists argue that not only are there alternative acceptable answers to most legal disputes, but there are alternative procedures of judicial decision-mak-

ing that are acceptable. See H.W. Arthurs, *Without the Law: Administrative Justice and Legal Pluralism in Nineteenth Century England* (Toronto: University of Toronto Press, 1985).

39. *Regina* v. *Morgentaler, Supreme Court Reports* 1 (1988): 30. See the discussion of the Morgentaler decision in Ian Greene, *The Charter of Rights*, 152 ff.

40. For example, see Charles Taylor, *Reconciling the Solitudes* (Kingston: McGill-Queen's, 1993).

41. A.V. Dicey, *Introduction to the Study of the Law of the Constitution* (London: Macmillan, 1885).

42. Dicey was also suspicious of written bills of rights because there was no need for them. Superior court judges could develop a common law "bill of rights" by applying the principle of the rule of law in conjunction with the principle of the equal application of the law.

43. McCormick and Greene, *Judges and Judging* (Toronto: James Lorimer & Co.), ch. 5. The "improvisers" (10 per cent of judges interviewed) reported that they had no standard approach to decision-making because all cases are different. The "strict formalists" (22 per cent) reported formalistic methods of decision-making that they felt led different judges to the same conclusions. The "pragmatic formalists" (44 per cent) compared the decision-making process to creating a check-list of items, assessing the shifting balance between the two sides, or to water rising to a level of probability. The "intuitivists" (24 per cent) relied more on a "gut feeling" or a "key moment" in a hearing.

44. Other factors that were controlled in this study included the law firm that submitted the application on behalf of the claimant, whether the application was substantive or pro forma, whether written submissions were included with the application, whether the minister responded to the application and if so whether the applicant responded to the Minister, whether the transcript from the Immigration and Refugee Board (IRB) hearing had been filed, whether the applicant or someone else swore the affidavit, whether a refugee hearing officer had participated in the IRB hearing, who the IRB tribunal members were, whether an issue of natural justice had been raised, whether a Charter of Rights issue had been raised, whether any novel points of law were raised, and whether the factual or credibility findings from the IRB were challenged.

45. A "blind" review refers to the fact that the independent expert had no knowledge of which judge had actually made the decision on the Federal Court of Appeal, or what that decision was. The expert was an experienced counsel, who has since been appointed to the judiciary.

46. There was no statistical difference between the proportion of cases "approved" by the independent expert on each judge's docket.

47. There were 2,341 applications for leave filed in the Federal Court of Appeal in 1990, and Ian Greene was able to collect relevant data on the outcome of 2,081 of these. The Court granted leave to 572 applicants (25%), and refused leave to 1,513 applicants (66%). Forty-four applications (2%) were withdrawn by the applicant, 171 (7%) were dismissed for non-perfection, and one case was granted a stay pending decisions in other proceedings about the applicant's immediate family. There was no clear record of disposition for 3 applications. The data collection took place between November 3 and 13, 1992, by Ms. Karen Atkin, a Ph.D. student at York University, who acted according to instructions from Greene.

48. Because we will never have a record of how the leave applications rejected by both the strict and liberal judges would have fared on a substantive appeal, it cannot be concluded that the "liberal" judges had a better or worse record of screening out cases without merit at the leave stage.
49. A possible remedy for this obvious injustice is to ensure that applications for leave that are rejected are reviewed by a second judge, who would have the power to reverse the negative decision.
50. In *Sentencing as a Human Process*, John Hogarth illustrates the impact of discretion on the sentencing behaviour of lower court judges.

Chapter 2

1. Patrick Boyer, *A Passion for Justice* (Toronto: The Osgoode Society for Canadian Legal History, 1994), 15.
2. Byrne Hope Sanders, *Emily Murphy: Crusader* (Toronto: Macmillan, 1945), 138.
3. Interview by Peter Gzowski on "Some of the Best Minds of Our Time," CBC Radio One, July 27, 1998, 8:00 p.m.
4. Bertha Wilson, "Will Women Judges Really Make a Difference?" (Osgoode Hall Law Journal 28, 1990).
5. One of the provincial appellate judges we interviewed confirmed that she had been approached by the Justice Department during the 1990s about a position on the Supreme Court, but had declined for family reasons.
6. *Canadian Encyclopedia Plus* (Toronto: McClelland & Stewart, 1997), "Disease."
7. See Doreen Barrie and Roger Gibbins, "Parliamentary Careers in the Canadian Federal State", *Canadian Journal of Political Science* 22 (1989): 137, and Allan Kornberg and William Mishler, *Influence in Parliament: Canada* (Durham, NC: Duke University Press, 1976) ch. 2.
8. A lawyer who considered himself or herself as primarily a solicitor would rarely appear in court. The work might consist, for example, mostly of business and real estate transactions, mortgages, and wills.
9. Interviews with an English Court of Appeal judge and a House of Lords judge by Ian Greene in May, 1992. These judges were surprised to learn that Canadian appellate judges tended not to see the need for specialized panels.
10. McCormick and Greene, *Judges and Judging*.
11. See Neil Nevitte, *The Decline of Deference*, for a discussion of the changing demographic nature of Canadian society.
12. For example, see Ian Bushnell, *The Captive Court* (Kingston: McGill-Queen's, 1992), and C. Neal Tate, "Explaining the Decision-Making of the Canadian Supreme Court, 1949-1985," *Journal of Politics* 51 (1989).
13. There is no difference between the appellate courts and elected parliamentarians with regard to skewed gender representation.
14. The propensity for high achievement does not set appellate court judges apart, of course, from high achievers in other professions such as medicine, accounting, or the academic world.
15. It was not always this difficult to get into law school. Most current appellate court judges graduated from law school in the 1950s, an era when the competition for entry was not as fierce as it is today.
16. See Michael S. Whittington and Richard J. Van Loon, *Canadian Government and Politics* (Toronto: McGraw-Hill Ryerson, 1995), 501 & 557.

17. The comparison uses data reported in McCormick and Greene, *Judges and Judging*, ch. 3.

18. Whittington & Van Loon, 558. It should be noted, however, that there have been three Ph.Ds in the Chrétien cabinet, meaning that the proportion of Canadian cabinet ministers with Ph.Ds is about the same as the proportion of appellate judges with this degree.

19. Whittington & Van Loon, 500. About two-thirds of Canadian MPs are business-men, lawyers, and other professionals.

20. The size of the judges' former law firms ranged from a sole practitioner firm (one judge) to 140 active lawyers (one judge). The mean size was 20, while the median size was 10.

21. *Canadian Encyclopedia Plus*, "Marriage and Divorce."

22. The proportion of appellate judges with children is higher than the national average, and the average family size is higher than the national average. How-ever, this may be because judges are older than the average adult Canadian, and therefore had their children at a time when families tended to be larger. Many of their children were part of the baby boom. (*Canadian Encyclopaedia Plus*, "Marriage and Divorce, " and "Baby Boom.")

23. Guy Bouthillier reports that 54 per cent of the judges appointed to the Quebec Court of Appeal up to 1972 had been cabinet ministers or elected members. William Klein found that a third of the superior court judges appointed in Ontario, Quebec, and Manitoba from 1905 to 1970 had been candidates for elected office. See Guy Bouthillier, "Materiaux pour une analyse politique des juges de la Cour d'appel," *La Revue Juridique Themis* (1971): 563, and William John Klein, *Judicial Recruitment in Manitoba, Ontario, and* Quebec, 1905-1970 (Ph.D. Dissertation, University of Toronto, 1975).

24. Allan Kornberg and William Mishler, *Influence in Parliament: Canada* (Dur-ham, NC: Duke University Press, 1976).

25. See Ed Ratushny, "Judicial Appointments: The Lang Legacy," in Allen Linden, ed. *The Canadian Judiciary* (Toronto: Osgoode Hall Law School, 1976).

26. At one time, all the provinces except Quebec had county or district courts. Beginning in the mid-1970s, the county and district courts were merged with the provincial superior trial courts through legislation passed by the relevant provin-cial legislatures.

27. Peter Russell, *The Judiciary in Canada*, 118.

28. Minister of Justice and Attorney General of Canada, "Federal Judicial Appoint-ments Process," mimeo., April 1994.

29. All judges in our sample were appointed to an appellate court after 1967, and only four who were promoted from a lower court were appointed to that court prior to 1967.

30. McCormick and Greene, *Judges and Judging*, 84-95.

31. Appellate court judges' salaries are set by the federal Judges' Act. At the time of writing, there is a bill before Parliament that would raise appellate court judges' salaries by about eight per cent. There is an independent salary review commission for federally-appointed judges that reports every three years, but it is up to Parliament to decide whether to accept the advice of the commission.

32. *Canadian Encyclopedia Plus*, "Social Class."

33. Several of the appellate judges had attended private schools.

34. See Walter Tarnopolsky, "The Evolution of Judicial Attitudes," in Sheilah Martin and Kathleen Mahoney, eds., *Equality and Judicial Neutrality* (Toronto: Carswell, 1987).

35. The proportion of women elected as members of Parliament or members of the provincial legislatures is now lower than the percentage of women on the Canadian appellate courts. See Lynda Erickson, "Entry to the Commons: Parties, Recruitment, and the Election of Women in 1993."

36. Ian Greene and David Shugarman argue that until Canadian political parties develop higher ethical standards, women and less well-established ethnic groups are likely to continue to be discouraged from seeking and achieving elected office. See Greene and Shugarman, *Honest Politics*.

Chapter 3

1. The major exception in Canada is refugee cases, as noted in Chapter 1.

2. These figures do not correspond to the provincial figures reported by Peter McCormick for 1989 in "Sentence Appeals in the Alberta Court of Appeal, 1985-1992," *Alberta Law Review* 31 (1993): 626-27. This paper reports data from a paper written with Mr. Justice W. D. Griffiths of the Court of Appeal for Ontario. However, it appears that these figures reflect "inscribed" appeals, rather than all appeals filed; see discussion of the funnel of appeals later in this chapter.

3. Smaller declines were registered in two provinces, 15 per cent in Manitoba and 7 per cent in Newfoundland.

4. This court was known as the Provincial Court (Criminal Division) before 1990 and the Ontario Court of Justice (Provincial Division) thereafter.

5. Figures are from the *Court Statistics Annual Reports* published by the Ontario Ministry of the Attorney General.

6. See Carl Baar, "The Business of the Courts," *Canadian Lawyer* 21 (1997): 12. And note that Ontario jury criminal courts received 4,853 indictments in 1989-90 compared with 2,838 in 1996-97, as reported in annual statistical reports cited in note 5 above.

7. "Report of the Attorney General's Advisory Committee on Charge Screening, Disclosure, and Resolution Discussions," Ministry of the Attorney General, The Hon. G. Arthur Martin, Chair (Toronto: Queen's Printer for Ontario, 1993).

8. If the initial trial is heard by a provincial court judge, the appeal is to a superior court judge. If the trial is heard by a lay judge — for example, a justice of the peace as in Ontario — the appeal is to a provincial court judge.

9. Note that Ontario's 1994-95 annual statistical report no longer separates board and tribunal appeals from small claims and superior court appeals, making it difficult to confirm this analysis.

10. At one time, the Court of Appeal for Alberta may have had the same tendency to make small changes in sentences. However, McCormick's data in "Sentence Appeals in the Alberta Court of Appeal, 1985-1992," 640-41, demonstrate that the Court of Appeal for Alberta "does not tinker."

11. Two of the Ontario appellate judges that we interviewed said that they believed that by being open to arguments for relatively small adjustments to sentences, they hoped they were encouraging appellants to behave better in prison than they might otherwise. This is because the appeal court would not be open to reducing a sentence unless the appellant had been well behaved while behind bars, and those appealing the length of a sentence knew that.

12. The provincial superior trial courts may be referred to as the Provincial Supreme Court, the Court of Queen's Bench, or, in the case of Ontario, the General Division of the Ontario Court of Justice.

13. For example, more precise data on the number of complex civil and serious criminal trials may indicate whether some provinces have more serious cases (and more trials) per capita, and whether this accounts for a higher rate of appeals. Tracing changes in the volume of appeals over time, as well as collecting more precise data on civil case-types, may also help.

14. Thomas Church *et al.*, *Justice Delayed: The Pace of Litigation in Urban Trial Courts, Executive Summary* (Williamsburg, VA: National Center for State Courts, 1978).

15. Carl Baar, "Judicial Independence and Judicial Administration in the *Tobiass* Case," *Constitutional Forum* 9:2 (1998): 48-54.

16. During the 1970s, the Ontario government was stymied in two attempts to reform the overall structure of courts administration. One strategy was abandoned after it became clear to the government that the majority of judges were opposed to it. Another approach was abandoned primarily because of opposition from the bar and administrators within the Ministry of the Attorney General. See Ian Greene, *The Politics of Court Administration: The Ontario Case* (Ph.D. dissertation, University of Toronto, 1983).

17. It should be remembered, however, that anywhere from 15 per cent to 40 per cent of the Supreme Court of Canada's annual case load is composed of appeals as of right in criminal cases. Most of these are disposed of in oral decisions. See "Statistics 1987 to 1997," *Bulletin of Proceedings: Special Edition*, February 16, 1998, Supreme Court of Canada.

18. We were delayed in collecting the data from Alberta because a new filing system was being implemented in the court locations in Calgary and Edmonton in the early 1990s, and as a result we were not able to gain access to a sample of files in a timely fashion.

19. Thus, one might expect future research on how appeal cases drop out between filing and hearing to find somewhat more cases proceeding all the way through the process.

Chapter 4

1. One Ontario judge we talked to went so far as to suggest that Alberta's practice might violate judicial independence. On the this practice, see Peter McCormick, "Conviction Appeals to the Court of Appeal of Alberta: A Statistical Analysis, 1985-1992," *Alberta Law Review* 31 (1993): 301, and "Sentence Appeals in The Alberta Court of Appeal."

2. Peter McCormick, "The Canadian Provincial Courts of Appeal: A Comparison of Procedures," paper prepared for the Canadian Judicial Appellate Court Seminar, Victoria, B.C., May 12-15, 1991 (Ottawa: National Judicial Institute: 1991), 3.

3. Occasionally, the judges will tell the litigants which side has prevailed in the appeal, and will say that the decision has been reserved, meaning that the reasons will come later. This happens in situations where the judges feel that there is an urgent need for the litigants to know the outcome. Most often, however, the litigants are simply told in court that the decision has been reserved, and they will have to wait for the entire written decision to learn of the outcome.

4. These questionnaires were analysed by Peter McCormick and the results were presented to the Canadian Appellate Court Seminar in 1991. They are reported in "The Canadian Provincial Courts of Appeal: A Comparison of Procedures."

5. It should be kept in mind that in addition to hearing cases in panels, appellate judges also hear "motions" sitting alone in their chambers. These motions deal with procedural matters preliminary to the hearing. For example, it is not uncommon for counsel for one of the parties in a civil suit to make a motion for an injunction to stop the other party from carrying out actions that the first party considers potentially harmful, pending the outcome of the appeal. We asked the judges what proportion of their time was spent hearing motions in chambers. The responses varied from 1 to 35 per cent, with an average of 10 per cent, with the highest proportions in the Quebec and Federal appeal courts. The Quebec court is unique because of its civil law case load, and the Federal court had an administrative law specialty, and these differences may help to explain the higher proportion of time spent hearing motions. The differences in the other courts can be accounted for in part by individual differences in how long it takes to consider motions, and in part by the fact that certain judges are willing to hear more than their fair share of motions.

6. In Alberta, the Court of Appeal is split between Calgary and Edmonton, and in Quebec it is split between Quebec City and Montreal.

7. Eighty-five per cent of the judges said that some thought of themselves as specialists in particular areas of the law, such as criminal law or human rights.

8. McCormick, "The Canadian Provincial Courts of Appeal: A Comparison of Procedures," 5.

9. Surprisingly, in Greene's earlier study of the attitudes of trial and appellate court judges, most judges did not object to "judge-avoidance" practices. They felt that it was important for litigants to come before judges they trusted. See Ian Greene, "The Politics of Court Administration in Ontario."

10. There is some evidence that some chief justices in prior decades may have attempted to influence the outcome of cases by "stacking" some of the panels. For examples in the Supreme Court of Canada, see Ian Bushnell, *The Captive Court: A Study of the Supreme Court of Canada.*

11. Seven-judge panels are possible, but only a few have been struck in recent history. (McCormick, "The Canadian Provincial Courts of Appeal: A Comparison of Procedures," 5.)

12. Reference re Bill 30, An Act to Amend the Education Act (Ont.), *Supreme Court Reports* 1 (1987): 1148.

13. The mean was 17 days, and the median (half the responses fall on either side of the median) was 14 days.

14. Only in the Supreme Court of Canada were the factums distributed two weeks in advance to everyone on the panel like clockwork.

15. The "median" response is numerically in the middle of all the responses. Thus, half of the responses to the question about preparation time were less than 2.5 hours, and half were greater.

16. Interview with an appellate judge in western Canada, 1994.

17. This difference in British Columbia is possibly a result of the fact that the B.C. appellate sees itself as a "very" hot court. The judges indicated to us that all are equally well-prepared at a basic level. However, some panels select a "lead" judge in advance of the hearing who begins to research the key issues identified

by the factums. In that sense, all the judges are not equally well-prepared because some judges have done extra work that might not have occurred at such an early stage in other provincial appellate courts.

18. These contrasting views are taken from interviews in 1994 with two judges in the same court — a court with a heavy case-load.

19. This is because the pre-hearing meetings in British Columtia are not mandatory, and some judges do not consider them useful.

20. See Baar, Greene, McCormick and Thomas, "The Ontario Court of Appeal and Speedy Justice." *Osgoode Hall Law Journal* 30 (1992): 261.

21. We were able to collect data on the time taken in hearings in Saskatchewan, Manitoba, Ontario and New Brunswick, and to some extent in Quebec. We found, for example, that two-thirds of the civil appeals took one hour or more.

22. The exception to this rule is for sentence appeals. The convict appealing the sentence has a right to come to the courtroom, and sometimes they take advantage of this opportunity, if for no other reason than to spend a day out of prison.

23. Ninety per cent of the judges we interviewed said that the lawyer for the respondent was very occasionally asked to speak first, but they said that this happened in only 1 or 2 per cent of the cases at most.

24. Reserved decisions include written reserved decisions, hand-written endorsements with brief reasons, and taped reasons. Non-reserved decisions include all decisions announced orally in court. In less than 2 per cent of the reserved decisions, the outcome is announced in court and the reasons are reserved.

24. A preliminary analysis indicates that a higher rate of reserving decisions in the provincial courts of appeal is not associated with a lower reversal rate at the Supreme Court of Canada level. The reversal rates of the penultimate appellate courts for 1987-1990 are as follows: Alberta, 33.3% (42 cases); British Columbia, 31.1% (74), Federal Court, Appeal Division, 44.7% (38); Manitoba, 48.8% (41); New Brunswick, 61.5% (13); Nova Scotia, 50.0% (14); Newfoundland, 22.2% (9); Ontario, 23.5% (98); Prince Edward Island 50.0% (2); Quebec, 58.9% (90); Saskatchewan, 33.3% (30). The overall reversal rate for the years indicated was 39.3%.

26. Intervenors are parties without a direct stake in the case but with a stake in the legal issues who have been given permission to present factums.

27. The Supreme Court of Canada sets a page limit of 40 pages on factums, although lawyers often apply for permission to submit a lengthier factum, and often receive it. Most provincial courts of appeal have limits to the length of factums as well, usually of about 30 pages.

28. Interviews by Ian Greene with one judge in the House of Lords, and one judge on the English Court of Appeal, June, 1992.

29. Nearly 40 states now have intermediate courts of appeal, and in the intermediate courts oral argument is the norm. It is in the final state appellate courts where there is usually no oral argument unless counsel apply to present their case orally. These applications are made and granted in a minority of cases.

30. McCormick and Greene, *Judges and Judging*.

31. These groups we labelled "strict formalists" (22 per cent of the judges), "pragmatic formalists" (44 per cent), and "intuitivists" (24 per cent). Only 10 per cent could not describe a particular process and we labelled them "improvisers." At the time, we did not realize that these improvisers tended to be over-represented

among the few appellate court judges that we interviewed as part of a larger sample of judges.

32. As we show in Chapter 8, determining the proportion of "winners" is much more complex than this statistic indicates. For example, there is the issue of the proportion of appeals filed that actually make it to a hearing. And in criminal appeals, the crown wins about two-thirds of its appeals, but this is because the crown usually will not appeal unless there is a very good chance of winning.

33. Only one judge said these conferences don't always occur — a judge on the Newfoundland Court of Appeal — although three others on the same court said that they do always occur. We suspect that the judge who said that they don't always occur had a long memory going back to the days when they did not, in fact, always occur.

34. The judges were asked to indicate on a scale from 1 to 5 the importance of whether a case represented a new area of law to the decision about whether to reserve. On this item the average response was 4.6 — the highest of all the items.

35. The judges were asked to indicate on a scale from 1 to 5 the importance of whether a case was a Charter case to the decision about whether to reserve. On this item the average response was 3.2.

36. On the scale from 1 to 5, the average response was 1.9.

37. On the scale from 1 to 5, the average response was 1.9.

38. On the scale from 1 to 5, the average response was 1.6.

39. It is interesting also that three-fifths of the appellate judges questioned said consensus is more likely on 3- than 5-member panels; the rest said that the panel size makes no difference. However, only .07 per cent of the cases in our sample were heard by panels larger than 3-judge panels. Across Canada, between 90 and 95 per cent of the decisions of the panels in the penultimate appellate courts were unanimous. In criminal cases, this proportion of unanimous decisions holds true for both sentence and substantive appeals, and for both summary conviction and indictable offenses.

41. One represented "not extensive at all," and 5 represented "very extensive."

42. Technically, of course, it is only decisions of the Supreme Court of Canada that must be final because there is no higher court to which they can be taken, and theoretically all provincial and federal appeal court decisions are capable of further appeal to the Supreme Court itself. In practice, however, only about one in every hundred of these decisions are appealed, so the "end point" designation is appropriate.

43. Marc Galanter "Why the 'Haves' Come Out Ahead."

44. John Wold, "Going through the motions: the monotony of appellate court decision making," *Judicature* 62 (1978-79): 58, and John Wold and Gregory Caldeira, "Perceptions of 'Routine' Decision Making in Five California Courts of Appeal," *Polity* 13 (1980): 334.

45. Some judges put the number of pointless appeals higher, others put it lower — it is probably more accurate, but a little less satisfyingly epigrammatic, to think of them as falling in a range between 20% and 50%.

46. *Singh et al.* v *Minister of Employment and Immigration, Supreme Court Reports* 1 (1985): 177.

Chapter 5

1. The author of this chapter, George J. Szablowski, wishes to thank Mr. Justice Melvin L. Rothman of the Quebec Court of Appeal, who read the first draft and offered extremely helpful comments. Of course, the author is solely responsible for its content and for any remaining errors and omissions.
2. Gerald L. Gall, *The Canadian Legal System*, 3rd ed. (Toronto: Carswell, 1990), 165-184.
3. See the discussion of the doctrine of precedent in this chapter, supra.
4. Neill Nugent, *The Government and Politics of the European Union*, 3rd ed. (Durham NC: Duke University Press, 1994), 227-228.
5. The literal translation is "community experience." This very important concept is part of the EC or EU legal tradition. It includes the entire body of laws, regulations and procedures developed by the EC or EU institutions from its inception to date; the founding treaties and all subsequent treaties and international agreements ratified by the member-states including all international legal commitments of the EC or EU; and all decisions of the European Court of Justice. States which intend to become new members of the EU (eg. Poland, the Czech Republic, and Hungary) must not only formally accept the *acquis* but also implement them internally within a specified time.
6. Francisco Granell, "The European Union's Enlargement Negotiations, with Austria, Finland, Norway, and Sweden" *Journal of Common Market Studies*, March, 1995: 117-141.
7. George J. Szablowski and Hans-Ulrich Derlien, "East European Transitions, Elites, Bureaucracies, and the European Community" *Governance*, July 1993: 304-324, and Nugent, 386.
8. George J. Szablowski, "Administrative Discretion and the Protection of Human Rights," in Richard A. Chapman, ed., *Ethics in Public Service*, (Edinburgh: University of Edinburgh Press, 1993), 59-75. See also Mark Janis, Richard Kay & Anthony Bradley, *European Human Rights Law* (Oxford: Clarendon Press, 1995), 65-88.
9. Barry Appleton, *Navigating NAFTA* (Toronto: Carswell, 1994).
10. Several respondents have confirmed their participation and interest in these activities.
11. These numbers include supernumerary judges.
12. See Table 5.1, which is a comparative report for January to December 1993-1994-1995 prepared by the clerks of the Court of Appeal of Montreal and Quebec.
13. From a letter dated June 26, 1991. Translation from the French by George Szablowski.
14. From an interview conducted on June 17, 1991.
15. From an interview conducted on June 18, 1991. Translation from the French by George Szablowski.
16. From an interview conducted on June 19, 1991. Translation from the French by George Szablowski.
17. From an interview conducted on June 17, 1991. Translation from the French by George Szablowski.
18. From an interview conducted on June 17, 1991. Translation from the French by George Szablowski.

19. From an interview conducted on June 21, 1991. Translation from the French by George Szablowski.

20. From an interview conducted on June 20, 1991. Translation from the French by George Szablowski.

21. From an interview conducted on June 21, 1991. Translation from the French by George Szablowski.

22. From an interview conducted on June 18, 1991. Translation from the French by George Szablowski.

23. From an interview conducted on June 17, 1991.

24. From an interview conducted on June 17, 1991.

25. From an interview conducted on June 21, 1991. Translation from the French by George Szablowski.

26. From an interview conducted on June 17, 1991.

27. From an interview conducted on June 18, 1991.

28. From an interview conducted on June 17, 1991.

29. From an interview conducted on June 18, 1991. Translation from the French by George Szablowski. The judge's point was that the judiciary is not part of the civil service, either structurally or from the policy perspective, and is not accountable to the government of the day or to officials in the federal or provincial ministries of justice.

30. Peter McCormick, *Canada's Courts* (Toronto: James Lorimer & Co., 1994), 70-72.

31. *Ibid*, 70.

32. *Ibid*, 71.

33. R.S. Brown, "Allocation of Cases in a Two-tiered Appellate Structure: The Wisconsin Experience and Beyond," *Marquette Law Review* 68 (1985): 189.

34. Rapport sur le fonctionnement des tribunaux judiciaires, mai 1990.

35. Rapport du comité de liaison - Barreau du Québec - Cour d'Appel, mai 1991.

36. Those which fall within the supervisory or error correcting function of the court of appeal, and those which merit the higher category of appellate function.

37. In fact, the joint committee adopted the opinion of Professor Patrick Glenn who dissented from the Gilbert Committee's recommendations, and it cited with approval the observations made in 1990 by Mr. Justice Robert Kerans of the Alberta Court of Appeal at a meeting of the Canadian Judicial Council held in Charlottetown, P.E.I. The members of the joint committee were: Madame Sylviane Borenstein, la Batonnèire of the Quebec Bar; Mr. Justice Louis LeBel, Quebec Court of Appeal; Me J. Vincent O'Donnell, Q.C.; Mr. Justice Melvin L. Rothman, Quebec Court of Appeal; and Me Carole Brosseau.

38. See John D. McCamus and Donald F. Bur, *Appellate Court Reform in Ontario: A Consultation Paper* (Toronto: Ministry of the Attorney General, 1994).

Chapter 6

1. "Statistics 1987 to 1997," *Bulletin of Proceedings: Special Edition*, February 16, 1998, Supreme Court of Canada.

2. W. Ian Binnie was appointed on January 8, 1998 to replace John Sopinka. Mr. Justice Sopinka died suddenly in late 1997. Michel Bastarache was appointed on September 30, 1997 to replace Gerald La Forest, who had retired.

3. The letters assigned to the judges do not indicate either seniority or the order of interviews. Rather, they are arbitrary so as to protect the anonymity of the judges.

4. Lorne Sossin, "The Sounds of Silence: Law Clerks, Policy-Making and the Supreme Court of Canada," *University of British Columbia Law Review* 30 (1996): 289.

5. *Ibid*, 289-290.

6. *Ibid*, 285.

7. It is possible for the court to receive as many as ten or twelve applicants from the larger law schools. A recommendation from the dean is essential if the applicant is to be considered.

8. Each judge receives all the applications, and decides how many applicants he or she wants to interview. One or two judges interview as many as forty, while others interview much smaller groups. There is usually an overlap between the applicants who are interviewed. Some are interviewed by several judges, while others may be interviewed by just one judge. The average number of candidates interviewed by each judge is probably around twenty.

9. According to Sossin, "Presently, employed clerks play a key role in culling the large number of applications received by the court to a manageable short-list of 'top' candidates, which is then submitted to the Justices for their final selection. ... Based on my experience, clerks tend to internalize the selection criteria by which they themselves have been privileged." "Sounds of Silence," 11.

10. The relative size of the corams was calculated from figures provided by the Supreme Court of Canada.

11. For statistics on average panel sizes for the various chief justiceships since World War II, see Peter McCormick, "The Supervisory Role of the Supreme Court of Canada: Analyis of Appeals from Provincial Courts of Appeal, 1949-1990," *Supreme Court Law Review* 3 (1992): 1 (2nd Series).

12. But note the concerns expressed in Andrew Heard, "The Charter in the Supreme Court of Canada: The Importance of Which Judges Hear an Appeal," *Canadian Journal of Political Science* 24 (1991).

13. The Supreme Court holds three sessions per year. The fall session begins in October and runs to December. The winter session runs from late January to March, and the spring session is from late April to the end of June. During these sessions, the court sits for two weeks of appeal hearings, followed by two weeks of non-sitting time, followed by two weeks of sitting time, and so on until the end of the term. During non-sitting weeks and between sessions, the judges work on their decisions, prepare for upcoming hearings, and consider leave to appeal applications.

14. Peter McCormick, "Judicial Career Patterns and the Delivery of Reasons for Judgment in the Supreme Court of Canada, 1949-93" *Supreme Court Law Review* 5 (1994): 2nd series.

15. See, for example, the article by Elliot Slotnick, cited in McCormick, *ibid.*

16. *Ibid.*, 37.

17. The judges were asked, "How important is it for a panel to try to avoid a dissent?" A 1 to 5 scale was used for replies, where 1 indicated "not at all important," and 5 indicated "extremely important." The average response from the eight judges was 1.9. Five judges chose 1, two chose 3, and only one chose 4.

18. An extreme form of this is the "plurality decision" where no single statement of "outcome plus reasons" is able to draw the signatures of a majority of the panel.

19. The judges were asked how important is it for a panel to avoid separate concurring decisions on a 5-point scale, where 1 represented "not at all important," and 5 "extremely important." The average response was 2.9 (one 1, three 2s, one 3, two 4s, and one 5.)

20. In practice, few dissents are ever cited except in later reasons for judgment by the dissenting judge himself or herself; see McCormick, "The Supreme Court Cites the Supreme Court."

21. Given the role of clerks in assisting with the drafting of judgments, one wonders whether "judgment writing assistance" courses might help to promote brevity and clarity in some Supreme Court decisions.

22. These three judges seemed to accept as a matter of course that they should cite relevent precedents not mentioned by counsel if these precedents were drawn to their attention by their research services. None of these precedents determined the outcome of the case; they merely provided additional ammunition for the result. If a precedent came to light that might affect the outcome of the case, these judges would have suggested that the precedents be drawn to the attention of counsel, and that counsel be given an opportunity to comment on their relevance.

23. Five judges were asked how important it was for them to take judicial notice of social or political facts not mentioned by counsel. A 1 to 5 scale was used, where 1 represented "not at all important," and 5 "extremely important." The average response was just 1.8.

Chapter 7

1. Martin Shapiro, "The Giving Reasons Requirement," *University of Chicago Legal Forum* (1992): 179; Frederick Schauer, "Giving Reasons," *Stanford Law Review* 47 (1995): 633.

2. *R. v. Daviault, Supreme Court Reports* 3 (1994): 63.

3. Jean Louis Goutal, "Characteristics of Judicial Style in France, Britain and the U.S.A.," *American Journal of Comparative Law* 24 (1976): 43, and Michael Wells, "French and American Judicial Opinions," *Yale Journal of International Law* 19 (1994): 81.

4. Baar *et al.*, "The Ontario Court of Appeal and Speedy Justice," 261.

5. *Supreme Court Reports* 1 (1988): 30.

6. Frederick Schauer, "Precedent," Stanford Law Review 39 (1987): 573.

7. Tyree, Greenleaf & Mowbray "The Problem of Precedent" in J.Gero & R.Stanton, eds., *Artificial Intelligence Developments and Applications*, (Amsterdam: North-Holland 1988).

8. H. Patrick Glenn "The Common Law in Canada." *Canadian Bar Review*, 74 (1995): 261.

9. Gordon Bale, "W.R. Lederman and the Citation of Legal Periodicals by the Supreme Court of Canada," *Queen's Law Journal* 19 (1994): 36.

10. Rene David and John C. Brierly, *Major Legal Systems in the World Today* (London: Stevens, 1990); Mirjan Damaska *The Faces of Justice and State Authority* (New Haven, CT: Yale University Press, 1986); Claire L'Heureux-Dube "By Reason of Authority or by Authority of Reason," *University of British Columbia Law Review* 27 (1993).

11. James G. Snell and Frederick Vaughan, *The Supreme Court of Canada: History of the Institution* (Toronto: University of Toronto Press, 1985), 180.

12. Gall, *The Canadian Legal System*, ch. 7.
13. McCormick, "Judicial Authority and the Provincial Courts of Appeal."
14. Russell, *The Judiciary in Canada*, 291.
15. Hogg, *Constitutional Law of Canada* (3rd edition), ch. 8.7 ff.
16. Henry Merryman, "Towards a Theory of Citations," *Southern California Law Review* 50 (1977): 400, and Lawrence M. Friedman *et al*, "State Supreme Courts: A Century of Style and Citation," *Stanford Law Review* 33 (1981): 798-9.
17. Ross Flowers, "Stare Decisis in Courts of Co-Ordinate Jurisdiction." *Advocates Quarterly* 5 (1984-85): 464.
18. *Ibid.*
19. *Ibid.*
20. See, for example, Merryman in "Towards a Theory of Citation" and Friedman in "State Supreme Courts."
21. For the more extended discussion of which this is the summary, see Peter McCormick "The Evolution of Coordinate Precedential Authority in Canada," *Osgoode Hall Law Journal* 32 (1994): 271.
22. Friedman, "State Supreme Courts."
23. Bushnell, *The Captive Court*.
24. Glenn, "The Common Law in Canada."
25. See Chapter 6 above, and Henry S. Brown, et al., "Leave to Appeal Applications: The 1991-92 Term." *Supreme Court Law Review* 4 (1993; 2nd series): 27.
26. G.V.V. Nicholls "Legal Periodicals and the Supreme Court of Canada." *Canadian Bar* Review 28 (1950): 427.
27. Peter McCormick "Do Judges Read Books, Too?" *Supreme Court Law Review* 9 (1998; 2nd Series): 463.
28. Bale, "Lederman and the Citation of Legal Periodicals," and Vaughan Black and Nicholas Richter, "Did She Mention My Name?: Citation of Academic Authority by the Supreme Court of Canada 1985-1990," *Dalhousie Law Journal* 16 (1993): 377.
29. *Supreme Court Reports* 2 (1978): 1198
30. *Supreme Court Reports* 41 (1909): 516
31. Hogg, *Constitutional Law of Canada*, ch. 8.7 ff.
32. *Supreme Court Reports* 2 (1985): 295; see also Greene, *The Charter of Rights*, 71-72.
33. *Supreme Court Reports* (1963): 651
34. *Supreme Court Reports* 1 (1985): 613
35. *Supreme Court Reports* 1 (1980): 471
36. Peter McCormick, "What Supreme Court Cases Does the Supreme Court Cite? Follow-up Citations on the Supreme Court of Canada, 1989-1993," *Supreme Court Law Review* 7 (2nd series, 1996): 452.
37. Peter McCormick, "The Supreme Court Cites the Supreme Court: Follow-Up Citation on The Supreme Court of Canada, 1989-1993," *Osgoode Hall Law Journal* 33 (1995): 452.
38. Merryman "Towards a Theory of Citations," and Friedman "State Supreme Courts."
39. Bora Laskin, "The Supreme Court of Canada: A Final Court of and for Canadians." *Canadian Bar Review* 29 (1951): 1038.
40. Peter McCormick "The Supreme Court and American Citations 1945-1994." *Supreme Court Law Review* 8 (2nd series, 1997): 527.

41. See Gerald Gunther's preface in *Learned Hand: The Man and the Judge*, (New York: Alfred A. Knopf, 1984).
42. See, for example, David P. Currie, "The Most Insignificant Justice: A Preliminary Enquiry," *University of Chicago Law Review* 50 (1983): 466, and Frank H. Easterbrook "The Most Insignificant Justice: Further Evidence," *University of Chicago Law Review* 50 (1983): 481.
43. See J.M. MacIntyre "The Use of American Cases in Canadian Courts," *University of British Columbia Law Review* 2 (1966): 478, and Ian Bushnell "The Use of American Cases," *University of New Brunswick Law Journal* 35 (1986): 157.
44. Glenn, "The Common Law of Canada."
45. See Neal Tate & Torbjorn Vallinder, eds., *The Global Expansion of Judicial Power* (New York: New York University Press, 1995), and Mary L. Volcansek, ed., *Judicial Politics and Policymaking in Western Europe* (London: Frank Cass & Co., 1992).
46. As we noted in Chapter 4, most appellate judges think of their primary audience as the litigants in the cases that come before them. To the extent that appellate judges perceive that their audiences are becoming more attuned to issues of internationalization, they may be more amenable to citing non-Canadian sources.

Chapter 8

1. See Table III (1995) in "1995 Statistics Re Delays: Courts of Appeal," (Ottawa: Canadian Judicial Council, last revised May 3, 1996).
2. This variable accounted for more of the differences in the pace of appeals than whether or not the accused was in custody during the appeal, or whether the crown or the accused brought the appeal.
3. If anything, the median time should be somewhat lower than the mean time, since a few excessively long cases would skew the results, increasing the mean time without having any effect on the median time.
4. Prince Edward Island did submit data, but had zero substantive appeals and only two combined conviction and sentence appeals. The median time for 13 sentence appeals was 135 days, slightly less than the mean of 153 days shown in Table 7.

Chapter 9

1. This chapter is based on Ian Greene, Carl Baar and Peter McCormick. "Law, courts and democracy in Canada," *International Social Science Journal* 152 (1997): 225, with permission of Blackwell Publishers Ltd. for UNESCO.
2. Bushnell, *The Captive Court.*
3. For example, see Brian Dickson, "Remarks by the Rt. Hon. Brian Dickson, P.C. on the Occasion of the Mid-Winter Meeting of the Canadian Bar Asociation," Saint John, New Brunswick, March 1, 1988.
4. See David Vienneau, "John Sopinka: The human face of justice," the *Toronto Star*, November 25, 1997, A1, A6. According to Mr. Justice Sopinka, "judges ought to take every opportunity to meet with the public and explain the workings of the judiciary."
5. *Valente* v. *The Queen et al.*, *Supreme Court Reports* 2 (1985): 673.
6. McCormick and Greene, *Judges and Judging*, 248.

7. Chief Justice Lamer summarized these kinds of concerns in an address to the Canadian Bar Association in August, 1998. See Edison Stewart, "Judge wonders how to right twisted rulings," the *Toronto Star*, August 24, 1998, A1.

8. *Regina* v. *Morgentaler, Supreme Court Reports* 1 (1988): 30.

9. David Marshall, *Judicial Conduct and Accountability* (Toronto: Carswell, 1995).

10. *OPSEU* v. *A.-G. Ontario, Supreme Court Reports* 2 (1987): 2.

11. McCormick, *Canada's Courts*, 97 ff.

12. McCormick and Greene, *Judges and Judging*, 211 ff.

13. Rainer Knopff, "Courts and Character" (paper presented to the annual meeting of the Canadian Political Science Association, Brock University, 4 June 1996), 22.

14. David Vienneau, "Explosive Issues hit Canada's high court," the *Toronto Star*, 1 July 1996, A1.

15. See Kelly Toughill, "Harnick defends his judge selections," the *Toronto Star*, January 22, 1997, A10.

16. McCormick, "Judicial Councils for Provincial Judges."

17. The Hon. Madam Justice J. MacFarland, Commissioner, "Report of a Judicial Inquiry Re: His Honour Judge W.P. Hryciuk, A Judge of the Ontario Court, Provincial Division" (Toronto: Ontario Judicial Council, 1993).

18. See "Appendix G: Report of the Canadian Judicial Council ... concerning the conduct of Mr Justice Jean Bienvenue...." in *Annual Report, 1996-97* (Ottawa: Canadian Judicial Council, 1997), 69.

19. *McKeigan* v. *Hickman, Supreme Court Reports* 2 (1989): 796.

20. Jackson and Tate, eds., *Comparative Judicial Review and Public Policy* (Westport: Greenwood Press, 1992) and Tate and Vallinder, eds., *The Global Expansion* of Judicial Power (New York: New York University Press, 1995).

21. See Robert Putnam, "Bowling Alone: America's Declining Social Capital," *Journal of Democracy* 61 (1995): 61, and *Making Democracy Work* (Princeton: Princeton University Press, 1993).

Chapter 10

1. Other critical factors include the content and style of the factum, the style and expertise of the counsel who appear before the judges, and systemic factors that determine who litigates and the reputation of litigants.

2. Hogg, *Constitutional Law of Canada*, 3rd edition.

3. As well, any provincially-appointed judge who applied for a promotion to an appellate court could be considered by the appropriate committee.

4. See Table 3.1.

5. Although an appeal of both conviction and sentence is handled as two separate proceedings before two different panels, a process which makes it hard to compare Alberta caseload figures with those of other provinces.

6. See, for example, Justice W.F. Sinclair, "Structural Reform: Creation of Provincial Supreme Courts: The View from Alberta," *Criminal Law Quarterly* 31 (1988): 43.

7. See McCormick, "Conviction Appeals to the Alberta Court of Appeal."

8. See McCormick, "Sentence Appeals in the Alberta Court of Appeal."

9. In Quebec, however, a single trial judge served as a more or less permanent ad hoc appeal judge for years, after which a practice of five-month ad hoc assign-

ments was abandoned in favor of a straightforward increase in the size of the appeal bench.

10. It is also the Alberta practice to use appeal court judges as ad hoc members of the provincial superior trial court, as caseload pressures require, although this is much less frequent, and applies only to appeal judges who have been elevated from the trial bench.

11. See Thomas B. Marvell, "State appellate court responses to caseload growth." *Judicature* 72 (1989): 282.

12. The Chief Justice is always senior, regardless of the length of service; and supernumerary judges never preside.

13. For the purpose of this comparison, we are including in the "reserved" category all non-oral decisions that result in written reasons, including bench memos, taped decisions and decisions delivered by way of an endorsement.

14. See Tables 4.1 and 4.2

15. The provinces have constitutional responsibility for the administration of the provincial appellate courts, thanks to section 92(14) of the Constitution Act, 1867.

16. These decisions are sometimes influenced by the advice of court administration staff. However, the judiciary has constitutional authority over administrative matters that affect judicial decision-making, as explained in *Valente* v. *The Queen et al.*, *Supreme Court Reports* 2 (1985): 673.

17. Mr. Justice David Marshall has suggested that one solution would be to empower the puisne judges to choose the chief justice from amongst their ranks for a limited term. After all, the puisne judges themselves may have greater insight into the administrative abilities of their colleagues than anyone else. Another approach would be the formation of a selection committee six months to a year prior to the end of a chief justice's retirement, and to ensure that this process would give due weight to the views of the puisne judges.

18. See Peter McCormick's paper "Judicial Power and Judicial Leadership on the Laskin Court, 1973-84: a statistical analysis," presented to the Canadian Political Science Association Annual Meeting, Ottawa, June, 1998.

19. Opinion of Mr. Justice William McIntyre, *Regina* v. *Morgentaler, Supreme Court Reports* 1 (1988): 30.

20. Maureen Mancuso, Michael M. Atkinson, André Blais, Ian Greene and Neil Nevitte. A *Question of Ethics: Canadians Speak Out* (Toronto: Oxford University Press, 1998).

Appendix

1. The result of this project was the article by Carl Baar, Ian Greene, Peter McCormick and Martin Thomas entitled "The Ontario Court of Appeal and Speedy Justice."

2. Colin Campbell and George Szablowski, *The Superbureaucrats*, xxx.

3. The Supreme Court judge who sits on the panel cannot be the one who heard the trial decision being appealed.

References

Appleton, Barry. *Navigating NAFTA*. Toronto: Carswell, 1994.

Arnup, John D. *Middleton: The Beloved Judge*. Toronto: McClelland & Stewart, 1988.

Baar, Carl. "The Business of the Courts," *Canadian Lawyer* 21:4 (1997): 12.

——. "Criminal Court Delay and the Charter: The Use and Misuse of Social Facts in Judicial Policy Making," *Canadian Bar Review* 72:3 (1993): 305.

——. "Judicial Independence and Judicial Administration in the *Tobiass* Case," *Constitutional Forum* 9:2 (1998): 48-54.

——. "The Zuber Report: The Decline and Fall of Court Reform in Ontario," *Windsor Yearbook of Access to Justice* 8 (1998): 105.

——. "Using Process Theory to Explain Judicial Decision-Making," *Canadian Journal of Law and Society* 1 (1986): 57.

Baar, Carl, Ian Greene, Martin Thomas, and Peter McCormick. "The Ontario Court of Appeal and Speedy Justice," *Osgoode Hall Law Journal*, 30:2 (1992): 261.

Baar, Carl, and Ellen Baar. "Diagnostic Adjudication in Appellate Courts: The Supreme Court of Canada and the Charter of Rights," *Osgoode Hall Law Journal*, 27 (1989): 1.

Bale, Gordon. "W.R. Lederman and the Citation of Legal Periodicals by the Supreme Court of Canada," *Queen's Law Journal* 19 (1994): 36.

Barrie, Doreen and Roger Gibbins. "Parliamentary Careers in the Canadian Federal State," *Canadian Journal of Political Science* 22 (1989): 137.

Beatty, David. *Constitutional Law in Theory and Practice*. Toronto: University of Toronto Press: 1995.

——. *Talking Heads and the Supremes: The Canadian Production of the Constitutional Review*. Toronto: Carswell, 1990.

Berg, Larry L., Justin J. Green, John R. Schmidhauser and Ronald S. Schneider. "The Consequences of Judicial Reform: A Comparative Analysis of the California and Iowa Appellate Court Systems," *Western Political Quarterly* 28 (1975): 263.

Black, Vaughan and Nicholas Richter. "Did She Mention My Name?: Citation of Academic Authority by the Supreme Court of Canada 1985-1990," *Dalhousie Law Journal* 16 (1993): 377.

Blom-Cooper, Louis and Gavin Drewry. *Final Appeal: A Study of the House of Lords in its Judicial Capacity*. Oxford: Clarendon Press, 1972.

Blumberg, Abraham. *Criminal Justice*. Chicago: Quadrangle, 1967.

Bogart, W.A. *Courts and Country: The Limits of Litigation and the Social and Political Life of Canada*. Toronto: Oxford University Press, 1994.

Bouthillier, Guy. "Matériaux pour une analyse politique des juges de la Cour d'appel," *La Revue Juridique Themis*, (1971): 563.

Boyer, Patrick. *A Passion for Justice: The Legacy of James Chalmers McRuer*. Toronto: The Osgoode Society for Canadian Legal History, 1994.

Brockman, Joan, and Dorothy Chunn, eds. *Investigating Gender Bias: Law, Courts and the Legal Profession*. Toronto: Thompson Educational, 1993.

Brown, Henry S., Brian A. Crane & Gordon Thompson. "Leave to Appeal Applications: The 1991-92 Term," *Supreme Court Law Review* 4 (1993; 2nd series): 27.

Brown, R.S. "Allocation of Cases in a Two-tiered Appellate Structure: The Wisconsin Experience and Beyond," *Marquette Law Review* 68 (1985): 189.

Bushnell, Ian. *The Captive Court: A Study of the Supreme Court of Canada*. Kingston: McGill-Queen's University Press, 1992.

——. "The Use of American Cases," *University of New Brunswick Law Journal* 35 (1986): 157.

Cairns, Alan C. *Reconfigurations: Canadian Citizenship and Constitutional Change*. Toronto: McClelland & Stewart, 1995.

——. *Charter versus Federalism: The Dilemmas of Constitutional Reform*. Kingston: McGill-Queen's University Press, 1992.

Canon, Bradley C., and Dean Jaros. "External Variables, Institutional Structure and Dissent on State Supreme Courts," *Polity* 1 (1970): 175.

Church, Thomas, Jr., *et al. Justice Delayed: The Pace of Litigation in Urban Trial Courts, Executive Summary*. Williamsburg, VA: National Center for State Courts, 1978.

Currie, David. "The Most Insignificant Justice: A Preliminary Enquiry," *University of Chicago Law Review* 50 (1983): 466.

Damaska, Mirjan. *The Faces of Justice and State Authority: A Comparative Approach to the Legal Process*. New Haven, CT: Yale University Press, 1986.

David, Rene and John C. Brierly. *Major Legal Systems in the World Today*. London: Stevens, 1990.

Dicey, A.V. *Introduction to the Study of the Law of the Constitution*. London: MacMillan, 1885.

Dworkin, Ronald. *Law's Empire*. Cambridge, MA: Harvard University Press, 1986.

——. *Taking Rights Seriously*. Cambridge, MA: Harvard University Press, 1977.

Easterbrook, Frank. "The Most Insignificant Justice: Further Evidence," *University of Chicago Law Review* 50 (1983): 481.

Eisenstein, James, and Herbert Jacob. *Felony Justice: An Organizational Analysis of Criminal Courts.* Boston: Little, Brown, 1977.

Erickson, Lynda. "Entry to the Commons: Parties, Recruitment, and the Election of Women in 1993," in Manon Tremblay and Caroline Andrew, eds., *Women and Political Representation in Canada.* Ottawa: University of Ottawa Press, 1998: 219.

Erickson, Richard, and Patricia Baranek. *The Ordering of Justice: A Study of Accused Persons as Dependents in the Criminal Process.* Toronto: University of Toronto Press, 1982.

Flowers, Ross. "Stare Decisis in Courts of Co-Ordinate Jurisdiction," *Advocates Quarterly* 5 (1984-85): 464.

Fouts, Donald E. "Policy-making in the Supreme Court of Canada, 1950-1960," in Glendon Schubert and David J. Danelski, eds., *Comparative Judicial Behaviour: Cross-Cultural Studies of Political Decision Making in the East and West.* New York: Oxford University Press, 1969.

Friedman, Lawrence M. *et al.* "State Supreme Courts: A Century of Style and Citation," *Stanford Law Review* 33 (1981): 773.

Galanter, Marc. "Why the 'Haves' Come Out Ahead: Reflections on the Limits of Legal Change," *Law and Society Review* 9 (1974-75): 95.

Gall, Gerald L. *The Canadian Legal System,* 3rd ed. Toronto: Carswell, 1990.

Gibson, James L. "From Simplicity to Complexity: The Development of Theory in the Study of Judicial Behavior," *Political Behavior* 5 (1983): 7.

Glenn, H. Patrick. "The Common Law in Canada," *Canadian Bar Review* 74 (1995): 261.

Glick, Henry, and Craig F. Emmert. "Stability and Change: Characteristics of State Supreme Court Judges," *Judicature* 70 (1986): 106, 229.

Goldman, S. "Voting Behavior on the United States Courts of Appeals Revisited," *American Political Science Review* 69 (1975): 491.

———. "Judicial Selection and the Qualities that Make a Good Judge," *Annals* 462 (1982): 112.

———. "Should There Be Affirmative Action for the Judiciary?" *Judicature* 62 (1979): 493.

———. "Voting Behavior on the United States Courts of Appeals, 1961-1964," *American Political Science Review* 10 (1966): 374.

Goldman, Sheldon, and Charles Lamb, eds. *Judicial Conflict and Consensus: Behavioral Studies of American Appellate Courts.* Lexington: University of Kentucky Press, 1986.

Goutal, Jean Louis. "Characteristics of Judicial Style in France, Britain and the U.S.A.," *American Journal of Comparative Law* 24 (1976): 43.

Granell, Francisco. "The European Union's Enlargement Negotiations with Austria, Finland, Norway, and Sweden," *Journal of Common Market Studies,* (March, 1995): 117.

Greene, Ian. "Are Canadian Judges Independent Enough?" in F.L. Morton, *Law, Politics and the Judicial Process in Canada, II.* Calgary: University of Calgary Press, 1993: 167.

———. *The Charter of Rights.* Toronto: James Lorimer & Co., 1989.

———. "The Courts and Public Policy," in Michael M. Atkinson, ed., *Governing Canada: Institutions and Public Policy.* Toronto: Harcourt Brace Jovanovich, 1993: 179.

———. "The Doctrine of Judicial Independence Developed by the Supreme Court of Canada, *Osgoode Hall Law Journal 26:1 (1988): 177.*

———. "Judges as Leaders," in Ron Wagenberg, Richard Price, and Maureen Mancuso, eds., *Leaders and Leadership in Canada.* Toronto: Oxford University Press, 1994.

———. "Judicial Accountability in Canada," in Philip C. Stenning, ed., *Accountability For Criminal Justice.* Toronto: University of Toronto Press, 1995: 355.

———. "The Politics of Court Administration in Ontario," *Windsor Yearbook of Access to Justice* 2 (1982): 124.

Greene, Ian, Carl Baar and Peter McCormick. "Law, courts and democracy in Canada," *International Social Science Journal* 152 (1997): 225.

Greene, Ian and David P. Shugarman. *Honest Politics: Seeking Integrity in Canadian Public Life.* Toronto: James Lorimer & Co., 1997.

Greene, Ian, and Paul Shaffer. "Leave to Appeal and Leave to Commence Judicial Review in Canada's Refugee-Determination System: Is the Process Fair?" *International Journal of Refugee Law* 4:1 (1992): 71.

Gunther, Gerald. *Learned Hand: The Man and the Judge.* New York: Alfred A. Knopf, 1984.

Harvey, Cameron ed. *Chief Justice Samuel Freedman: A Great Canadian Judge.* Winnipeg: Law Society of Manitoba, 1983.

Heard, Andrew. "The Charter in the Supreme Court of Canada: The Importance of Which Judges Hear an Appeal," *Canadian Journal of Political Science* 24 (1991).

Heumann, Milton. *Plea Bargaining: The Experiences of Prosecutors, Judges and Defense Attorneys.* Chicago: University of Chicago Press, 1978.

Hiebert, Janet L. *Limiting Rights: The Dilemma of Judicial Review.* Kingston: McGill-Queen's University Press, 1996.

Hogarth, John. *Sentencing as a Human Process.* Toronto: University of Toronto Press, 1971.

Hogg, Peter. *Constitutional Law of Canada*, 3rd ed. Toronto: Carswell, 1992.

Howard, J. Woodford. *Courts of Appeals in the Federal Judicial System.* Princeton: Princeton University Press, 1981.

Jackson, D.W. and C.N. Tate, eds. *Comparative Judicial Review and Public Policy.* Westport: Greenwood Press, 1992.

Janis, Mark, Richard Kay & Anthony Bradley. *European Human Rights Law*. Oxford: Clarendon Press, 1995.

Karlen, Delmar. *Appellate Courts in the United States and England*. New York: New York University Press, 1963.

Klein, William John. *Judicial Recruitment in Manitoba, Ontario, and Quebec, 1905-1970*. Ph.D. Dissertation, University of Toronto, 1975.

Knopff, Rainer. "Courts and Character." Paper presented to the annual meeting of the Canadian Political Science Association, Brock University, 4 June 1996.

———. *Human Rights and Social Technology: The New War on Discrimination*. Ottawa: Carleton University Press, 1990.

Knopff, Rainer, and F.L. Morton. *Charter Politics*. Scarborough: Nelson Canada, 1992.

Kornberg, Allan and William Mishler. *Influence in Parliament: Canada*. Durham, NC: Duke Univeristy Press, 1976.

Kornberg, Allan, William Mishler and Harold D. Clarke. *Representative Democracy in the Canadian Provinces*. Toronto: Prentice-Hall, 1982.

LaSelva, Samuel V. *The Moral Foundations of Canadian Federalism: Paradoxes, Achievements, and Tragedies of Nationhood*. Kingston: McGill-Queen's University Press, 1996.

Laskin, Bora. "The Supreme Court of Canada: A Final Court of and for Canadians," *Canadian Bar Review* 29 (1951): 1038.

Levin, Martin. *Urban Politics and the Criminal Courts*. Chicago: University of Chicago Press, 1977.

L'Heureux-Dube, Claire. "By Reason of Authority or by Authority of Reason," *University of British Columbia Law Review* 27 (1993): 1.

Llewellyn, Karl N. *The Common Law Tradition: Deciding Appeals*. Boston: Little, Brown, 1960.

MacIntyre, J.M. "The Use of American Cases in Canada Courts," *University of British Columbia Law Review* 2 (1966): 478.

Mancuso, Maureen, Michael M. Atkinson, André Blais, Ian Greene and Neil Nevitte. *A Question of Ethics: Canadians Speak Out*. Toronto: Oxford University Press, 1998.

Mandel, Michael. *The Charter of Rights and the Legalization of Politics in Canada*. Toronto: Thompson Educational, 1994.

Manfredi, Christopher P. *Judicial Power and the Charter: Canada and the Paradox of Liberal Constitutionalism*. Toronto: McClelland & Stewart, 1993.

Marshall, David. *Judicial Conduct and Accountability*. Toronto: Carswell, 1995.

Marvell, Thomas B. "State appellate court responses to caseload growth," *Judicature* 72 (1989): 282.

McCamus, John D. and Donald F. Bur. *Appellate Court Reform in Ontario: A Consultation Paper*. Toronto: Ministry of the Attorney General, 1994.

McCormick, Peter James. *Canada's Courts*. Toronto: James Lorimer & Co., 1994.

——. "The Canadian Provincial Courts of Appeal: A Comparison of Procedures," paper prepared for the Canadian Judicial Appellate Court Seminar, Victoria, B.C., May 12-15, 1991. Ottawa: National Judicial Institute, 1991.

——. "Case-load and Output of the Manitoba Court of Appeal, 1990," *Manitoba Law Review* 21 (1992).

——. "Conviction Appeals to the Court of Appeal of Alberta: A Statistical Analysis, 1985-1992," *Alberta Law Review* 31 (1993): 301.

——. "Do Judges Read Books, Too? Academic Citations by the Lamer Court 1991-6," *Supreme Court Law Review* 9 (2nd Series, 1998): 463.

——. "The Emergence and Evolution of Coordinate Precedential Authority in Canada: Interprovincial Citations of Judicial Authority, 1920-1992," *Osgoode Hall Law Journal* 32 (1994): 271.

——. "Judicial Authority and the Provincial Courts of Appeal: A Statistical Investigation of Citation Practices," *Manitoba Law Journal* 22 (1993): 286.

——. "Judicial Career Patterns and the Delivery of Reasons for Judgment in the Supreme Court of Canada, 1949-93," *Supreme Court Law Review* 5 (2nd series, 1994): 499.

——. "Judicial Citations, Judicial Influence and the Supreme Court of Canada, 1945-1994," paper presented to the Canadian Political Science Association Annual Meeting, Brock University, June 1996.

——. "Judicial Councils for Provincial Judges in Canada," *The Windsor Yearbook of Access to Justice* 6 (1986): 160.

——. "Judicial Power and Judicial Leadership on the Laskin Court, 1973-84: a statistical analysis," paper presented to the Canadian Political Science Association Annual Meeting, Ottawa, June, 1998.

——. "Party Capability Theory and Appellate Success in the Supreme Court of Canada, 1949-1992," *Canadian Journal of Political Science* 26 (1993): 523.

——. "Sentence Appeals in the Alberta Court of Appeal, 1985-1992: A Statistical Analysis of the Laycraft Court," *Alberta Law Review*, 31 (1993): 624.

——. "The Supervisory Role of the Supreme Court of Canada: Analyis of Appeals from Provincial Courts of Appeal, 1949-1990," *Supreme Court Law Review* 3 (2nd series, 1992): 1.

——. "The Supreme Court and American Citations 1945-1994: A Statistical Overview," *Supreme Court Law Review* 8 (2nd series, 1997): 527.

——. "The Supreme Court Cites the Supreme Court: Follow-Up Citation on The Supreme Court of Canada, 1989-1993," *Osgoode Hall Law Journal* 33 (1995): 452.

————. "What Supreme Court Cases Does the Supreme Court Cite? Follow-up Citations on the Supreme Court of Canada, 1989-1993," *Supreme Court Law Review* 7 (2nd series, 1996): 452.

McCormick, Peter, and Ian Greene. *Judges and Judging: Inside the Canadian Judicial System.* Toronto: James Lorimer & Co., 1990.

Merryman, Henry. "Towards a Theory of Citations: An Empirical Study of the Citation Practices of the California Supreme Court in 1950, 1960 and 1970," *Southern California Law Review* 50 (1977): 381.

Monahan, Patrick. *Politics and the Constitution: The Charter, Federalism and the Supreme Court of Canada.* Agincourt: Carswell, 1987.

Morton, F.L., Peter Russell, and Troy Riddell. "The First Decade of the Charter of Rights, 1982-1992: A Statistical Analysis of Supreme Court Decisions," paper prepared for presentation to the Annual Meeting of the Canadian Political Science Association, University of Calgary, June 12-14, 1994.

Murphy, Walter F., and C. Herman Pritchett, eds. *Courts, Judges and Politics.* New York: Random House, 1986.

Murphy, Walter F. "Courts as Small Groups," *Harvard Law Review* 79 (1996): 1565.

————. *Elements of Judicial Strategy.* Chicago: University of Chicago Press, 1964.

Nevitte, Neil. *The Decline of Deference.* Peterborough: Broadview Press, 1996.

Nicholls, G.V.V. "Legal Periodicals and the Supreme Court of Canada" *Canadian Bar Review* 28 (1950): 427.

Nugent, Neill. *The Government and Politics of the European Union,* 3rd edition. Durham, NC: Duke University Press, 1994.

Patterson, Alan. *The Law Lords.* London: Macmillan, 1982.

Peck, Sydney. "A Scalogram Analysis of the Supreme Court of Canada, 1958-1967," in Glendon Schubert and David Danelski, eds., *Comparative Judicial Behavior.* New York: Oxford University Press, 1969.

————. "The Supreme Court of Canada, 1958-1966: A Search for Policy through Scalogram Analysis," *Canadian Bar Review* 45 (1967): 666.

Porter, Mary Cornelia, and G. Alan Tarr. *State Supreme Courts: Policymakers in the Federal System.* Westport: Greenwood, 1982.

Putnam, Robert. "Bowling Alone: America's Declining Social Capital," *Journal of Democracy* 61 (1995): 61.

————. *Making Democracy Work.* Princeton: Princeton University Press, 1993.

Ratushny, Ed. "Judicial Appointments: The Lang Legacy," in Allen Linden, ed. *The Canadian Judiciary.* Toronto: Osgoode Hall Law School, 1976.

Rawls, John. *A Theory of Justice.* Cambridge MA: Harvard University Press, 1971.

————. *Political Liberalism.* New York: Columbia University Press, 1973.

Richardson, Richard, and Kenneth Vines. "Interpersonal Relationships on Three United States Courts of Appeals," in T.P. Jahinge and S. Goldman, eds., *The Federal Justice System: Readings in Process and Behavior.* New York: Holt, Rinehart and Winston, 1968.

Rohde, David. "Policy Goals and Opinion Coalitions in the Supreme Court," *Midwest Journal of Political Science* 36 (1972): 197.

Russell, Peter H. *The Judiciary in Canada: The Third Branch of Government.* Toronto: McGraw-Hill Ryerson, 1987.

——. *Leading Constitutional Decisions*, 4th edition. Ottawa: Carleon University Press, 1987.

——. "The Supreme Court Decision: Bold Statecraft Based, Questionable Jurisprudence." In Keith Banting and Richard Simeon, eds., *And No One Cheered: Federalism, Democracy and The Constitution Act.* Toronto: Methuen, 1983.

——. "Judicial Power in Canada's Political Culture," in M.L. Friedland, ed., *Courts and Trials: A Multi-disciplinary Approach.* Toronto: University of Toronto Press, 1975.

——. *The Supreme Court of Canada as a Bilingual and Bicultural Institution.* Documents of the Royal Commission on Bilingualism and Biculturalism. Ottawa: Queen's Printer, 1969.

Russell, Peter H., Rainer Knopff and F.L. Morton, eds. *Federalism and the Charter: Leading Constitutional Decisions*, 5th edition. Ottawa: Carleton University Press, 1989.

Sanders, Byrne Hope. *Emily Murphy: Crusader.* Toronto: Macmillan, 1945.

Schauer, Frederick. "Giving Reasons" *Stanford Law Review* 47 (1995): 633.

——. "Precedent," *Stanford Law Review* 39 (1987): 571.

Schick, Marvin. *Learned Hand's Court.* Baltimore: Johns Hopkins University Press, 1970.

Schmidhauser, John R. *Judges and Justices: The Federal Appellate Judiciary.* Boston: Little, Brown, 1979.

Schubert, Glendon. *Human Jurisprudence: Public Law as Political Science.* Honolulu: University Press of Hawaii, 1975.

Shapiro, Martin. "The Giving Reasons Requirement," *University of Chicago Legal Forum*, 179 (1992).

Slotnick, Elliot. Cited in McCormick, "Judicial Career Patterns."

Smiley, Donald V. *The Federal Condition in Canada.* Toronto: McGraw-Hill Ryerson, 1987.

Snell, James G., and Vaughan, Frederick. *The Supreme Court of Canada: History of the Institution.* Toronto: University of Toronto Press, 1985.

Sniderman, Paul M., Joseph F. Fletcher, Peter H. Russell and Philip E. Tetlock. *The Clash of Rights: Liberty, Equality, and Legitimacy in Pluralist Democracy.* New Haven: Yale University Press, 1996.

Sossin, Lorne. "The Sounds of Silence: Law Clerks, Policy-Making and the Supreme Court of Canada," *University of British Columbia Law Review* 30 (1996): 279.

Spaeth, Harold J. *Supreme Court Policy Making: Explanation and Prediction.* San Francisco: W.H. Freeman, 1979.

Songer, Don. "Consensual and Nonconsensual Decisions in Unanimous Opinions of the United States Courts of Appeals," *American Journal of Political Science* 26 (1982): 238.

Szablowski, George J. "Administrative Discretion and the Protection of Human Rights," in Richard A. Chapman, ed., *Ethics in Public Service.* Edinburgh: University of Edinburgh Press, 1993: 59.

Szablowski, George J. and Hans-Ulrich Derlien. "East European Transitions, Elites, Bureaucracies, and the European Community," *Governance* (July 1993): 304.

Tarnopolsky, Walter S. "The Evolution of Judicial Attitudes," in Sheilah Martin and Kathleen Mahoney, eds., *Equality and Judicial Neutrality.* Toronto: Carswell, 1987.

Tarr, G.A., and M.C. Porter. *State Supreme Courts in Nation and State.* New Haven: Yale University Press, 1988.

Tate, C. Neal. "Explaining the Decision-Making of the Canadian Supreme Court: Extending the Personal Attributes Model across Nations," *Journal of Politics* 51 (1989): 900.

———. "The Methodology of Judicial Behavior Research: A Review and Critique," *Political Behavior*, 5 (1983): 51.

Tate, C. Neal and T. Vallinder, eds. *The Global Expansion of Judicial Power.* New York: New York University Press, 1995.

Taylor, Charles. *Reconciling the Solitudes.* Kingston: McGill-Queen's University Press, 1993.

Tyree, Greenleaf, and Mowbray. "The Problem of Precedent," in J. Gero and R. Stanton, eds. *Artifical Intelligence Developments and Applications.* Amsterdam: North-Holland, 1988.

Ulmer, Sidney. *Courts, Law and Judicial Processes.* New York: The Free Press, 1981.

———. *Courts as Small and Not So Small Groups.* New York: General Learning Press, 1971.

Vienneau, David. "Explosive issues hit Canada's high court," the *Toronto Star*, 1 July 1996, A1.

Volcansek, Mary L., ed. *Judicial Politics and Policymaking in Western Europe.* London: Frank Cass & Co., 1992.

Walker, Thomas G., Lee Epstein, and William J. Dixon. "On the Mysterious Demise of Consensual Norms in the United States Supreme Court," *Journal of Politics* 50 (1988): 361.

Wasby, Stephen L. "Technology and Communication in a Federal Court: The Ninth Circuit," *Santa Clara Law Review* 28 (1988): 1.

———. "Communication in the Ninth Circuit: A Concern for Collegiality," *University of Puget Sound Law Review* 11 (1987): 73.

———. "Communication within the Ninth Circuit Court of Appeals: The View from the Bench," *Golden Gate Law Review* 8 (1977): 1.

Wells, Michael. "French and American Judicial Opinions," *Yale Journal of International Law* 19 (1994): 81.

Weiler, Paul. *In the Last Resort: A Critical Study of the Supreme Court of Canada*. Toronto: Carswell, Methuen, 1974.

Whittington, Michael S. and Richard J. Van Loon. *Canadian Government and Politics: Institutions and Processes*. Toronto: McGraw-Hill Ryerson, 1995.

Wilson, Bertha. "Will Women Judges Really Make a Difference?" *Osgoode Hall Law Journal* 28 (1990): 507.

———. "Decision-Making in the Supreme Court," *University of Toronto Law Journal* 36 (1986): 227.

Wold, John. "Going through the motions: the monotony of appellate court decision making," *Judicature* 62 (1978-79): 58.

Wold, John and Gregory Caldeira. "Perceptions of 'Routine' Decision Making in Five California Courts of Appeal," *Polity* 13 (1980): 334.

Index